Housing and
Economic Progress

PUBLICATIONS OF THE
JOINT CENTER FOR URBAN STUDIES

The Joint Center for Urban Studies is a cooperative venture of the Massachusetts Institute of Technology and Harvard University begun in 1959 to do research on urban and regional problems in a variety of disciplines. Its focus is basic research and policy applications of that research. Through this series of publications the Joint Center presents its principal findings on urban affairs.

Housing and Economic Progress

A STUDY OF THE HOUSING

EXPERIENCES OF BOSTON'S

MIDDLE-INCOME FAMILIES

Lloyd Rodwin

75505

HARVARD UNIVERSITY PRESS

& THE TECHNOLOGY PRESS

Cambridge, Massachusetts   1961

To Nadine and Sonya

Contents

Tables

Charts

Maps

Housing and
Economic Progress

CHAPTER 1

....

Introduction and Summary

We are accustomed to identify housing problems with slums and poverty and with what it is now our fashion to label somewhat coldly as the "low-income group." To say that this habit of thought is not quite accurate or very conducive to new insights may cause surprise in some quarters. Yet it is hardly an exaggeration. Most of our housing problems, and those of other countries, stem from economic progress, from rising income and inadequate market responses to such rises in income. Economic progress prompts or accentuates the growth of families, rising standards of demand, the desires and problems of ownership, shortages of housing, controversy over rent controls, debate about suburbia, the dilemma of our "gray" areas, and the current evangelical efforts to make our existing cities more delightful and efficient places in which to live.

These problems are much discussed today. Yet there is an unsuspected and revealing side to their history which has hardly been plumbed. The housing of the well-to-do has its biographers; and there are countless reports about the slum dwellers, the cholera epidemics, and the reform movements from the philanthropic efforts in the nineteenth century to the present programs of housing and urban renewal. But the housing problems of middle-income families, which may especially illuminate some of these contemporary issues, have no chroniclers and are shrouded in obscurity. The object of this book is to explore some of these neglected areas, using the past housing experiences of Boston's middle-income families as the basic source material.

Aside from sheer convenience, Boston was chosen for several reasons: (1) many excellent records, particularly state and federal census reports, were available; (2) Boston, being an older city, was well suited for historical analysis; (3) there was the opportunity of evaluating the theory of the structure and growth of residential areas, and a critique of this theory based in part on the interpretation of the experiences of Boston, and on the location decisions of its families of middle income; (4) there was little reason to suppose that any other community would provide more information for the specific studies contemplated.

Unfortunately, the Balkanization of the Boston metropolitan area was a handicap. Because of population and economic expansion the region has 65 small, independent cities and towns which adjoin each other and which coalesce into an independent economic entity. Of this aggregate, which contains about 2.9 million persons, Boston City is the largest and the central portion, with a population of approximately 725,000 in 1955. Map 1 provides a view of these multiple jurisdictions and the location of Boston City within the metropolitan complex. Data for the whole metropolitan area and for the city of Boston were not always available, and occasionally it was necessary to rely on information relating to one or the other. However, many of the basic trends developing outside of Boston City until 1900 likewise occurred within the underdeveloped areas of the city; and other metropolitan areas may have posed similar, though perhaps not so intricate, jurisdictional problems.

Of course, the evidence of a single metropolis can hardly be conclusive. On the other hand, national data would have been more difficult to obtain and possibly less meaningful or persuasive because of the regional variations and the crude averages. Be that as it may, the question whether Boston's housing experiences apply elsewhere can be answered only by further investigations of some other communities.

The principal theme of this book is that rising income and rising standards of demand, coupled with inadequate adjustments of housing supply in response to such rises in income and standards, are the sources of most of our vexatious problems of housing and neighborhood development. All of the studies in this book owe their origin, or are otherwise related, to this theme. Because of the variety of related themes, however, it may be helpful to the reader if we summarize the organization of these studies and the principal conclusions.

The book is divided into three parts. Part One contains Chapters 2–4. These examine statistically the changes in the housing conditions of Boston's middle-income families and some of the signifi-

Map 1. The Boston Standard Metropolitan Area

cant episodes and experiences associated with these changing conditions.

Chapter 2 concentrates on the data relating to the income of
middle-income families, the rents they paid, the proportion of rent
to income, and on the implications of these statistics for their housing standards for eight periods during the past century. On the basis
of these data, it is clear that although real income increased, housing
benefits were not reaped because of high prices. From 1846 to 1959
rents for new low-cost construction increased almost twice as much
as the corresponding increase of incomes. Only during World War
II and the postwar period under rent controls was this trend reversed, apparently only temporarily.

Given these trends, it is perhaps not surprising that the per
cent of income devoted to rent for new and existing housing increased rather than declined; and that, despite the inadequacies
in housing supply, conditions generally got better, though not so
much as might be expected. The improvements took two forms. A
more expensive dwelling, the one-family house, was aimed at, and
to some extent obtained, after the paring of all possible outlays.
More often, however, the higher standard of living produced by the
additional real income was reflected in the purchase of more space
and utilities and in shifts to a better environment.

Chapter 3 probes the same problems from other perspectives.
There are some striking episodes, both in the past and the present,
which highlight the statistical trends disclosed in Chapter 2. They
include the extraordinary growth of the building and loan movement; the fervid emotions aroused by the three-deckers; the growing dominance of the one-family house; and finally the shift in
public policy toward construction for ownership, as builder and
family preferences inclined steadily in that direction. The tale
begins with the history of building and loan associations. Although
they managed to grow and prosper, for many decades they failed to
achieve their original objective, which was to serve families of
"middling income." Average prices for homes financed by these
associations were beyond the price requirements of a large segment
of such families for most decades subsequent to 1890. But the development of a national mortgage credit system of banking in the
1930's and the revolution in contract terms for mortgage finance,
coupled with the housing shortage and the prosperity during and
following World War II, led to a major breakthrough in the 1940's.

Within a decade, the associations tripled their share of the total in the first-mortgage market, achieved a fivefold increase in the families served, and were for the first time making substantial progress in achieving the original goals of the movement.

During the period before World War I when the building and loan associations were more or less ineffectual, three-deckers enjoyed a huge success. They were criticized, of course, on several grounds, including their combustibility and high maintenance costs as well as their avoidance of legislative restrictions and their value-depreciating characteristics. But they were an improvement upon slums in terms of light, air, and environment; and they were cheaper than alternative types of construction. The three-deckers were finally squeezed out of the market in the early 1920's by high costs, rising standards of demand, and, more formally and belatedly, by restrictive zoning legislation. No substitute new middle-income housing took their place. Subsequently, one-family dwellings became the characteristic type of housing built. This trend grew out of the risks of rental housing construction, the increasing advantages and feasibility of owning, and the inclination of middle-income families, in the face of soaring costs and rising standards, to stretch still further their rental budget allowance to achieve the coveted tenure and environmental goals.

Following World War II, there was a substantial change in tenure attitudes. Easier credit arrangements and rising income placed a larger number of families in a position peculiarly susceptible to the pressures and allure of ownership, a factor which worried those who shaped public policy. Whereas in the 1920's home ownership was often recommended as a means of escaping the gouging landlord, in the 1940's rental housing programs were encouraged by most of the important public officials, albeit not particularly successfully. Among the factors responsible for this reorientation were the broadened interest in housing problems; the decline of faith in the efficiency of the free-market solutions; the desire to minimize risky home ownership commitments for young veterans and migrants, the dangers of which the depression of the 1930's had seared into the expert's consciousness; and the influence of the recommendations of the agencies, organizations, and "leadership" concerned with these housing issues.

Chapter 4, the final chapter of Part One, notes that the trends of rising income and inadequacies and shortages in housing production, when sufficiently exacerbated, provoke the controversial policy of rent control. But the effects of this policy can vary according to how it is applied. What may happen can be illustrated by comparing Boston's housing experiences with a free market and with rent control during two postwar periods: the first after World War I, characterized by housing shortages, increased income, and no rent controls; the second after World War II, with similar conditions except for the imposition of rent controls on existing housing until 1956. The evidence, although fragmentary, casts doubt on the popular thesis that such controls forced either a much greater shift in the tenure of rental housing, or more dampening of new construction, or less economical use of housing resources than would normally be the case. Important shifts in tenure occurred both with and without controls. The transfers reflected primarily the housing shortage and high income. Similarly, slow and insufficient production of rental housing is a result of many obstacles. It is doubtful whether the removal or the maintenance of rent controls on existing housing over a short-term period would affect the entrepreneur's decision to build, which depends essentially on market prospects. Finally, the exchange relationships under a free but very imperfect market are essentially inefficient and it is not possible on the basis of available evidence to say whether controls increase or diminish this inefficiency. In any case, the data indicate that there were more persons per room in tenant- than owner-occupied dwellings before controls were imposed and that on the basis of this criterion renters improved their position somewhat in relation to owners by 1956. However, most, if not all, of this reduction of intensity of space utilization might have occurred even without rent controls. More detailed examination of the data discloses no simple trend toward the use of more space by tenant or owner households of varying size. Percentagewise, during this period more tenant households, both large and small, occupied dwelling units with more rooms in some cases and with less rooms in other cases. The same pattern held for owner households. The data suggest that many larger households had difficulty in getting quarters of adequate size; and for both owners and tenants there was also a large increase of one- and two-person households, and in certain cases a substantial increase in the size of the dwelling units they occupied. Some of these trends were affected by rent controls, but much less than supposed. They were also familiar accompaniments of prosperity, and they were influenced by the size of the dwelling units supplied by the building industry. Probably we get the best indication of the net outcome of these variations generally by organizing the data on the basis of average rooms per household. From the standpoint of this criterion, both owner and tenant households occupied dwelling units with less rooms between 1950 and 1956, but the differences are small enough to be almost negligible. The main inference drawn from these data is that the attempt to achieve more economical use of space through higher prices implies putting pressure on low- and middle-income families who have less space; and this presumed result is based on the partially dubious assumption that many tenants will relinquish space rather than income.

Part Two, which contains Chapters 5 and 6, shifts the focus to the changes in Boston's residential land-use pattern resulting from the increase in population and income; and this review of land-use changes provides a basis for evaluating the adequacy of the principal effort to describe and explain the pattern of structure and growth of residential areas.

Chapter 5 surveys the history of Boston's residential areas and the effects of rising income in shaping this pattern. It shows how the increased population, both native in-migrant and foreign-born, plus expanding economic activities, created a need for more living space; and how the improving circumstances of the low-income native and foreign population sparked the desire for improved standards of living. Both forces prompted a search for a more satisfactory environment and made the relocation aspirations of middle-income families a key factor in transforming living patterns.

Starting about the turn of the century, a steady decline occurred in the population of the older districts within Boston, and steady increases in the surrounding outer areas. Improved yet cheapened transportation hastened the decentralization process and the emergence of blighted areas. Though these tendencies were evident to some extent in the past, the extraordinary population expansion tended to obscure the movements. However, this steady shift of population from the central area must be distinguished from the circular flow presumably characteristic of the changing housing requirements during the family cycle. The relatively permanent loss of population in the "inner cordon" of Boston is occurring because of deep-seated dissatisfaction with the existing environment. The pattern of departure is equally significant. The movements are

neither random nor haphazard. In the process of relocation, the
various nationality groups have formed residential patterns which
are clearly distinguishable despite the tendency for less concentration with the passage of time.

Taking these trends into account, Chapter 6 examines Hoyt's
generalizations on the nature and growth of residential areas, particularly their value for interpreting the history of Boston's neighborhoods and for approaching current policy problems involving
neighborhood change and improvement. In substance, Hoyt suggested that the organization of residential land uses occurs largely
in the form of sectors along the lines of transportation. High-rent
districts presumably shape the trend by pulling the entire city in
the same direction; and the expansion veers toward the edge of the
city largely because the growth of intermediate rental areas adjacent
to the "leaders of society" prevents expansion in other directions.
Upon analysis there appear to be several defects in Hoyt's theses,
including (1) the ambiguous formulation and use of the sector
concept; (2) the oversimplified version of class structure; (3) the
overdependence on upper-class "attractions" as a basis for interpreting shifts in residential location; (4) the inaccuracy of some of the
empirical generalizations; and (5) the potentially misleading reliance on residential trends more characteristic of the nineteenth-
century free-market.

To account for past and current trends, there is a need for a
more refined analysis of class structure and a greater emphasis on
the role of a functionally adequate physical and social environment,
as an influence on the location decisions of families. These additional
factors explain some of the moot and unsatisfactory points in Hoyt's
hypothesis: they furnish more illuminating clues to Boston's land-
use history and the location decisions of its middle-income families;
they provide a more adequate guide for policy decisions designed
to promote the most efficient use or reuse of *all* residential neighborhoods; and they suggest a more flexible approach for relieving
the housing pressures confronting minorities, thus moderating group
antagonisms and increasing the possibilities for mutual accommodation and tolerance.

Chapter 7, in Part Three, is the concluding chapter. It touches
on the relationships between the various middle-income housing
issues and how economic progress and rising standards of demand
led to changes in the character and image of the housing problem.

The feeling that these perplexing housing problems were a common issue affecting most groups, not just the poor, resulted in extensive public intervention, nationally and locally. Legislative measures proliferated in several directions during the 1930's in response to specific needs, and at the end of the following decade the separate programs were joined together in a "comprehensive approach" to the housing problem. But they lacked a strategy or a principle of stress and sacrifice. The book ends with a brief discussion of why such a strategy or principle may be needed and how a focus on the housing problems of middle-income families could become one means of evolving it in the future.

PART ONE:

....

THE HOUSING EXPERIENCE

OF BOSTON'S

MIDDLE-INCOME FAMILIES

....

CHAPTER 2

Income, Rent Levels, Expenditure Patterns, and Standards: 1846–1959

The housing conditions of Boston's middle-income families during the past century depended in part on how much they earned and how much of this income they wanted, or felt obliged, to spend for housing.[1] The conditions also depended on the kind of housing provided by the building industry, particularly its rent, volume, and quality. To get an inkling of what the housing conditions and trends were for such a lengthy period, we need to quantify and compare these factors. This is not an easy job. Comparable and appropriately classified data do not exist. At best one must lean on indirect evidence from sources of varying reliability. Several rash simplifying assumptions are also inescapable. Nonetheless, a stab at such estimates seems justified because of their possible usefulness in appraising the evolving housing situation of Boston's middle-income families.

ASSUMPTIONS AND PROCEDURES

Table 1 summarizes the basic data which were assembled; and Appendix A discusses in more detail the way in which these estimates were derived. But before examining the trends and implications they disclose, we should consider some of the assumptions and procedures upon which these estimates rest.

First is the term "middle-income families." For our purposes, it comprises those within the income range of the middle third of Boston's families—that is, we have divided the total number of families in Boston on the basis of income, so that the lower-income range contains one third of Boston's families and the middle-income range contains one third of Boston's families. For the earlier periods

when income distributions were not available, the families of mechanics, semiskilled and skilled workers, and the families of lower-
paid salaried and professional workers were assumed to be representative of the middle-income group. An advantage of this assumption is that it allows a fairly reliable identification of middle-income
families for diverse periods which can be used to supplement other
contemporary indices. Aside from its common-sense justification, the
assumption is in accord with the census classification of the socio-
economic scale of the labor force.[2] Also, it is clear from the earnings
of male workers by occupation in the 1940 and 1950 censuses that
the census categories for semiskilled and skilled workers make up
the bulk of the middle-income labor force.

To check on the adequacy of the housing provided, we determined the income ranges of the middle-income families. These income ranges were then compared with the rents that the middle-
third families were paying or would have to pay for existing and new
housing satisfying minimum standards of acceptability. To estimate
these income ranges was a hazardous task. But enough information
was unearthed to allow reasonable first approximations, and this information was checked and adjusted on the basis of other income
data available in a variety of studies. The analysis was restricted to
the rental market; and no distinction was possible for differences
which might prevail in rental submarkets, as, for example, differences in rent or supply characteristics of dwelling units in different
neighborhoods or types of structure. As a rule, the rents for each
period refer to dwelling units containing three or five rooms. They
are based on available studies for the period and were checked on
the basis of internal consistency, newspaper advertisements, and
other sources of information.

To judge the price adequacy of the housing provided for each
period, it was assumed that one sixth of income represented a
reasonable proportion for *shelter* rent. This proportion is hereinafter
referred to as the rent-paying capacity of the middle-income group.
The purpose of this normative ratio is to determine whether the
amount paid for rent was in line with this rent-paying capacity.
Several considerations influenced the choice of one sixth as the criterion. First, budget data for the two earliest periods indicated that
this proportion, and possibly less, was actually being paid for rent.
Second, it is a commonly accepted rule today that the proportion of
gross rent (i.e., shelter rent plus the cost of utilities) should not

exceed one week's salary, or 23 per cent of the income of the moderate-income groups.[3] Assuming that utilities average 5 per cent to 8 per cent [4] of income, shelter rent must be about 17 per cent to satisfy this norm; and since many workers are not employed 52 weeks a year, this proportion is fairly generous. Third, this ratio is based on family income, not just the principal wage earner's salary; and, therefore, it is in effect higher than would ordinarily be contemplated according to the rule of thumb.[5] Finally, the same rent-income ratio is maintained for each period surveyed, since the best available evidence indicates that as income increases the rent-income ratio tends to decline, or, in other words, that the expenditure for some of the other budget items, particularly sundries, tends to increase percentagewise.[6] By freezing the rent-income ratio we are in effect mediating between the "normal" tendency for the per cent of rent to income to decline and the possibility that changed standards and higher taxes might partially arrest the process.

Eight periods were selected for study: 1846, 1875–1884, 1885–1899, 1900–1914, 1920–1929, 1930–1939, 1946–1947, and 1956–1959. These periods were chosen partly because of the availability of data and partly because in several of the periods there were important changes in the housing situation. The information for all of the periods provides a summary over-all view of housing costs and middle-income trends for the past century.

Finally, we made two important assumptions in the interpretation of these data. These were, first, that a sufficient quantity of housing had been produced to serve the needs of those income groups able to afford the minimum-priced housing built; and, second, that we would accept the norms and judgments of the period studied concerning the quality of the housing produced. In short, the trends disclosed rest upon optimistic premises. To the extent that the premises were unrealistic in whole or part for any of the periods surveyed, the probability is that a less favorable housing situation actually prevailed for middle-income families.

SUMMARY OF TRENDS

Chart 1 (based on Table 1) indicates that beginning about 1885 there was generally a greater percentagewise increase of rents in new and existing houses than in total family income. From 1846 to 1939, rents in existing dwellings increased about 181 per cent, compared to an increase of 124 per cent in family income. Rents for

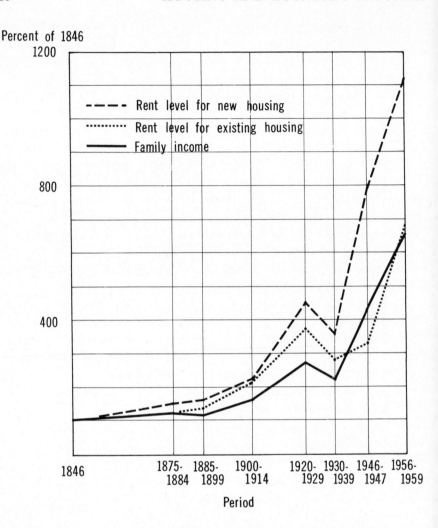

Chart 1. Per cent change of midpoints of estimated income of middle-income families and per cent change of estimated rent levels for existing and new minimum standard housing in Boston, by selected periods, 1846–1959
Source: Table 1

new low-cost construction increased 261 per cent during the same period.[7] Only during World War II and the postwar period under rent control was this trend reversed. By 1947, income had increased approximately 328 per cent, whereas rents for existing dwellings had risen only 219 per cent. Rents for new construction, however, which were not subject to controls, had risen 690 per cent. Rent

TABLE 1. *Ranges, midpoints, and per cent increases of the midpoints of estimated family income; annual rent-paying capacity; rent levels for existing minimum-standard housing and for new minimum-standard housing of middle-income families in Boston; and rent as per cent of income for existing and new minimum-standard housing, by selected periods, 1846–1959*

Years	Estimated family income[a]			Annual rent-paying capacity[b]		Rent levels for existing minimum-standard housing				Rent levels for new minimum-standard housing			
	Range	Mid-point	Mid-point as % of 1846	Range	Mid-point	Range[a]	Mid-point	Mid-point as % of 1846[c]	Rent (7) as % of income (2)	Range	Mid-point	Mid-point as % of 1846[c]	Rent (11) as % of income (2)
	(1)	(2)	(3)	(4)	(5)	(6)	(7)	(8)	(9)	(10)	(11)	(12)	(13)
1846	$ 584–934	$ 759	100	$ 97–156	$127	$ 91–156	$124	100	16	$ 90–175	$ 133	100	18
1875–1884	700–1200	950	125	117–200	159	100–215	158	127	17	156–247	202	152	21
1885–1899	693–1109	901	119	116–185	151	132–204	168	135	19	180–264	222	167	25
1900–1914	874–1622	1248	164	146–270	208	144–372	258	208	21	168–420	294	221	24
1920–1929	1560–2683	2122	280	260–447	354	348–576	462	372	22	480–720	600	451	28
1930–1939	1300–2100	1700	224	217–350	284	276–420	348	281	20	420–540	480	361	28
1946–1947	2500–4000	3250	428	417–667	542	312–480	396	319	12	900–1200	1050	790	32
1956–1959	4000–6000	5000	659	667–1000	834	564–1128	846	682	17	1200–1800	1500	1128	30

a See Chap. 2 and Appendix A for derivation.
b Rent-paying capacity is based on one sixth of income. It refers to shelter rents. For further discussion, see Chap. 2.
c These derived rents apply to three- to five-room dwelling units.

controls ended in 1956; and in the decade starting with 1947, rents for existing housing rose almost 114 per cent, whereas income only increased 54 per cent during the same period. Rents for new construction rose only 43 per cent during the decade, which is understandable if one considers that such construction had not been subject to price controls since the end of the war.

These cost trends are supported by other evidence, notably the Boeckh indices for Boston's residential construction costs. Data are available for a composite of one- to six-family structures as far back as 1913. The indices do not include land, builders' overhead, and profit; but they are partly designed to eliminate the effects of changing levels of building activity and changes in the type or characteristics of the units. Chart 2 (based on Table 2) indicates that during three periods of prosperity, construction costs outdistanced increases in median income by a substantial margin. Moreover, the increases from 1913 to 1958 and for the decades between, both for frame and brick residences, are roughly the same as the increases in Table 1 for about the same periods.

Assuming that the data are reliable, rents for existing low-priced construction of minimum standard were within the annual rent-paying capacity of the middle-income families for the first three and the last two periods. Existing rents were fairly high relative to income just before the shortage of the 1920's, highest during the shortage, and still high, but somewhat lower, during the depression. Rents for new construction seem to be moving fairly steadily beyond the reach of the rent-paying capacity of middle-income families, particularly since World War I. This apparently growing inability of the housing industry to produce minimum-standard dwellings for rent within the customary price range of middle-income families doubtless retarded the filtration process. For houses to filter down to low-income families, there must be a surplus of houses and a relative decline of value to a moderate enough price level to enable these families to benefit from the houses both in terms of price and type of accommodation. Filtration generally becomes increasingly ineffectual for income groups appreciably below the point where it is supposed to begin. Price inadequacies at the middle-income level would necessarily reduce the number of dwellings which could decline in value and reach lower-income families.[8]

Percent change

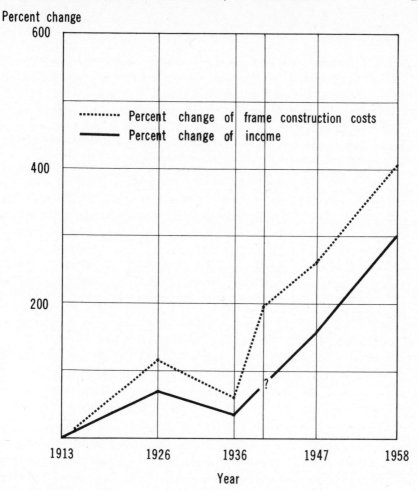

Chart 2. Per cent change since 1913 of midpoints of estimated income of middle-income families and frame construction costs in Boston by selected periods, 1913–1958
Source: Table 2

EXPENDITURE PATTERNS

The data in Table 1 may also be used to measure the proportion of rent to income for existing or new construction. They show an increase in the proportion of income required for shelter rent by middle-income families in Boston, for both new and existing housing, up to World War II. The trend continues up to the present for new construction, but there is a drop in the rent-income ratio for existing housing, ascribable, of course, to rent controls.

TABLE 2. *Amount and per cent change of median income of Boston's middle-income families, and index and per cent change of construction costs in Boston, by selected years, 1913–1958*

| Year | Estimated median income of middle-income families[a] | | Boeckh index of construction costs[b] for— | | | |
| | | | Frame residence[c] | | Brick residence | |
	Amount	% of 1913	Index	% of 1913	Index	% of 1913
1913	$1248	100.0	56.3	100.0	58.1	100.0
1926	2122	170.0	120.2	213.5	119.8	206.2
1936	1700	136.2	88.9	157.9	91.9	158.7
1947	3250	260.4	203.8	362.0	202.5	348.5
1958	5000	400.0	284.7	505.7	295.1	507.9

  [a] See Table 1.
  [b] The Boeckh index data were computed from Boeckh, E. H., and Associates, Inc., *A Study in Relative Construction Costs, Boston, Mass.*
  [c] In certain interim years the cost index was higher. For example, in 1920 it was 137.7.

We have some other evidence which tends to confirm the trends disclosed in Table 1. For example, the only systematic study of income expenditure for families of Boston's skilled workingmen before 1900 is the 1876 survey of the Massachusetts Bureau of Statistics of Labor, which shows an average of 15 per cent of family income paid for rent.[9] Evidence on rent-income ratios for the period following 1900 does not indicate a per cent decline of expenditures for housing. The Special Commission on the Necessaries of Life, set up following World War I to study the rising cost of living and the housing shortage, developed a cost-of-living index using a weight of 17.7 per cent for rent and 5 per cent for fuel, a total of approximately 23 per cent. The weight given to shelter rent apparently indicated the best prevailing judgment as to the reasonable proportion of rent expenditure to total income for the immediate prewar period. In 1924, during the height of the shortage, the commission found few families paying less than 25 per cent. In 1931, the Division of the Necessaries of Life (successor agency to the Special Commission) shifted the shelter-rent weight to 21.8 per cent. A later Bureau of Labor Statistics study in 1934–1935 of expenditure patterns for the Boston metropolitan area indicated a rent expenditure of 21.4 per cent to 20.0 per cent for the $1200–$2100 income bracket, the middle-income range for this decade, and a fuel, light, and refrigeration expenditure of 9.4 per cent to 8.3 per cent. During World War II and for a few years afterwards, the proportion of rent to income for existing housing dropped to 12 per cent because of rent controls; but the ratio for new housing rose to 32 per cent. By the 1956 to 1959 period, the rent-income ratio for existing housing rose to 17 per cent; and the same ratio for new housing declined to 30 per cent (see Table 1). Save for the depression and rent-control periods, therefore, the per cent of rents to income for the middle-income families of Boston apparently did not decline.[10]

How can we explain these trends? On the basis of several studies of consumer-expenditure patterns, it is generally believed that the per cent of income devoted to shelter rent generally diminishes as income increases. In other words, families get better housing and pay more for it in dollars, but the rent represents a smaller proportion of their income. Since real income has been rising for Boston's middle-income families, the per cent of income devoted to rent might be expected to decrease even though their housing standards have been rising. This tendency would be further reinforced if housing became, as some people suppose, a less important item for family expenditure.[11] It seems, however, that the disproportionate rise in housing costs, and the persistent housing shortage, particularly for medium- and low-priced housing, probably are responsible for reversing the anticipated decreases in the per cent of income devoted to rent. In short, although the income of families is increasing and they may be getting better housing, they are paying more for it in dollars and in proportion to their income. Of course, it is possible that a major variation occurred in the proportion of income that families wished to spend for various purposes. But this appears doubtful. The fact that the per cent decline was not simply arrested but reversed suggests that other forces, such as higher costs, were largely responsible, rather than the desire for improved housing standards.

Housing Standards

Nonetheless, because of higher income, housing conditions did improve. This progress occurred even though some reductions in housing costs were achieved largely by lowering standards in some particular, such as resort to inexpensive land, smaller units, cheaper materials, less space, and simpler exteriors. Of course, these pared-down standards were not just the result of cost inflation and expensive operating charges: they also show the influence of compact design, decreasing family size, and the effort to cater to the new market by providing the higher-standard and more expensive one-family house for the top middle-income families.

For the bulk of the middle-income families, however, the improvement in their housing had to be made available in some other way, since new housing was often beyond their means. Given the rise of income, what form was housing progress likely to take? Probably the more obvious advances could be expected in improved environment, housing equipment, and services. From the mid-nineteenth century onwards the movement out of the older parts of the city (discussed in more detail in Chapter 5) attests the urge to improve the housing environment as income increases. The period from 1918 through 1920 also witnessed a great demand for housing with modern conveniences: for bathrooms in apartments, fireproofing, steam heat, and cold and hot water. Increased expenditure for utilities (gas, electricity, and refrigeration) is another illustration of this trend.

Though increased services and the shift to the suburbs have been noted in housing literature, little attention has been paid to the parallel phenomenon of the increased number of rooms. Probably one explanation is the commonly accepted fact that the size of dwellings, really the size of the larger dwellings, has dramatically decreased. But room crowding and families living in one room were serious problems throughout the past century. The Boston Tenement House Committee in 1846 recommended building a greater proportion of two- rather than three-room units since the poor could afford no more.[12] In the 1890's, Robert Woods found it useful to distinguish between skilled and unskilled workers largely by the number of rooms they could afford.[13] And prior to World War I, the "room sweating" problem in central Boston occupied the chief attention of housing reformers.

Chart 3 (based on Table 3) indicates that between 1890 and 1950–1956 there was a reduction in the per cent of families living in two, three, and four rooms but a considerable increase in the per cent of families living in five, six, and seven or more rooms. The trend is even more obvious if it is remembered that: (1) fewer rooms or less space might well have been expected as a result of reduced family size; (2) many families leave the city limits when

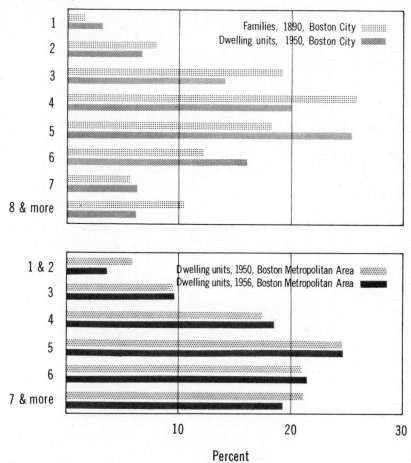

Chart 3. Per cent of families in Boston City by rooms per family in 1890 and per cent of dwellings in Boston City and Boston metropolitan area by size of dwelling in 1950 and 1956

Source: Table 3

TABLE 3. *Number and per cent of families in Boston City by number of rooms per family in 1890, and number and per cent of dwelling units in 1950 in Boston City and in 1950 and 1956 for the Boston metropolitan area, by number of rooms per dwelling unit*

| Number of rooms | Families occupying specific number of rooms,[a] 1890, Boston City | | Dwelling units having specified number of rooms, 1950 | | | | Dwelling units having specified number of rooms, 1956, Boston metropolitan area | |
| | | | Boston City | | Boston metropolitan area | | | |
	Number	% of total[c]	Number	% of total[c]	Number	% of total[c]	Number	% of total[c]
1	1,053	2	6,809	3[b]	10,185	2	36,441 }	5 }
2	5,695	8	14,603	7	26,182	4		
3	13,876	19	31,338	14	62,353	9	72,024	10
4	18,661	26	44,599	21	116,604	18	137,177	19
5	13,002	18	56,694	26	162,753	25	189,957	26
6	7,965	11	35,961	16	138,896	21	154,503	21
7	4,042	6	14,103	7	139,195 }	21 }	143,756 }	19 }
8 +	7,371	10	13,781	6				
Not reported	—	—	4,191	—	11,244	—	2,830	—
Total	71,665	100	222,079	100	667,412	100	736,688	100

[a] The breakdown for 1890 does not provide these data by dwelling units. The number of families in 1890 is the closest parallel to the number of dwellings in 1950 and the results should be reasonably accurate. For the census definition of family in 1890, see Eleventh Census, U.S., 1890, vol. 1, part 1, pp. clxxxviii–clxxxix.

[b] This increase reflects the fact that Boston is one of the largest rooming-house centers in the country. Boston's high percentage of single rooms is accounted for partly by the large number of educational institutions in the area and partly by the decline of several upper-class neighborhoods, followed by the conversion of homes into boarding houses.

[c] The percentages are based on the total reporting units.

Sources: Computed from the Bureau of the Statistics of Labor, *Twenty-Second Annual Report*, p. 351; Seventeenth Census, U.S., 1950, *Housing*, vol. 1, part 3, Table 19, pp. 21:23, 21:25; and Bureau of the Census, *1956 National Housing Inventory*, vol. 3, Table 1, p. 11.

they seek larger quarters; (3) the tremendous increase in equipment for dwelling units plus the builders' drive toward economy in construction costs has tended to put a premium on units with fewer rooms.

The change in housing conditions since World War II provides an even more dramatic illustration of these trends. In 1940, more than one out of every five dwelling units in Boston City and the Boston metropolitan area needed major repairs or lacked running water, a private bath, or a private toilet.[14] In 1956, only 8 per cent of the occupied units lacked hot water, a private bath, or toilet; and only 4 per cent were dilapidated.[15] True, these data do not include those houses which might be considered substandard because of high densities, lack of light and air, inadequate heating and lighting, and substandard neighborhoods. Also, about 23 per cent of the families who rented dwelling units in 1956 were paying more than 30 per cent of their income for rent; and more than 19 per cent of the families who owned homes lived in units whose value was three times annual income or higher, which suggests very dangerous financial burdens.[16] We are certainly not so well off housingwise as we might expect to be with our rising income.[17] Accepting all of these important reservations does not alter the fundamental fact that despite the cost-income discrepancies, and the inadequacies of the filtration process, there has been impressive housing progress.

CHAPTER 3

Middle-Income Housing:
Past and Present

The rising income of middle-income families in Boston during the past century, coupled with the slackening production of moderate-priced housing, generated fresh housing issues.[1] Although housing conditions improved, cost inflation and inadequate supply aroused broadened concern with housing. The history of the building and loan associations, the sprouting of the three-deckers, the shift toward the one-family house, and the changing tenure attitudes are some examples. By sifting these experiences, we can acquire some novel historical perspectives for diagnosing the changing character of middle-income housing and the direction of the dominant trends.

BUILDING AND LOAN ASSOCIATIONS

The initial ideal set by the founders of the building and loan associations (or cooperative banks, as they are known in Massachusetts) was to help independent workingmen get suitable homes. During the nineteenth century, money was scarce and commanded high rates.[2] Construction of water, sewerage, and street systems, of canals and railroads, of office buildings, factories, plant equipment, and so on, created an insatiable demand for capital. The banking system, geared primarily to the provision of credit for commerce and industry and even for land speculation,[3] did not provide the kind of consumer credit required for home building. The development of building and loan associations, both in Europe and the United States, reflected this growing need for reasonably priced housing loans. The aim of these associations was to secure the necessary capital by mutual savings and to furnish loans to members at reasonable rates, the latter being lowered still further by dividend returns to all members sharing in the venture. In effect these associations (together with savings banks) were social inventions designed to provide for the small surplus that skilled workers and middle-income families had earned which could not be ploughed back, as in the past, into land or business.[4]

In its early period, the movement inspired considerable hope and fervor. Labeled "the Workingman's Way to Wealth," [5] it stressed the virtues of cooperation and emancipation from landlords. It began as, and claims to be, a middle-income movement. In their first annual report (1857) the Massachusetts Insurance Commissioners stated:

The ostensible purpose of loan and fund associations is to supply the means by which the middle-classes of our community, particularly mechanics and laborers, whose income and sole means of support are derived from their daily toil, may procure for themselves and those dependent on them, a homestead, by the payment at frequent times of but little more than they are usually required to pay in rent.[6]

But they were not really workers' societies as Engels caustically observed:

nor is it their main aim to provide workers with their own houses. On the contrary, . . . this happens only very exceptionally. The building societies are essentially of a speculative nature . . . their chief aim is always to provide the savings of the *petty bourgeoisie* with a more profitable mortgage investment at a good rate of interest, with the prospects of dividends as a result of speculation in real estate.

The sort of clients these societies speculate on can be seen from the prospectus of one of the largest of them. . . . There is no mention of workers, but rather of people of limited income, clerks and shop assistants, etc., and in addition it is assumed that, as a rule, the applicants already possess a piano. In fact, we have to do here not with workers, but with petty bourgeois and those who would like and are able to become petty bourgeois; people whose income gradually rises as a rule, even if within certain limits, such as clerks and employees in similar occupations.[7]

There was ample justification for Engels' barbed observations about their speculative character. Most of the original associations were temporary organizations established for a relatively short period to serve only their members. Often they were organized on the initiative of local real estate or insurance agents to expand their

other business and gradually get actual compensation from managing the association itself. Many of the associations made glowing
promises of fabulous returns to lenders and modest rates to borrowers. The financial legerdemain necessarily involved in such schemes
was severely criticized by the Insurance Commissioners responsible
for supervision of these banks. Among the practices especially be-
rated were the high concealed rates of interest (sometimes ranging
between 20 per cent and 40 per cent), the steep premiums and fines,
the risks involved in the mechanism, and the loss of interest by
lenders if and when they chose to borrow. It is not surprising that
the early associations in Massachusetts, as elsewhere, soon fizzled
out in a wave of speculation. Between 1855 and 1866 (after which
year all but three of the associations in the state had disappeared),
about a thousand families benefited from the program.[8]

In 1877 new enabling legislation was passed by the General
Court, largely due to the efforts of Josiah Quincy. Again the aim
was to help "the man of moderate means" and "to render the middle-
classes of Boston a house-owning instead of a house-renting people." [9] All the important newspapers backed the legislation, one of
them declaring its enactment to be "the beginning of a new day for
the middle class." [10] This second effort took root. Except for the
decade of the 1930's, the number of banks, shares, loans, and assets
significantly increased.[11]

The new associations provided for regular repayment of principal over a period of eleven to twelve years. The amortization procedure required installment purchase of shares in the association
equal approximately to the value of the loan. Completion of these
payments resulted in "matured" shares which could be converted
into cash to liquidate the obligation. The two most marked changes
in the operation of the associations since their early speculative
period were, first, the establishment of their permanent status with
incentives for savers to invest without obligation to build; and,
second, the shift, particularly since the turn of the century, from
"share accumulation" loans to "direct reduction" loans, partly to permit mortgage loans without shareholding, and partly to avoid the
mounting criticism and borrower resistance to the higher effective
rates of the associations by making interest payable on the amount
of the mortgage loan still outstanding. Another less publicized
change was the gradual triumph of the policy of higher dividends
for investors over lower interest rates for home builders, "because all

members had savings invested while only some wanted to build,"[12] and partly because the higher proportion of investments in mortgages made it possible for the associations to pay higher rates of return than competitors such as savings banks, with their more diversified portfolio. This policy was an important element in establishing building and loan associations as serious competitors in the total savings depository market.[13]

But although the building and loan associations were "successful," it is only recently that the movement's principal objective seems conceivably within its grasp. For many decades the objective was frustrated even though the associations substantially increased their share of the total market. In 1890, for example, they had only 1,947 borrowers, or 2 per cent of the Boston families. By 1940, the building and loan associations held 20,610 first mortgages, or 15 per cent of a total of 135,626 first mortgages on one- to four-family properties in the Boston Metropolitan District. Despite this success, they served less than 2.5 per cent of the total families in the area; and many of the families served were not in the middle-income group.[14] During this period, the most that could be claimed is that many families secured homes by taking advantage of the resources of these associations, and that a significant innovation in building finance, the amortization principle, had been pioneered by them; but in the last analysis, the program tended to reach only the upper segments of its presumed market.

An example of ownership costs in Boston in 1880, cited by R. T. Paine to illustrate the prospects offered by building and loan associations, points up the unguarded optimism of the early proponents. On a five-room house, the value of which in 1880 was estimated to be $1600, monthly payments of $14, instead of the $17 customarily charged for rented flats, were considered possible. Savings in vacancy losses, repairs, and management were assumed. The substantial equity required, however, eliminated many potential purchasers. Paine's estimates also ignored repair bills, fuel, and interest on equity, not to mention such factors as diminished mobility and potential loss of savings. Also overlooked was the higher effective rate of interest, a result of two factors: possible fines, forfeitures, and other fees; and the fact that during the period of the loan, interest was generally computed on the principal, although repayments of the capital occurred and the total loan may not have been received because of the discounting of the initial premium.[15]

We can get some indication of how adequately the building and loan associations served their contemplated market in subsequent periods by checking the actual value of the new houses financed by the building and loan associations (Table 4). Using the average value of first-mortgage loans on real estate as an index, and assuming that the proportion of mortgage to property value is 65 per cent,[16] it is possible perhaps to approximate these values from data included in the annual reports of the Commissioner of Banks. In Chart 4 (based on Table 5), these values are summarized and compared with the income range of middle-income families for different periods. Unfortunately these data are available only up to 1940.

TABLE 4. *Number of building and loan associations in Boston City; number, total amount, and average amount of first-mortgage loans held by these associations; and estimated approximate average value of new houses financed, by selected years, 1880–1940*

Year	No. of associations[a]	No. of 1st-mortgage loans[a]	Total amount of 1st-mortgage loans[a]	Average amount of first-mortgage loans[a]	Estimated approximate average value of new houses[b]
1880	3	79	$ 90,400	$1,144	$1,760
1890	14	1,118[c]	1,790,582	1,601	2,464
1900	18	2,618	4,946,973	1,890	2,908
1910	21	5,140	11,588,485	2,255	3,469
1914	34	7,858	18,190,973	2,314	3,560
1925	50	23,126	86,792,236	3,753	5,774
1928	52	30,233	126,275,789	4,177	6,426
1935	46	25,971	86,857,950	3,344	5,145
1940	38	24,150[c]	75,262,711	3,116	4,739

[a] These data were computed from the reports of building and loan associations submitted to the Commissioner of Banks of Massachusetts.

[b] The average amount of first-mortgage loans was assumed to represent 65 per cent of the value of the average new dwellings financed by the building and loan association. For further discussion of this point, see chap. 3, note 16.

[c] These figures differ slightly from those on p. 29. There were a total of 1,947 borrowers in 1890 whereas the figure 1,118 in this table refers only to first mortgages; and the estimate in the text of 20,610 first mortgages covers only one- to four-family properties whereas the estimate of 24,150 in this table includes all first mortgage loans. For the census sources of the data on p. 29, see footnote 14 of chapter 3.

Source: Reports of the Commissioners of Savings Banks, Commonwealth of Massachusetts, for the years indicated.

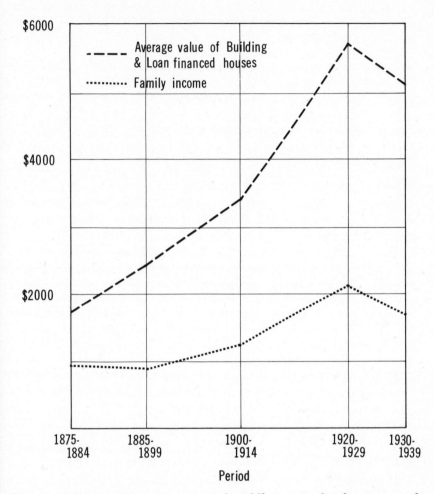

Chart 4. Midpoints of income ranges of middle-income families compared to the average value of new houses financed by building and loan associations in Boston for selected periods, 1875–1939
Source: Table 5

The trend confirms the suspicion that a large proportion of the houses were priced outside the middle-income market. Assuming that the value of a house should be no more than two times annual income, or even two and one half times annual income, and that the required down payment did not eliminate the largest share of the market, the building and loan associations might have met the price requirements of the middle-income families only in the first decade after the passage of the 1879 legislation. Thereafter, the prices of the houses they financed suggest that the associations tended on the

TABLE 5. *Income range of middle-income families compared to the approximate average value of new houses financed by building and loan associations in Boston, by selected periods, 1875–1939*

Period	Income range of middle-income families			Approximate average value of new houses financed by building and loan associations[a]	Ratio of average value of new houses to midpoint of income range (per cent)
	Lower limit	Mid-point	Upper limit		
1875–1884	$ 700	$ 950	$1200	$1760	185
1885–1899	693	901	1109	2464	272
1900–1914	874	1248	1622	3469	278
1920–1929	1560	2122	2683	5774	272
1930–1939	1300	1700	2100	5145	303

[a] Certain years were selected from which to compute the total amount and number of first-mortgage loans for the purpose of deriving an estimate of the approximate average value of new houses financed by building and loan associations. These years were 1880, 1890, 1910, 1925, and 1935.

Source: Tables 1 and 4.

average to accommodate families in the penumbral zone between the top brackets of the middle- and the lower brackets of the upper-income families. Though the requirements of these families were otherwise unprovided for and sufficiently important to justify the service, undoubtedly they were not the same market originally envisioned. Apparently the resources mustered by the "cooperative" mechanism and the easier payment schedule which the amortization policy made possible simply did not reduce costs sufficiently before 1940; but there was none the less enough of a demand for home mortgage funds to allow the associations to burgeon by catering to the requirements of the more well-to-do families within their reach.

In 1932, however, the nation set up a national mortgage credit reserve. Known as the Home Loan Bank System, it created the basis for a more flexible and expanded program of home mortgage financing modeled on the Federal Reserve System. Treasury stock subscriptions provided most of the initial financing. Eleven district banks were established and were supervised by a Home Loan Bank Board. Member institutions, primarily building and loan associations, could go to these district banks and, using their mortgages as collateral, borrow additional capital when their funds had been exhausted. To induce the public to deposit and buy shares in the associations, the government insured the deposits and even chartered federal associations. One of the aims of the system was to unfreeze the frozen portfolios of the mortgage banks and to stimulate construction; but in the first few years the net effect was like having "a small tea kettle full of hot water to pour upon the iceberg of frozen home loans."[17] Neither entrepreneurs nor bank officials were particularly eager to make investments during the depths of the depression. Liquidity, security, and survival were the key concerns. Nevertheless, an extraordinary mechanism had been created to increase the resources and activities of the building and loan associations when conditions changed and profit-making opportunities beckoned.

The 1930's also witnessed a revolutionary change in the contract terms of home finance. Instead of the traditional system of short-term, renewable mortgages with junior financing, high interest rates, and expensive renewal charges, the federal government adopted and extended the basic ideas of the building and loan associations, providing for amortized loans originally for fifteen and twenty years, and later for still longer periods. The federal government also added the policy of small down payments and high loans relative to value. These mortgage terms were imposed by the federal government when it came to the aid of banks and home owners in the 1930's. About one million loans and about three billion dollars of mortgage debt were refinanced through the Home Owners Loan Corporation (1933), and a system of federal mortgage insurance was devised for financial institutions providing home mortgage credit (1934). The innovations had a limited influence during the 1930's; but they opened vast opportunities for mortgage credit expansion when circumstances proved more favorable.[18] The housing shortage and the substantial rise of income during and following World War II provided these favorable circumstances, and the activities of the building and loan associations boomed. The tremendous demand for capital for more profitable nonresidential investments absorbed part of the resources of the competitors of the associations, thus further augmenting the demand for the services of the associations.

Unpublished records for 1947–1948 in the office of the Massachusetts Commissioner of Banks indicate that the average value of first-mortgage real estate loans made by building and loan associations in Boston City during 1947–1948 was $6388.[19] Since probably not more than one third of the mortgages made during this period were under G.I. financing (permitting loans up to 90 per cent of the value of the house), the average value of the homes financed was approximately $8375. This estimate, if correct, fixes the average value of new houses at about 258 per cent of average annual income during this period, a price–income ratio which, coupled with more liberal amortization policies, suggests that the associations were beginning to reach a larger segment of the middle-income market.

This trend evidently continued. By 1950, the associations held 85,011 first mortgages, or 48 per cent of the total of 180,156 first mortgages on all owner-occupied properties in the metropolitan area. Translated in terms of mortgage debt, they held approximately 359 million dollars of first mortgages, or 42 per cent of all the outstanding first mortgages. The associations also occupied about the same position for owner-occupied properties with one dwelling unit. In other words, within a decade the associations had tripled their share of the total in the first-mortgage market. They also served about 13 per cent of all the households in 1950, thus achieving a fivefold increase since 1940. Even though many of the families served were probably not in the middle-income bracket, it is clear that the associations were now making more substantial progress in achieving their original goals, albeit partly as a result of the encouragement and assistance of the federal government and partly the result of war and postwar prosperity.[20]

THE THREE-DECKER

Prior to World War I, the very same groups which the building and loan associations were supposed to benefit flocked to the so-called "three-deckers." Lack of knowledge about the associations might have been partly to blame, yet that explanation is hardly satisfactory. Most people quickly take advantage of opportunities open to them, especially those so optimistically publicized as the building and loan associations. In any case, the three-decker certainly did not flourish because of public acclaim. Why then did the three-decker develop, and what accounts for its spread?

As one might expect with so controversial a phenomenon, its origin is disputed and shrouded in mists. According to one fanciful interpretation, the three-decker was a mistake made by an architect and by builders who came from Fall River where they had built two story and a half houses with mansard roofs. His estimate was less than he could build them for and he persuaded the party who was developing this little tract that instead of building a mansard roof he should carry the walls up vertically and put a flat roof on it, thus giving more room in the upper story. That is the birth of the three decker . . . a building of three floors, all the floors the same area and each floor occupied by one family with no spare room in the attic.[21]

A less apocryphal version of history would emphasize the increasing building costs and the growing anti-slum and anti-tenement campaign in the second half of the nineteenth century. Boston and other cities enacted new legislative restrictions, among the more important of which were stricter height limits and lot coverage controls, as well as fireproof and sanitary requirements. The revised legislation aimed to outlaw the worst evils and thus compel minimum standards. As defined under the new code, a "tenement" referred to any house occupied by more than three families living independently and cooking on the same premises, or more than two families above the first story. The changed requirements led to price mark-ups of at least 10 per cent and 12 per cent, and perhaps more.[22] Rather than risk the possibility of overpricing their market by erecting costly new legal tenements, builders and petty contractors resorted to two-family and three-family houses as inexpensive and altogether legal alternatives. Easy to put up, cheaper to sell, in several respects relatively better places in which to live, these structures sprouted almost everywhere.

The three-decker, which was the dominant type in the city of Boston, was detached or built in rows or pairs. To get the greatest return on capital, lot and block coverage was usually high. Separate entrances through public hallways in front and usually in back were provided to each self-contained dwelling. The types varied greatly, of course, but

a fairly representative dwelling with five rooms and a bath room would contain a small private hallway leading on one side into the parlor, bedroom and dining room, the last with its windows opening on to an open piazza or balcony . . . one of the most desirable features of these houses; on the other side the hallway leads into a second bedroom and the bathroom, and at the end is the door leading to the kitchen, at the other side of which is the entrance from the back stairway. Such a dwelling would probably be fitted with a gas range with hot water fittings.[23]

In 1890 there were 6,313 three-family units in Boston, or 12 per cent of the total number of structures; by 1895, or three years following the tightened 1892 law, there were 8,454 such units, an increase to approximately 14.4 per cent. More than 30 per cent of the *new* structures built were three-deckers. A little more than twenty years later, Mayor Peters informed a national housing conference held in Boston that "We are a city of wooden three-family homes. Almost half of our 76,000 dwellings are of this type."[24] Presumably it was not until the first comprehensive zoning ordinance was passed in 1924 that this "product of the land shark and the jerry builder was effectively outlawed."[25]

Building limits, land values, and lack of space barred the three-decker from the inner central area. Almost any other free, open land was available. A superior environment beckoned in the outer areas and cheaper transportation facilitated relocation. Hence, when the building boom commenced, most of the remaining suburban districts within Boston—i.e., Brighton, Dorchester, Roxbury, and Jamaica Plain, as well as parts of East Boston, Charlestown, and of course many areas outside Boston—were swamped with these structures.

Another characteristic of this type of construction was that it could be adapted by the speculator to cover not only acres of vacant land but also the remaining green islands within the city. Small vacant spaces were quickly converted into "choice" sites adjacent to and essentially parasitic on already well-built and fairly open neighborhoods. Unlike the tenement slum, which at least in its worst manifestations was more or less rooted to certain areas of the city, these mobile slum carriers could and often did turn up almost anywhere throughout the region. Fire and disease had quickened the interest of community leaders in the slums of the past. Now substantial property values were at stake. No neighborhood seemed "safe."

All sorts of objections, relevant and irrelevant, were leveled against the three-deckers. They included complaints about the deceptive salesmanship, the undue emphasis on the glory of being a home owner, the lack of detail about subsequent costs and charges, and, of course, the absence of a private back yard. Far more serious, the three-deckers were clearly a fire hazard, dangerous to both occupants and surrounding properties. The Massachusetts Civic League declared that "even with two staircases it is a dangerous fire hazard, but when provided with only one it is a crime against humanity."[26] The National Board of Fire Underwriters promptly raised its charges for these houses. Dramatic and ominous evidence of the threat was furnished by the Chelsea fire "with its ten million loss and its thousands homeless in 1908, and the Salem, Massachusetts, fire with its fourteen million loss and its ten thousand homeless in 1914."[27] Three-deckers were also costly to the individual and society. As a long-run investment, they presumably were more expensive for the owner, if not the builder. Higher insurance, maintenance, and especially depreciation charges were supposed to wipe out any apparent advantages from lower initial costs or tax payments. Their impact on surrounding property values was notorious and aroused the most fervid emotions of property owners and their organizations. Dorchester and Roxbury, in particular, have been cited as examples of the great fall in values associated with the sprouting of these flimsy wooden tenements.[28] Moreover, few slum types, including even the cheaper varieties, flaunted their sheer ugliness more brazenly—if not initially—with the first signs of untidiness or neglect.

Granting most of these points, why then was the three-decker such a success, at least from a merchandising point of view? Apparently all the finespun economic arguments could not gainsay the fact that it was, after all, a poor man's house, a poor man's investment, and a poor man's bargain. If it worried many as being a potential incinerator, it impressed a great many more as superior to the tenement dungeons; and surely it was an improvement in terms of light, air, cleanliness, and neighborhood.[29] Its inexpensive construction also made the houses easier to sell and to buy. The builder with a relatively small investment could unload his product at a handsome profit, using the persuasive sales appeal of the first year's revenues at full tenancy, with optimum neighborhood conditions and the temptation of practically rent-free ownership.

If we assume that the families housed in these units were a broad middle-income group, then within that category the owners can be regarded as the top layer, enjoying the status of ownership, while the tenants represented the lower two thirds of that broad income category. If the area became too run-down, owners could unload, tenants could move, and the houses could accommodate still lower-income groups. Here indeed was a housing solution which gave some substance to one version of "filtering up," namely, better and often new houses and neighborhoods to which the lower-income families with rising income could move. Top middle-income families had the opportunity of petty ownership and investment; and the bulk of the middle-income families had light, air, more space, and a better environment. The "Dorchesters" of Boston were indeed the middle-income "suburbs." Whatever other arguments may be raised, it is clear that a better alternative was not available.[30]

World War I interrupted all construction; and the postwar housing crisis and soaring prices reflected the pressures imposed by curtailed building, increased families, rural migration, and the expansion of effective demand as a result of the war economy. Several marked changes were noticeable in the type of houses provided when building commenced. Most experts contend that the zoning law of 1924 substantially checked the three-decker. Actually, considerable latitude for such construction was possible because of the establishment of General Residence districts and the loose interpretation of residential areas allowing use of 35 foot heights. Moreover, from the evidence available it appears that the three-decker began to decline as the major type of small rental house construction in the city of Boston as early as 1917. Following 1918, it dropped percentagewise below the two-family house; and except for 1920, when the two-family house record was equaled, it has remained significantly behind ever since.[31]

Why did this change occur? No direct evidence is available, but two factors seem to be particularly relevant. By 1918 three-deckers may have oversaturated their market, both quantitatively and as a result of organized pressure against this type of construction.[32] Even more important, the price inflation may have eliminated the old market. With soaring costs, the necessary down payments and carrying charges for the two-decker were only barely within reach of potential purchasers. For instance, the price for the average three-decker was about $6400 a decade earlier. But after the war two-deckers cost from $6200 to $7600, and three-deckers cost more than $11,000. A further factor consistent with this view is that the zoning law was only passed in 1924. Apparently the previous supporters who had withstood many assaults slackened in the fight, and zoning achieved another equivocal victory.[33]

THE TREND TOWARD THE ONE-FAMILY HOUSE AND OWNERSHIP

The ending of the three-decker construction program left a serious and unfilled gap in the supply of moderate-priced houses. Multiple risks made investment in rental housing a speculative venture, less and less attractive to the builder. Changing neighborhoods, work stoppages, higher costs, relative illiquidity of investment, frequent oversupply in terms of effective demand, heavy fixed charges, high property taxes, and government controls constantly threatened equity investments. Under such circumstances, the ordinary builder tries to risk little money, skim the cream of the market, and avoid long-term commitments. When rental housing is built the returns often tend to be based on financial legerdemain, "milking" of the properties, and speculation in land values. The last has become so ingrained throughout American history that it is now, according to one keen observer, an essential ingredient of the American character.[34]

Since home ownership was also the socially compulsive ideal, highly favored by the tax system and by families with children, rising income, and middle-class aspirations, there was a strong surge toward the one-family house and ownership. Charts 5 and 6 (based on Tables 6 and 7) record these trends. Between 1890 and 1920 about 31 per cent of the dwelling units erected in the Boston metropolitan area were detached one-family units, compared to 54 per cent in the period from 1920 to 1940. For Boston City the percentages were 12 and 20 respectively. If the period from 1940 to 1956 were included the disproportion would be even greater, since more than 60 per cent of the housing built during this period consisted of detached one-dwelling units.[35]

A higher proportion of almost all types of apartment dwelling units, except those in two-family houses and in apartment houses for ten or more families, was built before 1920. But even for large apartment houses, the number of dwelling units provided was numerically small compared to those provided during the previous decades in the popular rental properties (see Tables 6 and 7). For example, in the Boston Metropolitan District between 1920 and 1930, about 13,000 dwelling units were built in houses accommodating ten or more families, compared to approximately 18,000 dwelling units in three-family houses between 1890 and 1899, 27,000 between 1900 and 1910, and 20,000 between 1910 and 1919. For Boston City 8,000 dwelling units were built between 1920 and 1930 in apartment houses for ten or more families, compared to 15,000 in dwelling units for three-family houses built between 1900 and 1909, and 10,000 between 1910 and 1919.

Moreover, while the production of one-family dwellings increased, the proportion of rented one-family dwellings to total one-family dwellings in Boston City dropped from 65 per cent to 35 per cent between 1845 and 1940. For the metropolitan area the percentage of rented one-family dwellings was 27 in 1940, 11 in 1950, and 7 in 1956.[36]

The per cent of total houses owned for the greater Boston area fluctuated from 32 in 1890 to 43 in 1930, 37 in 1940, 43 in 1950, and 47 in 1956.[37] In Boston City, which felt the chief impact of the foreign immigration, the per cent of ownership was 18 in 1890 and 17 in 1910. It then climbed to 26 per cent by 1930; but during the depression a decline occurred, reaching 21 per cent by 1940, followed by an increase to 25 per cent in 1950 (Chart 7 based on Table 8).

Even more telling were the new financial techniques developed to enlarge the ownership market. Between 1890 and 1950 the per cent of families owning homes in the city of Boston and holding title free of mortgage was almost halved; or, to put it differently, of the total families owning, the per cent holding encumbered titles nearly doubled (Chart 7). Only one third, approximately, of the owner-occupied one-family homes in the city of Boston and the metropolitan area were without mortgages in 1950.[38] And it is hardly surprising that the sharpest increases in ownership occurred after both world wars, periods marked by increased income, serious shortages, and high costs.

As costs move higher, moreover, there appears to be an increasing advantage in the government innovations during the past two decades in the financial terms for ownership. By amortizing a loan for twenty-five to thirty years, it is frequently easier, in terms of monthly or annual outlays, to own than rent. Smaller down payments, income tax advantages, preferential assessments on local property taxes, and other factors contribute to this advantage. Although the ultimate cost of ownership may be substantially higher when the total interest payments are counted, the family does not seem to mind as long as it is getting a better house at a lower monthly cost more or less within its reach. The substantial volume of construction during the last decade can be explained only by the fact that "more liberal mortgage credit terms . . . [have] to a very

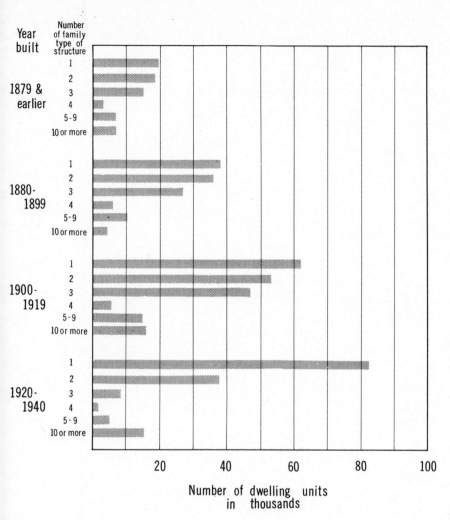

Chart 5. Number of urban and rural nonfarm dwelling units in the Boston Metropolitan District in 1940 by type of structure and year built
Source: Table 6

large extent blunted the impact of the staggering increase in building construction costs and in the prices of existing homes. As everyone knows, the annual carrying costs of the residential mortgage debt, in spite of higher debt-to-value ratios, have not risen nearly as fast as either construction costs or mortgage debt because of lower interest rates and longer contract terms."[39]

The movement in the direction of greater ownership can there-

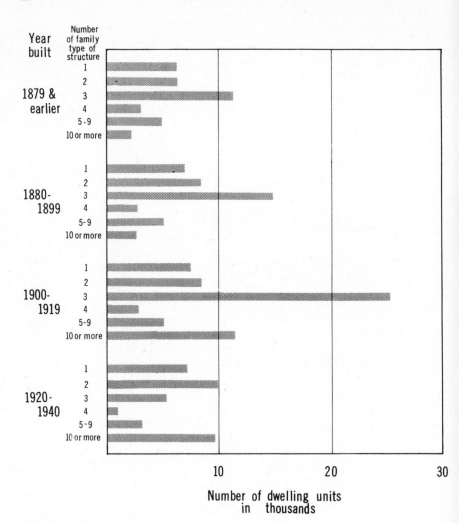

Chart 6. Number of dwelling units in Boston City in 1940 by type of structure and year built
Source: Table 7

fore be expected to continue. A high percentage of tenancy still exists both in Boston City and the metropolitan area, and rising income tends to produce increased ownership. But ownership status, however desirable, can be dangerous, especially ownership that is forced because of the absence of alternative housing, or because of lack of choice of tenure for one-family houses, or because high prices for rental housing make it desirable to skimp a little more in

TABLE 6. Number and per cent of urban and rural nonfarm dwelling units in the Boston Metropolitan District in 1940, by type of structure and years built

Years built	All dwelling units[a]	1-family structures		2-family structures		Dwelling units built in— 3-family structures		4-family structures		1-4-family structures with business		5-9-family structures		10-family and over structures	
		Number	% of total	Number	% of total	Number	% of total	Number	% of total	Number	% of total	Number	% of total	Number	% of total
1935–1940	17,394	14,062	81	950	5	225	1	248	1	79	1	965	6	801	5
1930–1934	24,784	17,662	72	4,145	17	518	2	268	1	105	—	307	1	1,734	7
1925–1929	65,736	31,233	48	19,885	30	3,440	5	925	1	210	—	2,452	4	7,544	12
1920–1924	45,456	19,780	44	13,091	29	4,394	10	634	1	397	1	1,604	4	5,519	12
1910–1919	94,648	30,900	33	25,200	27	19,826	21	2,059	2	1,054	1	6,171	7	9,266	10
1900–1909	108,703	30,971	29	28,069	26	26,944	25	3,742	3	2,564	2	9,084	8	7,072	7
1890–1899	81,950	25,100	31	23,304	29	17,814	22	3,832	5	2,257	3	6,574	8	2,998	4
1880–1889	44,456	13,237	30	12,652	29	9,164	21	2,396	5	1,650	4	3,752	9	1,540	4
1879 and earlier	92,286	30,235	33	23,411	25	17,390	19	5,556	6	4,047	4	8,144	9	3,290	4
Not reporting	72,841	19,611	27	18,779	26	15,272	21	3,192	4	1,753	2	7,189	10	6,939	10
Total	648,254	232,791	36	169,486	26	114,987	18	22,852	4	14,116	2	46,242	7	46,703	7

[a] The totals include a negligible number of "other dwelling units": 1935–1940, 64; 1930–1934, 45; 1925–1929, 47; 1920–1924, 37; 1910–1919, 172; 1900–1909, 257; 1890–1899, 71; 1880–1889, 65; 1879 and earlier, 213; not reporting, 106.
Source: Sixteenth Census, U.S., 1940, Housing, Characteristics by Type of Structure, Table C-1, p. 161.

TABLE 7. *Number and per cent of dwelling units in Boston City in 1940, by type of structure and years built*

Years built	All dwelling units[a]	Dwelling units built in—												
		1-family structures		2-family structures		3-family structures		4-family structures		1-4-family structures with business		5-9-family structures		10-family and over structures	
		Number	% of total	Number	% of total	Number	% of total	Number	% of total	Number	% of total	Number	% of total	Number	% of total
1935–1940	2,684	1,034	39	330	12	71	4	48	2	13	1	572	21	614	23
1930–1934	5,016	1,954	39	1,590	32	301	6	13	—	22	1	145	3	986	20
1925–1929	15,916	2,750	17	5,377	34	2,336	15	136	9	31	2	1,538	10	3,736	24
1920–1924	12,138	1,270	11	2,648	22	2,637	22	180	2	90	1	1,070	9	4,237	35
1910–1919	28,294	2,736	10	4,853	17	9,978	35	637	2	358	1	3,094	11	6,613	23
1900–1909	40,934	4,731	12	7,675	19	15,358	38	1,818	4	1,393	3	5,019	12	4,907	12
1890–1899	27,709	4,332	16	5,309	20	9,774	35	1,836	7	1,205	4	3,311	12	1,922	7
1880–1889	15,651	2,599	17	3,231	21	5,163	33	1,064	7	898	6	1,830	12	847	5
1879 or earlier	36,625	6,359	17	6,307	17	11,204	30	3,097	9	2,327	6	4,990	14	2,171	6
Not reporting	26,547	3,489	13	5,082	19	8,554	32	1,527	6	922	4	3,694	14	3,234	12
Total	211,514	31,254	15	42,402	20	65,376	31	10,356	5	7,229	4	25,263	12	29,267	14

a The totals include a negligible number of "other dwelling units": 1935–1940, 2; 1930–1934, 5; 1925–1929, 12; 1920–1924, 6; 1910–1919, 25; 1900–1909, 33; 1890–1899, 20; 1880–1889, 19; 1879 or earlier, 100; not reporting, 45.
Source: Sixteenth Census, U.S., 1940, *Housing, Characteristics by Type of Structure*, Table B-1, p. 160.

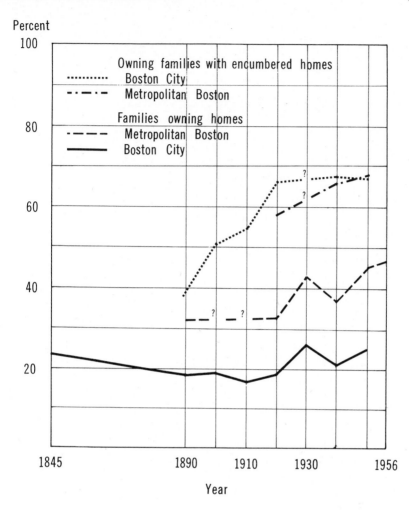

Chart 7. Per cent of families owning homes and per cent of owning families
with encumbered homes in Boston City and metropolitan Boston, 1845–1956
Source: Table 8

order to secure some of the added prestige, extra space, emotional
afflatus, and other real or fancied advantages of ownership. Heavy
financial risks and burdens are sometimes involved: budget expenditure patterns can be distorted, family savings squandered, mobility
unduly curbed, and job opportunities lost. Prestige and social status
may also be frustrated, with grave personal consequences. All of
which explains why the tenure issue is one of the leading and increasingly sensitive problems of housing policy.

TABLE 8. *Number and per cent of families renting, owning homes, and owning encumbered homes in Boston City, by selected years, 1845–1950*

Year	Total number of families[a]	Families owning homes		Families owning homes free of encumbrance		Families owning encumbered homes		Number of families unknown whether owning free or enc.	% of owning families		Families renting homes		Number of families unknown whether own or rent
		Number	% of total[b]	Number	% of total[b]	Number	% of total[b]		Owning free	Owning enc.	Number	% of total	
1845	19,175	4,465	23	—	—	—	—	—	—	—	14,710	77	48
1890	89,661	16,512	18	10,102	11	6,410	7	82	61	39	73,101	82	4,926
1900	114,705	20,696	19	9,944	9	10,395	10	357	49	51	89,083	81	1,892
1910	139,700	23,496	17	10,540	8	12,731	9	225	45	55	114,312	83	1,995
1920	164,785	30,132	19	9,998	6	19,609	12	525	34	66	132,658	81	2,998
1930	179,200	46,014	26	—	—	—	—	—	—	—	130,188	74	2,594
1940	199,987[c]	41,236	21	12,494	6	26,300	13	2,442	32	68	156,157	79[d]	—
1950	218,103[c]	54,266	25	15,934[d]	7	32,756[d]	15	1,786[d]	33	67	163,837	76[d]	—

a The definitions of family in census reports vary somewhat for different periods.

b The percentages are based on the number of families for whom the information is known. The same proportions may be assumed to apply to the remainder. In any case, with the possible exception of the data for 1900, the differences are unlikely to affect the percentages significantly.

c These data are for total occupied dwelling units.

d For 1950, the total number of families owning homes is larger than the total of its components, *i.e.,* of families owning free and encumbered and of families whose ownership status is unknown. The figure is larger because the data for the components are only available for one- to four-dwelling unit structures without business.

Sources: Federal, Commonwealth, and Boston censuses for the years listed.

It is an issue, moreover, that is characteristically identified with the housing situation of the middle-income group. For the rich there is no tenure problem. The poor, on the other hand, have no alternative, since the question of tenure has become subordinated to the first requirement of decent dwellings. Middle-income families, however, are in the penumbral zone where alternatives first become possible. It is for these groups that the changing income status, cost trends, and limited housing supply creates or intensifies the problem. It is for these groups that the incentives are real, the pressures importunate, and the risks, therefore, slighted. It is perhaps all the more important for these groups that public policy should do more than just grease the path to ownership.

CHANGING TENURE ATTITUDES

Despite, or possibly because of, the trend toward ownership, public policy began to veer in the opposite direction. The shift in posture becomes dramatically evident if we compare the approach to the housing shortages following World War I and World War II. During both periods, houses built for sale or rent, because of high construction costs and the greater profits, served generally the higher-income groups. Few new dwelling units were available in the price range which the middle-income groups could afford. The war and postwar prosperity intensified the existing trends in the direction of rising income, soaring costs, and reduced supply of moderate-priced housing. As might have been expected, the pressures were felt mostly by the low- and middle-income families.

Two or three main housing policies emerged during the shortage of the 1920's. First and foremost, strong government action or controls were anathema. Rent controls were scoffed at, even by the Special Commission established to study the problem: the experience of Diocletian's period was cited to evidence their futility.[40] Instead, credit stringency aroused much attention. Plans to tap national banks for mortgage financing, to mobilize and expand building and loan association resources, and even to secure federal credit or postal savings were hopefully discussed. Though the United States had become a great creditor nation, money was going to more profitable sources such as nonresidential construction, European and South American loans, retooling, financing of new industries, or expansion of old ones. The Boston City Planning Board tried to attract private capital into housing but found there was no interest "partly

due to the condition of the money market and partly to the fact that
any plan which presented itself possessed neither the advantages of
a good business enterprise nor the meritorious features of a philanthropic proposition."[41]

Public distress, however, did produce mild legislation. In 1919
the Special Commission on the Necessaries of Life was created to
threaten public exposure and remonstration if extortionate rents
were sought. Increases of 25 per cent or more were presumed to be
unreasonable, and consequently 25 per cent increases became the
mode. A stay of eviction notice could also be secured, and fines imposed for failure to furnish customary services. But a 1917 constitu-
tional amendment which apparently gave the mayor the discretion-
ary power of deciding when the government could intervene to
build in cases of emergency was interpreted out of existence. Mayor
Peters heeded the Attorney General, who advised him that the law
referred only to acts of God, floods or destruction, and not simply to
a housing shortage.[42]

As a *basic solution* tenants were urged to buy homes and so
escape the gouging landlords. Ownership was extolled as never before. Builders found it profitable to construct houses to sell to families whose rent had been excessively raised. Local finance and building companies devised schemes to make it even easier for people to
own. The federal government, through the Department of Labor,
collaborated both by endorsing the program and by furnishing mil-
lions of brochures to beguile tenants into ownership status. The
shortage completely refocused the interest of the community and
nation on housing. "Previously," a prominent official observed,
". . . any discussion of the housing situation implied questions of
sanitation, of an insufficient amount of light and air, and of overcrowding in rooms and on the land. Translated as it has now become by necessity into a question of housing shortage it has been
receiving attention at the hands of practically every group of citizens
in the community."[43] Because of the concern with the new problems,
the more importunate needs of lower-income groups were neglected.
Instead a solution was devised, geared to middle-class aspirations
and goals. Rarely did a policy seem more beneficient to its proponents. As many of the lower- and middle-income groups were to be
drawn toward ownership, thus rescuing them from the "greedy"
and "foreign" landlord who did not understand "our customs,"[44]
they were at the same time advancing toward an American ideal.

Equally pleasant as an afterthought was the observation that the vacancies would relieve the pressures and help lower rents for those remaining as tenants.

Few warning notes were sounded about the risks of inflated costs, excessive financial commitments, and forced ownership. It was more or less assumed that the most efficient solutions would be achieved through the normal mechanism of the market.[45] For example, the Special Commission on the Necessaries of Life declared in 1920:

> The Commonwealth is facing a serious situation. New houses are necessary but new houses cost much more, and they will not be built unless the builders can see rental returns which justify the investment. Rents on existing property if raised to equality with rent on new property will show excessive returns to the owner. If rents are raised, valuations will also rise with the result that the value of the basic commodity—real estate will be inflated because of the *temporary* inflation of building material prices. A remedy suggested is the exemption of new buildings from taxation except the land, for a period of five to ten years; but this is unconstitutional. It is doubtful also if a law fixing rentals on valuation would be within our constitution. *The situation will eventually work its way out.*[46]

Some aspects of the shortage were in fact deemed beneficial. Thus the same commission made the following observation in 1923:

> It is estimated that from 80 per cent to 90 per cent of this new construction is being built for or will be sold to home owners. As a result of this housing shortage, the unhealthy drift toward tenantry is being arrested. The Commonwealth will be benefited by the increased number of home owners.[47]

To the commission's surprise and discomfiture, the shortage continued year after year. Rents were raised, though the commission declared after investigation that the percentage increases were generally far higher than necessary. The commission also found it "interesting to note" that most new construction was proceeding for income levels where vacancies were appearing; deplored the fact that many of the homes were shoddily built, expensive to operate and heat, "and probably destined to cause much trouble to their owners"; even began to doubt whether the problem of providing new construction at rents between $20 and $40 a month could be solved at existing cost levels; and requested extension of the mild legislation on the books based on the requests of almost all the heads of the cities of Massachusetts.[48] Real estate people generally disapproved, save for a small minority who served on rent boards, and the commission was shortly thereafter eliminated.[49]

A marked reversal in tenure attitudes occurred following World War II. Again the middle- and low-income families were in distress due to the postwar shortages, soaring costs and prices, and the higher profits obtainable by building more expensive homes. Many drastic government powers were recommended and brought into play, including rent controls, public building and renewal programs, and advocacy of rental housing.[50]

Forced ownership increased, but it was not, at least officially, regarded as a panacea for inflated rents, or as a desirable status for most of the newly returned veterans, or as a justifiable risk for many of the lower- and middle-income groups.[51] President Truman urged that 1947 be considered a rental housing year. Federal officials began to think about and act on rental housing investment and urban renewal. These declarations and policies were endorsed by government officials and reports in Massachusetts and Boston and supplemented by legislative action.[52]

But why this new orientation? Is there an explanation for the change? A precise answer is not possible, but some estimate of the relevant factors can be ventured. After both wars the housing problem was of crisis proportions. But the shortage following World War II was probably more intense. Some of the reasons for this situation were the prolonged failure to build moderate-priced housing during the 1920's, the stagnation of the 1930's, the very limited construction during the war, coupled with the sustained period of war and postwar prosperity, and finally the jump in rents of new construction of more than 200 per cent since 1939. Low- and middle-income families were once again the most seriously affected.

Though this situation prompted recourse to governmental measures, one reason for the shift in outlook seems to be a secular change in attitude toward the market economy. Maladjustments are no longer regarded as very temporary phenomena, and there is much less patience with the price mechanism as an effective or fair regulator of supply and demand: hence the ready inclination to search for solutions by influencing or "tampering" with market incentives. The emphasis on urban renewal and the more receptive attitudes in the postwar period to rental housing are simply concrete illustrations of this change. The new approach is all the more remarkable because today housing for ownership is often cheaper on a monthly basis than equivalent accommodations for rent; and because rental housing goes counter to cherished values and symbols of American society, including those income groups for whom the policy is adopted.

The experience of the 1930's, too, had imbedded itself deeply in the public consciousness and is partly responsible for the change. Considerable efforts were made then to assist victims of mortgage foreclosures and to stimulate construction through a national credit reserve and mortgage loan insurance. These policies were continued during and after the war, and today the government is subject to heavy contingent liabilities as a result of these commitments. The possibility of overextension and overvaluation of loans has made federal officials understandably more sensitive to the risks of ownership.

Equally important has been the influence of the national movement for better housing, particularly the leadership of the public housing groups. As a militant and purposeful minority, the effects of their criticism far outweighed their significance in numbers. Their arguments, in the light of the experience of the 1930's, had a portentous, almost prophetic force; and their moral earnestness still exuded some of the evangelism of the early New Deal, especially as instanced by their concern for the welfare of the lower- and middle-income families. Supporting them, also, was the institutional heritage of the 1930's, the national and local housing agencies, private and public, whose function it had become to study the housing developments and suggest appropriate policies. Problems that before the 1930's were ignored or hardly discussed were now debated and reacted to with vigor. Persistent, organized support was mustered before congressional and legislative committees, and emotional diatribes as well as closely reasoned analyses were presented to public forums with local and national audiences.

Another factor has been the broadening population base of housing policy. What was previously considered a problem only affecting slums and the lowest-income families now embraces other groups and physical areas of the community. Indirectly, in the form of urban renewal and employment policy, and directly, in the form of rising living standards and housing shortages, the issues have changed their guise. Charity, philanthropy, and acceptance of the results of market phenomena gave way first to "muckraking," then to changes in strategy and social policy. In line with this trend was the advocacy by Washington officials of a *comprehensive* housing program as a basis for postwar housing policy, a position which was destined to arouse interest in proposals for middle-income housing and the redevelopment or renewal of central areas. This concern was further stimulated by the logic of events. If the depression focused the major housing interest on the problems of slums and poverty, then the war and postwar prosperity have directed attention to shortage, high prices, the dearth of rental housing, and the need for rebuilding and renewal in central areas. The emergence and the slow recognition of these difficulties confronting middle-income families has already changed and promises to change still further the orientation of housing policy in directions scarcely anticipated in the 1930's; and not least of these changes are the initial, wary reactions to the tenure issue.

In short, the risks involved for middle-income groups, the foreclosures of the 1930's, the influence of liberal housing leadership, the interest in serving the *whole* market, the minority criticisms of federal ownership policies, and to some extent even the new urban renewal programs for central areas seem to be responsible for a greater official emphasis, or at least lip service, in favor of rental housing. An important issue now looms as a consequence of this tentative change in sentiment. Will the "directed" market approaches provide more or less satisfactory solutions? The answer to this question is highly controversial. Certainly, however well-intentioned the new outlook is reputed to be, it is still questionable whether effective means for securing suitable and reasonably priced rental housing have yet been devised.

....

CHAPTER 4

Boston's Experience with and
without Rent Controls

Perhaps the most inflammatory aspect of the tenure issue concerns rent controls.[1] They are admittedly inadequate measures: partial, negative, and stopgap. In general, they are enacted when there is intense dissatisfaction with the pricing and allocation solutions of the market mechanism in periods of rising income and severe housing shortage. Their main aim is to curb the advance of rents until housing supply is more in line with demand. But the policy generally breeds sharp criticisms on the grounds that it is misguided, and that the results are in many ways detrimental to the interests of the middle- and low-income groups. Several prominent writers have specifically declared that rent controls accelerate the shift of houses from tenancy to ownership status, discourage the production of housing, and result in an inefficient use of housing resources and an uneconomical use of space.[2] Despite the virulence of the controversies, pro and con, one can find almost no adequate empirical tests of the conflicting claims. This neglect is all the more surprising since some relevant data based on the experiences of communities following World War I and World War II are available for this purpose. Actually the effects of this policy vary according to how it is applied; and a revealing insight into what may happen can be gotten by comparing Boston's housing experiences during these two periods.*

TENURE SHIFTS IN A FREE MARKET

Following World War I, Boston, like other cities, experienced a critical housing shortage. Income rose, but construction lagged.

---

* Appendix B provides a theoretical analysis of the same problems.

As already noted, fundamental reliance was placed on market adjustments to deal with the situation. In the absence of government control, rents and sale prices rose sharply. According to the Consumer's Price Index for Moderate Income Families of the Bureau of Labor Statistics, rents rose from 76.5 in 1914 to 117.8 in 1925, or approximately 54 per cent.[3] Price increases for new houses during the same period averaged about 100 per cent.[4] Old houses also had risen in value. Only 23.6 per cent of the owner-occupied houses were valued below $5,000 in 1930, whereas there were 39.3 per cent in 1920; and 32.2 per cent over $10,000 in 1930 compared with 11.2 per cent in 1920. These buoyed-up values prevailed even though both the Consumer and the Wholesale Price indices for Boston showed a substantial decline for the years 1928–1930 compared to the price levels in 1920.[5]

A considerable scramble for apartments occurred. Those who could not find homes or who could not afford the high rent levels doubled up. Others with more income vied to outbid the next fellow. An apparently frequent practice of landlords during the period seems to have been the service of eviction notices on blocks of houses. Potential ex-tenants were then allowed to make new rent offers for their apartments. This practice sometimes took place several times during the year. Often notices were served during the winter after the tenants had purchased their coal (which was scarce and expensive), thereby catching them in a relatively immobile situation. Many families paid an exorbitant percentage of their income—sometimes as much as 25 to 40 per cent—for rent.[6]

Higher rents also intensified the pressure to buy and to sell, and the tendency to view the responsibilities of ownership with relative optimism. Before and after the 1921 depression the general disposition was to believe that the country was on a continually rising economic spiral. Many borderline families who could with some strain on their resources meet the ownership requirements probably underestimated the responsibilities involved, especially since the national and local campaigns in favor of this step received endorsement from all respected groups in society. For many families, moreover, ownership was not more expensive than tenancy. There is evidence that a large proportion of the new owners did buy for this reason. In 1923, and then again as late as 1925, the Special Commission on the Necessaries of Life reported "that nearly all of new construction is being sold to or being built by victims of high rents."[7]

There is little direct information concerning the number of houses, particularly single-family houses, that shifted tenure. If the prevailing speculative fever constitutes partial evidence, it was probably high. Frequent references were made in the reports of the Special Commission to the tactics of speculators who raised rents several times in the course of a few months and then sold the properties on the basis of the high income. Sales of individual units of apartment houses in increasing numbers brought demands for legislative investigation and supervision. "One of the favorite devices of the promoter of such a scheme," it was reported, "is to force up rents to show a profit upon an inflated valuation, then tenants are ordered to move out or buy their apartments. There are often several mortgages on the property. The equity is split up into shares and each tenant must buy the shares which represent his apartment."[8]

Unfortunately, there are no reliable data to indicate the extent of these practices. Probably the majority of the landlords treated their tenants reasonably, but the small minority who acted otherwise coerced many to move, to pay extortionate rents, or to take refuge in ownership, if possible; and there were many tenants who were never victims but who constantly feared that they might be next. Though the temper of the times was clearly set against controls, the consequences of the shortage were serious enough to make the Special Commission on the Necessaries of Life thankful that rent riots and bloodshed did not occur in Boston, as was the case in other cities.[9]

Data on tenure trends in the 1920's are available only for the city of Boston. They indicate that by the end of the decade ownership had jumped from 18.5 per cent to 26.1 per cent. (See Table 8.) Actually, the figures only indicate the net changes. Since 1926 the effects of inflated valuations and excessive financial commitments had made themselves felt in a much heavier foreclosure rate.[10] The speculative apartment-house boom later in the decade also obscures somewhat in an over-all average the ownership shifts that occurred from 1920 to 1925. And most of the building of new homes took place in suburban areas. Therefore, the increase of ownership in Boston proper, where multifamily units were generally built, further underlines the scale of the change in tenure. The figures are even more interesting if it is remembered that the remodeling and creation of small apartments, induced by high rents and sanguine profit expectations, might have offset some of the trend toward ownership.

Despite the absence of records indicating the changes that occurred, it is possible and perhaps useful to hazard a rough approximation of the actual tenure shifts. The total increase in ownership between 1920 and 1930 is known. If the number of dwelling units which were built for ownership between 1920 and 1930 could be determined, the difference between this figure and the total increase in ownership between 1920 and 1930 would constitute the number of net transfers from tenancy to ownership.[11]

The proportion of dwelling units built for owner occupancy is not available. However, we can venture some estimates of these proportions. Useful bench-mark data for this purpose are the known percentages of owner-occupied dwelling units, by type of structure for 1940, 1950, and 1956. These existing percentages can be compared with the maximum possible owner-occupancy percentages, assuming that private or cooperative ownership of individual apartments is a negligible phenomenon. Thus, 100 per cent owner occupancy is possible for dwelling units in one-family structures, 50 per cent for two-family structures, 33⅓ per cent and 25 per cent for three- and four-family structures respectively, and 20 per cent or less for five- and more family structures. Actual owner-occupancy percentages, as Table 9 indicates, were naturally lower. The proportion of new dwellings built during the 1920's for owner occupancy will lie somewhere between the ranges of these two groups of percentages.

To avoid overstatement of the number of transfers that occurred, the proportion of newly built dwelling units which are assumed to be occupied by the owners should be higher rather than lower than the proportion of newly built dwelling units which actually were occupied by the owners. Therefore, we are deliberately influencing the direction of error when we estimate that the proportion of such newly built owner-occupied dwelling units was approximately 95 per cent for the one-family detached house, 45 per cent for the dwelling units in two-family structures, 25 per cent for the dwelling units in three- and four-family structures, and 5 per cent for the dwelling units in apartment structures for five and more families. These estimates, although crude, will give us a rough

TABLE 9. *Ratio of owner-occupied dwelling units to total dwelling units, 1940 and 1950, and estimated number and per cent of dwelling units built for ownership in Boston City, 1920–1929, by type of structure*

Type of structure	Ratio of owner-occupied dwelling units to total dwelling units (per cent)		Per cent of dwelling units built for ownership		Total number of dwelling units built 1920–1929 (5)	Estimated number of dwelling units built for ownership 1920–1929 (col. 4 × col. 5) (6)
	1940 (1)	1950 (2)	Maximum (3)	Estimated (4)		
1-family	71	87	100	95	4,020	3,819
2-family	28	41	50	45	8,025	3,611
3–4-family	13	18	25–33	25	5,410	1,353
5-family and more	2	4	20 or less	5	10,581	529
Total					28,036	9,312

Source: Cols. 1 and 5: Sixteenth Census, U.S., 1940, *Housing, Second Series, General Characteristics*, Table 4, p. 9; *Characteristics by Type of Structure*, "Regions, States, Cities of 100,000 or more and Principal Metropolitan Districts," Tables B-1 and C-1, pp. 160–161. Col. 2: Seventeenth Census, U.S., 1950, *Housing*, vol. 1, part 3, Table 17, p. 21–14.

indication of the number of dwelling units which shifted their tenure.

Table 9 indicates that 28,036 dwelling units were built between 1920 and 1930. Of these, 4,020 were one-family dwelling units, 8,025 were dwelling units in two-family structures, 5,410 were dwelling units in three- and four-family structures, and 10,581 were dwelling units in structures containing five and more families. If our estimated percentages are applied to the total dwelling units of each type erected during the decade, then the probable maximum total number of dwelling units built for owner occupancy was approximately 9,312. Owner-occupied units, however, increased from 30,132 to 46,014 from 1920 to 1930 or 15,882.[12] The difference between the increase in total owned dwelling units and the number of dwelling units built for owner occupancy is 6,570 and represents the increase in ownership attributable to the net shifts in tenure. The shifts add up to 41 per cent of the total increase in owned units. The proportion is quite large. If the assumptions employed in this analysis are reasonably correct, then the evidence, at least for Boston's experience during the 1920's, tends to cast doubt on the view that high rents in a free market will significantly curb the pressure for rental dwelling units to shift their tenure.

POSTWAR CONSTRUCTION IN A FREE MARKET

Few dwelling units were built in the city of Boston in 1918 due to the war. And though rents and sales prices rose, only 481 dwelling units were built in 1919 and 320 in 1920. Approximately 878 were built in 1921, which also represented a very low volume of construction, despite the fact that the 1920 record was more than doubled. During this period the pace of all types of construction was sluggish. (See Chart 8 based on Table 10.)

"Banks and large financial organizations," it was reported, "are not willing to finance large-scale building operations at present costs. Prices have not sufficiently liquidated. Consequently construction has begun on the basis of the construction of one- or two-family houses which are sold before others are commenced."[13]

Following the postwar recession, the amount of residential construction rose sharply and steadily. Although the number of new dwelling units in multifamily houses increased, and although the dwelling units in this type of structure were the most numerous in the city of Boston, percentagewise the multifamily house steadily

Permits issued

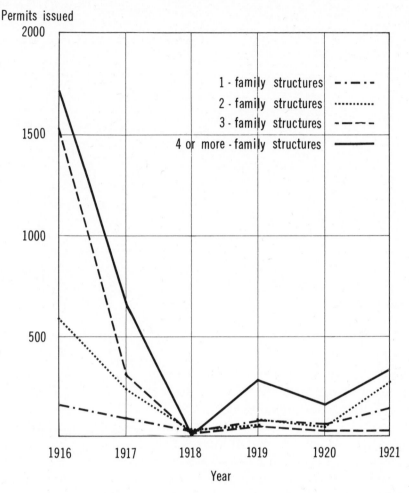

Chart 8. Number of building permits by type of structure, issued in Boston, 1916–1921
Source: Table 10

declined as construction of other housing, particularly two-family houses, took hold. During the second half of the decade, the rate of construction was high except for a slump first in 1926 and then again in 1929, the latter year marking the decline preceding the depression of the 1930's. The building of two-family structures proceeded at a firm pace, averaging about 34 per cent of the total new building in Boston City for 1925–1929 (Chart 9 based on Table 11). The number of one-family houses built in the city during this

TABLE 10.   *Number and per cent of dwelling units, by type of structure, for which building permits were issued in Boston, 1916–1921*

Year	Total number of dwelling units	Dwelling units built in—							
		1-family structures		2-family structures		3-family structures		4- or more family structures	
		No.	% of total	No.	% of total	No.	% of total	No.[a]	% of total
1916	3965	155	4	582	15	1509	38	1719	43
1917	1293	84	7	234	18	318	25	657	51
1918	37	15	41	16	43	6	16	0	—
1919	481	74	15	76	16	52	11	279	58
1920	320	63	20	50	16	51	16	156	49
1921	878	138	16	266	30	135	15	339	39

[a] This column was computed by subtracting total dwelling units from the totals for one-, two-, and three-family units.

Source: Computed from Boston Building Department, "Annual Statistical Reports," 1916–1921.

period was small, amounting to about 17 per cent of the total. Three-family structures, which enjoyed a slight spurt in 1925, averaged generally about 15 per cent of the total volume. Though the per cent distribution of dwelling units in structures with five and more families declined approximately 11 per cent during the second half of the decade, these dwelling units still represented the modal units for Boston City for the entire decade.[14]

For the Boston metropolitan area, however, the one-family house was clearly the basic building type during the 1920's averaging at least 46 per cent[15] of the total dwelling units erected (Chart 9). Structures with two dwelling units were second, comprising about 30 per cent of the total new construction; structures with five and more dwelling units were third, with about 16 per cent of the total; and dwelling units in three- and four-family structures trailed behind the rest with a total of 9 per cent.

In summary, all building following the war was definitely retarded, probably due to the dislocation, uncertainties, and cost maladjustments of the industry. When construction did commence, the building of one-family houses took priority for the metropolitan area as a whole. Within Boston City, however, the building of one-family

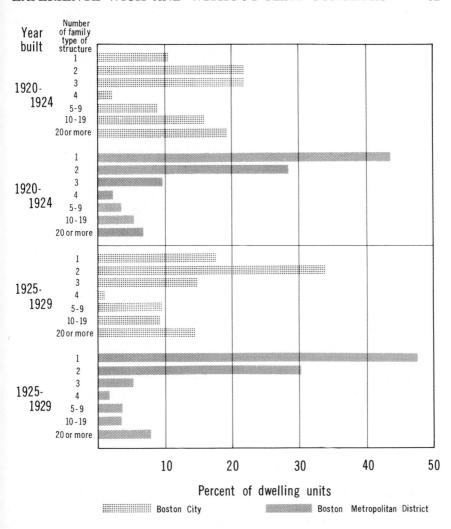

Chart 9. Per cent of dwelling units by type of structure in Boston City and Boston Metropolitan District built during 1920–1924 and 1925–1929 Source: Table 11

houses was both tardy and negligible, which indicates that the observation by Naigles that single-family houses were the unchallenged construction type during the 1920's requires at least a locational qualification.[16] All types of building, including single- and two-family houses as well as multifamily construction, reached high levels near the end of the decade. Since prices for all types of new construction were generally steep, only the top income groups or

TABLE 11. *Number and per cent of dwelling units in Boston City and Boston Metropolitan District built during 1920–1924, 1925–1929 and 1920–1929, by type of structure*

Type of structure	Dwelling units built in Boston City[a]						Dwelling units built in Boston Metropolitan District[a]					
	1920–1929		1920–1924		1925–1929		1920–1929		1920–1924		1925–1929	
	Number	% of total	Number	% of total	Number	% of total	Number	% of total	Number	% of total	Number	% of total
1-Family	4,020	14	1,270	11	2,750	17	51,013	46	19,780	44	31,233	48
2-Family	8,025	29	2,648	22	5,377	34	32,976	30	13,091	29	19,885	30
3-Family	4,973	18	2,637	22	2,336	15	7,834	7	4,394	10	3,440	5
4-Family	437	2	270	2	167	1	2,166	2	1,031	2	1,135	2
5-9-Family	2,608	10	1,070	9	1,538	10	4,056	4	1,604	4	2,452	4
10-19-Family	3,355	12	1,908	16	1,447	9	4,736	4	2,414	5	2,322	4
20-Family and more	4,618	16	2,329	19	2,289	14	8,327	8	3,105	7	5,222	8
Total[b]	28,036	100	12,132	100	15,904	100	111,108	100	45,419	100	65,689	100

[a] The data are based on dwelling units in Boston in 1940 by year built.

[b] The total does not include the category "Other Dwelling Places." There were also approximately 27,000 dwelling units in Boston City and 73,000 in the Boston metropolitan area which did not report the year built. A considerable percentage of these unreported units were probably built before 1920.

Source: Sixteenth Census, U.S., 1940, *Housing, Characteristics by Type of Structure*, "Regions, States, Cities of 100,000 or More and Principal Metropolitan Districts," Tables B-1 and C-1, pp. 160–161.

those able to pay rents of $40 a month or more were directly served.[17]

Therefore, on the basis of Boston's experience, the claim that absence of controls speeds building programs during an early post-war adjustment period appears dubious. On the contrary, the evidence indicates that construction was retarded because of cost distortions and industrial maladjustments. Second, even in a period when the illusion of ever-rising land values was still a strong influence on the incentives for construction of rental housing, the absence of controls did not reverse the pressure for one-family houses as the dominant type. Third, it is possible that some building, especially high-cost construction, may have been stimulated by the free market, due to the pressure on families to leave older but not necessarily cheaper houses; and some building may have occurred which would not have taken place if there had been fears and misapprehensions on the part of builders concerning restrictive government policies. These contentions cannot be checked.

EFFICIENCY, SPACE UTILIZATION, HOUSING SHORTAGE, AND A FREE MARKET

There is general acceptance of the fact that the housing market is imperfect and inefficient. In addition, a housing shortage places landlords in a quasi monopolistic position; and economists generally contend that quasi monopolistic agreements are inefficient. The imposition of terms with few real alternatives for the purchaser is conducive to friction and resentment. Even minor matters are unlikely to be resolved in a mutually satisfactory way. For example, it is painfully evident in time of shortage that many tenants hesitate to make even trivial requests because of fear of the consequences. In a sense, the creation of a tribunal in Massachusetts, the Special Commission on the Necessaries of Life, was an uncertain response to this situation. It intervened and helped to settle amicably, if possible, issues between landlords and tenants involving both monetary and nonmonetary questions. Its job was to discourage landlords from taking undue advantage of their situation and to tackle problems growing out of the failure of landlords to provide customary services, as well as the more explosive situations involving exorbitant rent hikes.[18]

Though higher prices reduced demand and thus provided for

more "economical" use of space, even in the 1920's the severity of the housing shortage was attributed to "extravagant" living and the demand for "modern improvements."[19] Many officials hoped that the depression of 1921 would ease the problem somewhat. Vacancies and lower rents did in fact occur—but in higher-rent apartments; the crisis intensified for the low- and middle-income families. Even more families searched and bid for the less expensive apartments. Old firetraps and slums which had been partially emptied for the first time during the war years were filled once again. Often "no improvements were made—the rent was largely determined by the amount that the tenant who was unable to bargain or move could be forced to pay."[20]

Despite the "economical" use of space, there was still evidence of serious shortage in 1925, according to the last report of the Special Commission on the Necessaries of Life. There were still many complaints of excessive increases of rent, "vacate" notices followed by increases of rent, "colonization" or doubling up of families, and objections to children. In many cases, the high rents served less to reduce the space used than to enrich speculators interested in bolstering inflated sales prices with jacked-up revenues. Not space, but various budget expenditures were often reduced. The Special Commission on the Necessaries of Life observed that many families were paying more than 25 per cent of their income for shelter, some paying "as high as 40 per cent . . . while few are paying less than 25 per cent."[21]

Judging from Boston's experience, therefore, the view that the automatic and impersonal price mechanism apportions space efficiently and economically requires several qualifications. The evidence indicates that because of the inelasticity of supply symptoms of shortage will persist for many years even in a free market. Discrimination against groups deemed less desirable by the landlord occurred precisely because many families needed accomodations. To a large extent, the situation degenerated into a freezing of space but a lowering of real income. For some families, economy of space meant overcrowded conditions in resuscitated slums. Higher-income groups received the first relief from new building and the first relief in the form of vacancies and rent reductions when deflationary trends developed. The position of the lower-and some middle-income groups worsened because of reduced income and an intensified shortage. Income was redistributed largely from lower- and middle-income groups to their landlords;[22] and space economies were imposed primarily on tenants, rather than on owners, who probably had more space to economize.

Rent Control Patterns in Boston

During World War II there were government controls on the prices and rents of existing houses. There were also similar controls on new houses and on the prices and allocation of materials. Following the war, most of the controls were abandoned except those on the rents of existing houses. However, these measures did not constitute a rent freeze. They permitted rent increases in order to compensate for increased costs and for new improvements. Given these relatively flexible measures, what were their effects on tenure shifts, new construction, and the efficiency of space allocation?

Tenure Shifts Under Rent Control

There were several factors affecting tenure, other than rent controls, which distinguished the housing shortage following World War II from the shortage of the 1920's. A relatively normal housing situation had prevailed before World War I, whereas there were signs of a growing shortage nationally and locally by the end of the 1930's.[23] Population growth and shifts, increased income, and retarded construction fundamentally accounted for the tightened market. Then increased income resulting from the defense, war, and postwar prosperity placed extraordinary pressures on housing resources in the direction of steeper rentals, higher sale prices, and the trend toward ownership. The new financing possibilities developed during the 1930's and 1940's aided and abetted these trends. Lengthened amortization periods, lower down payments and interest rates, elimination of secondary financing, Federal Housing Administration insurance, and finally the veterans housing legislation eased the path to ownership. Perhaps the only counterweight to these forces was the depression hangover of pessimism and skepticism which gripped many financial institutions and potential home owners in regard to undertaking long-term commitments based on slender resources and uncertain prospects.

Since the mid-twenties the income of families in the moderate bracket rose 133 per cent, though rising prices nullified much of the gain. Rents for new construction in the Boston area jumped about 150 per cent from 1925 to 1959.[24] Though we lack reliable indices of sale prices during this period for existing housing, a recent study suggests that in 1947 they were on the average slightly higher for old houses than for new ones having comparable space because of speed of acquisition as well as superior location and construction.[25] This situation continued well into the 1950's according to knowledgeable realtors. Control of rents in existing houses, however, kept average rent increases for moderate-income families down until the initial relaxation of the controls in 1947; and it was not until December 31, 1956 that rent controls ended for all of Massachusetts, including Boston.[26]

Since there was a significant increase of income after 1940, better quarters were sought and secured by many; but others were rooted to their existing homes because of the absence of reasonable alternatives. There was much pressure on rental housing because the prices for sales housing were often far beyond the present or anticipated incomes of low- and middle-income families. Rent controls undoubtedly prevented steep rent rises and the accompanying speculation. Yet the income of landlords, especially those owning multifamily properties, increased considerably (though not proportionately to other groups) as a result of 100 per cent occupancy and lower decorating, maintenance, and other costs.[27]

Despite the advantages of lower rents in controlled dwellings, increased real income prompted many middle- and upper-income families to carry out their ownership goals. Other families, often newcomers to the area fed up with overcrowding and apartment hunting, strained resources to the limit and also purchased. Census estimates indicate that, in 1946, 38 per cent of the married veterans in the Boston area did not have separate living quarters.[28] Many veterans used their G.I. privileges, ignoring the bond they signed, hoping that resale profits might be possible or that the government would shoulder the losses, if necessary. Still other families could not or would not take the risk. Many families paid "key money" or "bonuses" to landlords for the privilege of obtaining an apartment. Illegalities flourished, and doubling-up increased.

Under these conditions, how much of a shift toward ownership actually did occur? For Boston City, the proportion of families owning homes increased from 21 per cent in 1940 to 25 per cent in 1950, a rise of 4 per cent; for the metropolitan area during the same period the per cent of owners rose from 36 to 43, a 7 per cent increase.[29] The sample survey of the national housing inventory by the Bureau of the Census in 1956 indicates that the increase in the per cent of ownership since 1950 for the metropolitan area was another 4 per cent.[30] Unfortunately, there are no comparable figures for the Boston metropolitan area during the decade 1920–1930, and there are as yet no data for tenure changes in Boston City following 1950. But if we confine the comparison of ownership trends in two postwar periods to Boston City, we find that the per cent increase of ownership under rent controls in the 1940's is almost half the rise of 7.6 per cent which occurred during the decade of the 1920's. The reason probably is that the lower number of owners forced to buy during the 1940's because of evictions or high rents, and the disinclination or inability of many to purchase at high values, largely offset such additional sales as may have been occasioned by the onus of controls. At any rate, the data available on net tenure changes in Boston City indicate that shifts of tenure did not increase more rapidly under rent controls than during the 1920's without controls. If they had, and it is indeed surprising that they did not, the exceptional conditions referred to earlier in this section would account for at least some of the additional increase of ownership. Also, since rent controls were imposed in 1942, many shifts in tenure probably occurred between 1940 and 1942.

We can attempt a quantitative estimate of the houses that shifted tenure from 1940 to 1956, the year controls ended. The same procedure used for the decade of the 1920's may be employed. However, the previous estimate could only be made for the city of Boston, whereas the data for 1950 and 1956 are only available for the metropolitan area.[31]

The procedure, it will be recalled, was to estimate the number of units, by type, which were built for owner occupancy and then to substract this figure from the total increase of owner-occupied units for the period under review. Ownership percentages for new construction similar to those employed for the 1920's can be assumed, i.e., 95 per cent, 45 per cent, 25 per cent, and 5 per cent for one, two, three and four, and five and more family units respectively. Table 12 indicates that 85,496 dwelling units were added between 1940 and 1956. If we apply the ownership percentages to the new dwelling units, by type, we get an estimate of 35,187 as the number of units built for owner occupancy between 1940 and 1956. Subtracting this figure from 126,280, the total increase of owner-occupied units during this period, leaves 91,093 owned units result-

TABLE 12. *Ratio of owner-occupied dwelling units to total occupied dwelling units, 1940, 1950, and 1956, and estimated number and per cent of dwelling units built for ownership in metropolitan Boston, 1940–1956, by type of structure*

| Type of structure | Ratio of owner-occupied dwelling units to total occupied dwelling units (per cent) | | | Per cent of dwelling units built for ownership | | Total number of dwelling units | | New dwelling units added, 1940–1956 | Estimated number of dwelling units built for ownership, 1940–1956 (col. 5 × col. 8) |
	1940 (1)	1950 (2)	1956 (3)	Maximum (4)	Estimated[a] (5)	1940 (6)	1956 (7)	(8)	(9)
1-Family[b]	71	87	91	100	95	230,788	262,036	31,248	29,685
2-Family[b]	28	41	42	50	45	185,638	181,618	(−4,020)	} 3,235
3-4-Family	13	18	22	25–33	25	141,821	154,760	12,939	
5-Family and more	2	4	3	20 or less	5	92,945	138,274	45,329	2,267
Total	—	—	—	—	—	651,192	736,688	85,496	35,187

[a] See text for a discussion of these percentages.

[b] The 1950 Census had a classification called one- and two-family dwelling units, semi-detached. The category included units in semi-detached structures containing one dwelling unit and those in similar structures containing two dwelling units. Because of the ambiguity as to the actual type, one-third were assigned to the one-family units, two-thirds to the two-family units. One-family attached units were included in the one-family category.

Source: Columns 1 and 6: Sixteenth Census, U.S., 1940, *Housing, Second Series, General Characteristics*, Table 4, p. 9; Column 2: Seventeenth Census, U.S., 1950, *Housing*, vol. 1, part 3, Table 17, p. 21:14; Column 7: 1956 National Housing Inventory, vol. 3, part 3, Table 1, p. 11.

ing from net transfers, or approximately 72 per cent of the total increase in ownership.

Although we cannot compare the per cent of transfers for the city of Boston and for the metropolitan area, both are substantial. The higher rate of transfers for the metropolitan area was to be expected for two reasons, quite aside from the fact that stronger pressures toward ownership prevailed after World War II. First, in developing these estimates, the same percentages of dwelling units built for ownership were used for Boston City and the metropolitan area. This assumption probably led to an overstatement of transfers for the 1940–1956 period. This is because the percentage of houses built for ownership, by type of structure, was probably higher for the metropolitan area. If we used higher percentages, the net transfers of tenure would be correspondingly reduced. Second, the greatest number of shifts of tenure occurs in one- and two-family units, and these are largely concentrated in the suburban areas. In metropolitan Boston 33 per cent of the housing consists of one-dwelling-unit detached structures and 27 per cent of two-family units, compared to 11 per cent and 21 per cent, respectively, for Boston City.[32]

Despite the limitations of the data, one may conclude that the tendency toward shifts of tenure remains high both with and without rent controls. Lifting of rent controls on existing houses eliminates few, if any, of these forces and may even intensify them. If sufficient social justification exists for arresting the process, measures must be adopted to minimize the need and ability to purchase as well as the lure of windfall profits in the sale of houses.

POSTWAR CONSTRUCTION UNDER RENT CONTROLS

The effect of rent controls on new construction in Boston is less clear, partly because of the limitations of the data and partly because we have no basis for gauging how much construction might have occurred without the unfavorable climate of controls. We know that the market was large and that controls did not apply to new construction. We know, too, that the pattern of building which developed during the early years after World War II was comparable to the pattern of the early 1920's, and that the relative volume of construction was about the same during the two periods. These trends at the very least cast some doubt on the easy assumption that rent controls significantly impede construction.

Thus, construction in Boston City following World War I did

not achieve any volume before 1922, that is, not until the fourth year of peace. The total number of dwelling units built for the four years following World War I was 5113, compared to 5153 for the same number of years following World War II.[33] That this is so is surprising. A much larger proportion of the dwelling units were built in peripheral areas in the 1940's and 1950's compared to the 1920's. Therefore, the building of almost the same number of units for Boston City during these two periods indicates that the 1940–1949 volume is relatively high.

New dwelling units for Boston City were also made available through conversions. From 1946 through 1956, a total of 4946 new dwelling units were placed on the market this way, an average of approximately 495 dwelling units each year.[34] During the three years after the ending of rent controls in 1956, the average number of conversions dropped to about 325 per year. Unfortunately, no record exists of the number of conversions that occurred during the 1920's.

Data on construction for the metropolitan area are more relevant but more elusive. About 35,000 dwelling units were built between 1945 and 1949 according to the 1950 Census.[35] In contrast to this performance, about 45,500 dwelling units were built for the metropolitan area between 1920 and 1924.[36] However, these two postwar periods are not directly comparable. The figure of 45,500 is probably high for comparison purposes by at least 5,000 or 6,000 units, because the poor record of 1919 was omitted whereas the high volume of construction of 1924 was included.

We also have some data for comparing the amount of housing erected from April 1950 to December 1956 with that erected from 1920 to 1929, i.e., the record achieved at the height of the building boom during the "roaring twenties." For the ten-year period from 1920 to 1929 a total of 111,108 dwelling units were built: 45,419 dwelling units from 1920 to 1924; and 65,689 from 1925 to 1929. The average was approximately 11,000 dwelling units a year, or about 9,000 each year during the first period, and 13,000 a year during the second. These data, since they are based on census records of the year built, include units made available through conversions and other means; but they probably understate the volume since they do not include units lost through demolitions and mergers between 1920 and 1930.[37] The sample survey of the national housing inventory indicates that 91,000 dwelling units were built during the 6¾ year period from 1950 to 1956, giving an annual average production rate of 13,500. Of these, new dwelling units erected totaled 69,300 units, or a rate of about 10,300 a year; conversions, approximately 15,000 units, or 2,200 a year; and other sources supplied about 7,000 additional units, or 1,000 a year.[38]

The total new units provided per family or household appears roughly the same for the two periods. It is true we do not know precisely how much the number of households increased during the 1920's compared to the increase in the 1950's. But an estimate based on the population increase in the Boston Standard Metropolitan Area and average family size during the 1920's suggests that the increase in households was roughly the same as the 1950's or somewhat larger during the earlier period.[39]

The record on rental housing is less favorable. During the 1920's about 40 to 50 per cent of the dwelling units built were probably for rent.[40] Of the total new dwelling units created in the Boston metropolitan area between 1950 and 1956 only 35 per cent were for rent, according to the sample survey of the 1956 housing inventory. Even this volume of rental units would not have been achieved, without the special encouragement provided by the federal government's rental housing insurance program.[41] This decline, however, cannot be cavalierly ascribed to rent controls. It is altogether possible that, even if there had been a free market following World War II, a smaller proportion of dwelling units would have been built in this period than in the one following World War I. There is a long-term trend in the direction of ownership which reflects both consumer and builder preferences. We know that since the 1920's rental investment incentives have faded, the old faith in perpetually rising land values (and perpetually increasing population) in the central area has disappeared, strong fears have prevailed concerning future competition and risks (including rent control), and builders have been determined not to tie up much capital in rental housing developments unless they could "mortgage out." For these reasons, it is remarkable that Boston's record following World War II was as good as it actually was.

EFFICIENCY, SPACE UTILIZATION, HOUSING SHORTAGE, AND RENT
    CONTROLS

As indicated in Appendix B, aside from the normal imperfections of the housing market, quasi monopolistic elements still existed under rent controls. More equal bargaining positions, however, were achieved. The relative inability of tenants to find alternative accommodations was matched by the relative inability of landlords to take advantage of the situation. But tension and friction still occurred due to the constraints which each party on occasion exploited.

With both higher income and rent controls one could expect less crowding. The evidence confirms this expectation. A survey which the Census conducted in 1947 indicated that 6 per cent of the total households and 14 per cent of the veterans' households contained husband-wife sub-families.[42] By 1950, however, less than 3.3 per cent of the occupied dwelling units in the city of Boston and 2.2 per cent in the metropolitan area had 1.5 or more persons per room.[43] There was also a decrease from 1940 to 1950 in the number of occupied dwelling units in the metropolitan area containing more than 0.76 to 1.00 persons per room (Chart 10, based on Table 13). Another indicator is the median number of persons per occupied unit. For the metropolitan area it was 3.1 in 1956 and 3.2 in 1950, compared with 3.3 in 1947 and 3.9 in 1940.

These general trends are common knowledge. What is disputed, however, is the extent to which these same trends might have occurred without rent control, simply as the result of increased income. Though we cannot resolve this question, we can examine the situation of both renters and owners, and some of the details of the changes in the way they used space. Such an examination should shed some light on the charge that renters used space inefficiently under rent controls and that a free market might have induced less "extravagant" use of space.

On the whole there was less space in tenant-occupied than in owner-occupied units in 1940. Relatively, twice as many renters had more than 1.00 persons per room; and about 73 per cent of the owner-occupied units had 0.75 or less persons per room, compared to 56 per cent of the tenant families (Chart 10).

How did this pattern of space utilization fare under controls? In general, there was less crowding (Chart 10). From 1940 to 1950 the percentage distribution of units with one or more persons per room dropped 2 per cent for both owner- and tenant-occupied units. Renters, too, improved their position somewhat in relation to owners. Proportionately, there were 2 per cent more owner-occupied dwelling units with 0.76 to one person per room, compared to a decrease of 2 per cent for tenant-occupied units; and, relatively,

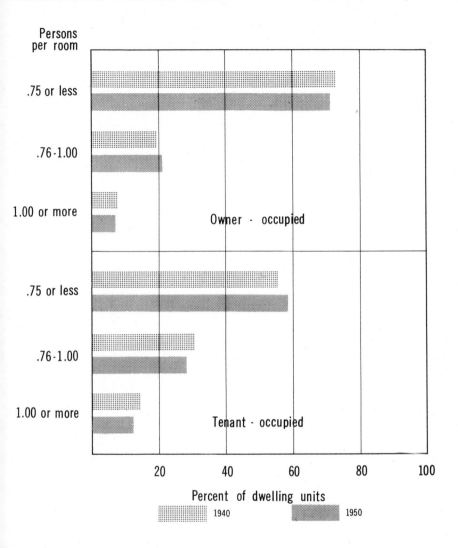

Chart 10. Per cent of owner-occupied and tenant-occupied dwellings by persons per room, 1940 and 1950
Source: Table 13

there were fewer owner-occupied units with 0.75 or less persons per room and somewhat more tenant-occupied units in this category.

These gross data, however, are still not precise enough to explain the character of the variation in the pattern of space utilization. Tables 14 and 15 provide more of these details. They show the households of different size for owners and for tenants and the dwelling units of different size in which they lived for the years

TABLE 13. *Number and per cent of owner-occupied and tenant-occupied dwelling units in Boston Standard Metropolitan Area, 1940 and 1950, by the number of persons per room*

Number of persons per room	Owner-occupied dwelling units				Tenant-occupied dwelling units				All dwelling units			
	1940		1950		1940		1950		1940		1950	
	Number	% of total	Number	% of total	Number	% of total	Number	% of total	Number	% of total	Number	% of total
0.75 or less	157,915	73.0	199,900	71.6	211,146	55.5	205,190	58.1	369,061	61.8	405,090	64.0
0.76 to 1.00	41,635	19.2	58,230	20.9	115,474	30.2	100,030	28.4	157,109	26.3	158,260	25.0
1.00 or more	16,904	7.8	16,755	6.2	54,951	14.4	43,505	12.3	71,855	12.0	60,260	9.5
Not reported	—	—	3,650	1.3	—	—	4,910	1.4	—	—	8,560	1.4
Total	216,454	100	278,535	100	381,571	100	353,635	100	598,025	100	632,170	100

Source: Sixteenth Census, U.S., 1940, *Housing, Second Series, General Characteristics*, "Massachusetts," Table 10, p. 25; and Seventeenth Census, U.S., 1950, *Housing*, vol. 2, part 2, Table A-7, p. 26–9.

TABLE 14. *Total owner and total tenant households in dwelling units by number of rooms, classified by number of persons in dwelling units by number of rooms, Boston Standard Metropolitan Area, 1950 and 1956*

Number of rooms	Total households				1 person				2 persons				3 persons			
	Owner		Tenant		Owner		Tenant		Owner		Tenant		Owner		Tenant	
	1950	1956	1950	1956	1950	1956	1950	1956	1950	1956	1950	1956	1950	1956	1950	1956
1–2	1,835	1,418	33,820	29,948	650	716	16,025	18,110	670	227	12,770	7,971	195	475	3,545	3,152
3	5,055	5,487	56,530	60,540	1,150	1,604	10,335	14,051	2,125	2,434	24,580	29,433	1,040	978	13,165	11,634
4	25,075	36,818	84,975	93,356	2,025	5,342	6,235	13,105	8,475	12,317	24,700	29,758	6,550	7,610	22,600	23,112
5	56,105	82,556	97,815	96,863	2,770	4,401	3,780	5,835	14,865	23,516	22,790	26,839	14,680	21,974	25,540	17,746
6[a]	82,140	102,104	75,585	68,857	2,975	5,579	2,080	3,163	17,150	20,676	12,820	11,215	18,560	20,056	16,935	14,644
7 +	104,675	116,504			3,375	5,030			17,845	19,892			20,190	23,210		
NR[b]	3,650	585	4,910	789	690	244	1,385	—	985		1,600	248	670	237	760	—
Total	278,535	345,472	353,635	350,353	13,635	29,916	39,840	54,264	62,115	79,062	99,260	105,464	61,885	74,540	82,545	70,288

Number of rooms	4 persons				5 persons				6 and more persons			
	Owner		Tenant		Owner		Tenant		Owner		Tenant	
	1950	1956	1950	1956	1950	1956	1950	1956	1950	1956	1950	1956
1–2	150	—	940	715	85	—	330		85	—	210	
3	450	471	5,835	4,203	180	—	1,785	765	110	—	830	454
4	5,090	6,038	18,755	17,119	1,865	3,927	8,195	7,028	1,070	1,584	4,490	3,234
5	12,750	16,804	22,535	22,595	6,540	9,353	12,925	11,871	4,500	6,508	10,245	11,977
6[a]	19,730	26,161	17,580	18,953	12,905	16,713	12,415	10,398	10,820	12,919	13,755	10,484
7 +	22,000	22,662			17,125	22,455			24,140	23,255		
NR[b]	595	104	625	488	400	—	320	53	310	—	220	—
Total	60,765	72,240	66,270	64,073	39,100	52,448	35,970	30,115	41,035	44,266	29,750	26,149

[a] For tenant households this category represents 6 and more rooms.
[b] Not reported.
Source: Seventeenth Census, U.S. Housing, Vol. II, Part 2, Table A-5, pp. 26–27 and 26–28.

TABLE 15. *Per cent and total owner households and total tenant households classified by number of persons in dwelling units, by number of rooms, Boston Standard Metropolitan Area, 1950 and 1956*

Number of rooms	Total households				1 person				2 persons				3 persons			
	Owner		Tenant		Owner		Tenant		Owner		Tenant		Owner		Tenant	
	1950	1956	1950	1956	1950	1956	1950	1956	1950	1956	1950	1956	1950	1956	1950	1956
1–2	.7	.4	9.6	8.5	4.8	3.2	40.1	33.4	1.1	.3	12.8	7.6	.3	.6	4.3	4.5
3	1.8	1.6	16.0	17.4	8.4	7.0	25.9	25.9	3.4	3.1	24.7	28.0	1.7	1.3	16.0	16.6
4	9.0	10.6	24.0	26.6	14.9	23.2	15.6	24.2	13.6	15.6	25.0	28.2	10.6	10.2	27.4	32.9
5	20.1	23.9	27.7	27.6	20.4	19.4	9.5	10.7	23.8	29.8	23.0	25.5	23.7	29.4	31.0	25.2
6ᵃ	29.4	29.6	21.4	19.6	21.8	24.3	5.5	5.8	27.6	26.2	12.9	10.6	30.0	27.0	20.4	20.8
7+	37.8	33.7			24.7	22.0			28.7	25.1			32.7	31.2		
NRᵇ	1.3	.2	1.4	.2	5.0	.9	3.5	—	1.6	.2	1.6	.2	1.1	.3	.9	—
Total	100	100	100	100	100	100	100	100	100	100	100	100	100	100	100	100

Number of rooms	4 persons				5 persons				6 or more persons			
	Owner		Tenant		Owner		Tenant		Owner		Tenant	
	1950	1956	1950	1956	1950	1956	1950	1956	1950	1956	1950	1956
1–2	.2	—	1.4	1.1	.2	—	.9	—	.2	—	.7	—
3	.7	.7	8.8	6.6	.5	—	5.0	2.5	.3	—	2.8	1.7
4	8.4	8.4	28.2	26.8	4.8	7.4	22.7	23.3	2.6	3.6	15.1	12.4
5	21.0	23.3	34.0	35.2	16.7	17.8	36.0	39.4	11.0	14.7	34.4	45.8
6ᵃ	32.4	36.2	26.6	29.6	33.0	32.0	34.5	34.5	26.4	29.2	46.3	40.1
7+	36.3	31.3			43.7	42.9			58.7	52.5		
NRᵇ		.1	.9	.7	1.2	—	.9	.2	.8	—	.7	—
Total	100	100	100	100	100	100	100	100	100	100	100	100

ᵃ For tenant households this group represents 6 and more rooms.
ᵇ Not reported.
Source: Computed from Table 14.

1950 and 1956. The trends are summarized in Chart 11. These data do not lend themselves to quick generalizations. First, they may not be fully characteristic of the entire control period. Probably there was less crowding at this time because more housing had become available and the end of the shortage was in sight. Nonetheless, the pattern of changes that occurred is of interest. For example, the chart does not show a simple trend toward the use of more space

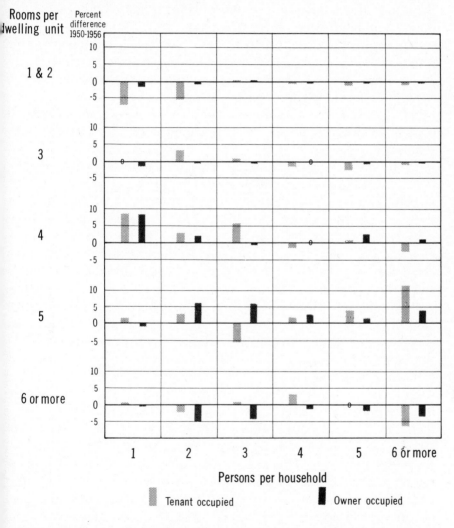

Chart 11. Difference from 1950 to 1956 in per cent of total owner-occupied households and in total tenant-occupied households in Boston Standard Metropolitan Area, by number of persons in dwelling units, by number of rooms
Source: Tables 14 and 15

by tenant or owner households of varying size. It indicates, rather, that in some cases tenants used somewhat larger units (one-person households using proportionately more four-room dwelling units, and four-person households using proportionately more dwelling units with five, six, or more rooms); and that in some cases tenants used smaller units (two-person households occupying proportionately fewer six-room units; three-person households occupying fewer five-room units; and six or more person households occupying proportionately fewer six or more room units). Similarly, owners in some instances occupied more space (one-person households using proportionately more four-room units; and two-person households using more four- and five-room units); and sometimes owner households occupied less space (five-person households occupying proportionately more four-room units; and six-person households occupying proportionately fewer dwelling units of seven and more rooms).

The data suggest, too, that many larger households had difficulty in obtaining accommodations of adequate size; and that, largely because of the shift in rental tenure to ownership, the proportion of owner households with three to six and more persons increased, whereas the number of tenants in these categories decreased. For both owners and tenants, there was also a large per cent increase of one- and two-person households; and in certain cases there was a substantial increase in the size of the dwelling units they occupied. Some of these trends were influenced by rent control, but probably much less than supposed. They are familiar accompaniments of prosperity, and they were also influenced by the type of dwelling units supplied during this period.[44] For, given a housing shortage, the type of dwelling units supplied does not simply reflect household requirements; it also inescapably shapes the occupancy characteristics. Thus, from 1950 to 1956 the greatest increases in supply for owners came in four- and five-room units, which rose 1.4 per cent and 3.6 per cent respectively; but units of seven and more rooms declined 4.4 per cent. Tenant-occupied dwelling units had increases in three- and four-room units of 1.8 per cent and 2.5 per cent respectively, and approximately a one per cent decline in the percentage of one-, two-, five-, six-, and seven-room dwelling units. These sizes of the dwelling units supplied probably reduced the opportunities for obtaining more space on the part of large households, whether owners or tenants; and they increased the opportunities for smaller households to obtain more space, whether owners or tenants.

The upshot of these trends is probably best summarized in Chart 12 (based on data assembled in Table 16). It shows the average number of rooms per household for owner households by size and for tenant households by size. It also compares these data with the average number of rooms per household for all owner households and all tenant households. These data indicate that the owner

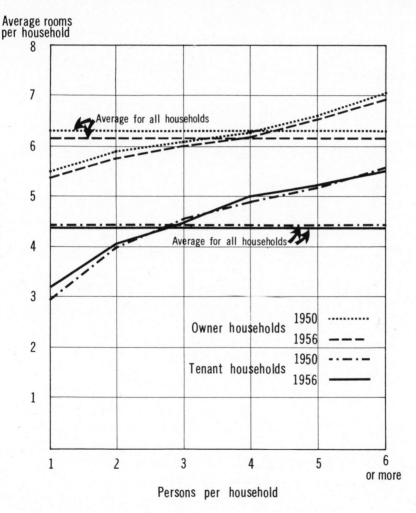

Chart 12. Average rooms per household in total owner and total tenant households in 1950 and 1956 in Boston Standard Metropolitan Area, by number of persons per household

TABLE 16. *Total number of household rooms, total number of households, and average number of rooms per household, by number of persons per household, for owner and for tenant households, Boston Standard Metropolitan Area, 1950 and 1956*

Number of persons per household	Year	Total no. of household rooms[a]		Total no. of households		Average number of rooms per household	
		Owner	Tenant	Owner	Tenant	Owner	Tenant
1 person	1950	71,845	114,213	12,945	38,455	5.52	2.97
	1956	123,259	173,599	22,672	54,264	5.44	3.20
2 persons	1950	361,707	391,524	61,130	97,660	5.92	4.01
	1956	455,716	427,649	79,062	105,216	5.76	4.06
3 persons	1950	373,873	372,714	61,215	81,785	6.11	4.56
	1956	447,651	315,790	74,303	70,288	6.03	4.49
4 persons	1950	377,865	321,256	60,170	65,645	6.28	4.89
	1956	445,580	318,613	72,136	63,585	6.18	5.01
5 persons	1950	255,257	184,051	38,700	35,650	6.60	5.16
	1956	342,391	157,349	52,448	30,062	6.53	5.23
6 and more persons	1950	290,080	164,169	41,725	29,530	7.07	5.56
	1956	307,081	144,425	44,266	26,149	6.94	5.52
Total	1950	1,730,627	1,547,927	274,885	348,725	6.30	4.44
	1956	2,121,678	1,537,425	344,887	349,564	6.15	4.40

[a] These data are derived from Tables 14 and 15. The number of household rooms in each category of household size (persons per household) was obtained by multiplying the number of households by the number of rooms in the dwelling units they occupied. (For example, if there were 1000 two-person households occupying three-room dwelling units, they are said to occupy 3000 household rooms). The total household rooms per household size was obtained by adding the number of household rooms in dwelling units of different size. However, the Census data for one- and two-room dwelling units were lumped together for 1956, but not for 1950. Therefore, in making these computations we applied the proportion of one- to two-room dwelling units in existence in 1950 to the 1956 data. These proportions ranged from 1.2 to 1.9. On the same basis dwelling units of seven and more rooms were counted as 6.4- to 6.7-room units; and dwelling units of seven and more rooms were counted as 7.9- to 8.2-room units. This procedure was followed for owners and tenants by household size, both for 1950 and 1956. Finally, the average number of rooms per household

households had more space, i.e., an average number of rooms per household of 6.30 in 1950 and 6.15 in 1956, compared with 4.44 and 4.40 for tenants for the same periods. Owner households had about one fifth more rooms in 1956 than in 1950 whereas those of tenants diminished slightly. But as the chart indicates, there are very small differences between owners and tenants from 1950 to 1956 in the average number of rooms per household for households of different size. The differences are never more than 0.1 or 0.2 for owners or tenants. However, if the chart shows any tendency at all, it is for tenants to be using slightly more space and for owners to be using slightly less space. This trend is in line with the similar tendency disclosed by the data on persons per room.

To sum up: given a severe housing shortage and increased income, Boston's experiences with and without controls do not bear out the simple view that rent controls force a much greater shift in the tenure of rental housing, or a dampening of new construction, or much more uneconomical and inefficient use of housing resources than would normally be the case. Basic shifts in tenure occur both with and without controls. These transfers are attributable primarily to other deep-seated forces, such as a seller's market and higher income. Similarly, slow and inefficient production of rental housing is a result of many obstacles. It is doubtful whether either the removal of reasonable rent controls on existing housing or their maintenance over a short-term period would affect the entrepreneur's decision to build, which depends essentially on market prospects. Finally, the exchange mechanism for housing under a free but imperfect market is essentially inefficient. It is reckless to pontificate on whether controls increase or diminish this inefficiency. In any case, the data indicate a trend toward less crowding, and both increases and decreases in the intensity of the use of space in Boston during the period of rent controls. It is not possible to say which increases are extravagant and which decreases are not. On the whole the position of tenants in relation to owners improved, but owners were less crowded to begin with; and also a large proportion of the dwellings with more rooms were vacated by tenants with smaller families. Finally, if there had been no rent controls, it is likely that the brunt of the economies would have fallen largely on tenants, who have less space, and it is not at all certain how much of the net effect would have been to redistribute space rather than income.

PART TWO:

BOSTON'S RESIDENTIAL
GROWTH AND DEVELOPMENT:
HISTORY AND THEORY

CHAPTER 5

Residential Growth and Development

Part One of this book focused on the economic progress of middle-income families and some of the issues that emerged in supplying adequate housing for them. Part Two now shifts the focus to the impact of economic progress in determining the structure and growth of Boston's residential areas. For as Boston's population and income grew, significant changes occurred in its residential patterns. A glance at the history of land use in Boston will help to establish what they were and the role of rising income and rising standards of demand in shaping them. This summary perspective will provide a basis for an evaluation in the next chapter of the existing generalizations on the growth and structure of residential areas, and the implications of these ideas for urban policy.

BOSTON'S RESIDENTIAL GROWTH AND STRUCTURE

1750–1830

Prior to 1775, Boston's North End was the "court end" of town where the governor, his officials, friends, and other well-to-do families lived. Between 1790 and 1810 new fashionable areas in-habited by the wealthier merchants and tradesmen also began to develop on Beacon and Cotton hills, the Fort Hill–Pearl Street areas, and along Summer, Winter, Franklin, and High streets. The market center was at Dock Square and most manufacturing located around the Mill Pond.[1]

By 1830, land uses had become more differentiated. Faneuil Hall constituted the market center; upper Washington Street contained the dry goods district; Fulton Street, the shoe and leather enterprises; State Street was the financial center; and the area south of the business district served warehouses and hardware establishments.[2] The North End, following the departure of the British officials and their Tory adherents, started on its decline. Skilled artisans subsequently occupied the area, but it soon was overrun by somewhat the same low-income groups and disreputable "dives" that gave notoriety to the northern slope of Beacon Hill.[3] Middle-income groups lived in parts of the West End, the North End, and in many of the streets near the central business area. The most fashionable residential districts were Beacon Hill, the Bowdoin and Pemberton Square area on the west, the Fort Hill–Pearl Street district to the south, and also along Tremont Street and Temple Place.[4]

Of course, the town was still quite small, and this specialization of land uses occurred within a short walking distance of the center (Map 2). Though meager evidence is available, it appears that the main lines of differentiation were on the basis of income and to a lesser extent occupation and national origin.[5] The movement by the new upper classes west and south to Beacon Hill, Bowdoin Square, and Fort Hill initiated the first important reorientation of residential areas. It was a response to the population, business, and commercial expansion, and to the growing dissatisfaction with the cramped and older quarters of the North End.[6]

1830–1890

The influx of the migrant and foreign population plus rising income created pressures for more space. The native in-migrants came from declining areas unable to meet the competition from the more fertile western territories,[7] and from smaller communities losing their inhabitants during the first half of the nineteenth century to the larger and rapidly growing manufacturing cities. The great Irish exodus in the 1840's, stimulated by depressed agricultural conditions and the potato blight in Ireland, more than doubled the number of Irish in Boston within a decade. By comparison, normal population expansion, rural in-migration, and the general flows of non-Irish immigrants shrank in significance; and the tide only began to ebb in the 1850's.[8]

The need for space was met by crowding and by more intensive use of land, by the continued reduction or grading of Boston's hills, by the further filling of the coves, and by suburban expansion and annexation.[9] Existing residential areas altered drastically in response to these forces. With the mass arrival of the Irish, the Fort Hill district and the North End became the immigrant center of the city. The Irish newcomers were packed into dark,

A	Beacon Hill	G	Franklin Street	M	Fulton Street
B	Cotton Hill	H	High Street	N	State Street
	Pemberton Square	I	Dock Square	O	Tremont Street
C	Fort Hill	J	Mill Pond	P	Temple Place
D	Pearl Street	K	Faneuil Hall	Q	Bowdoin Square
E	Summer Street	L	Washington Street	R	The "Neck" Area
F	Winter Street			S	Scollay Square

Map 2. Boston: 1844
Source: The Boynton Map of 1844, map engraved by G. W. Boynton and printed by S. N. Dickinson, owned by the Boston Athenaeum

damp, and crowded hovels, rooms, cellars, sheds, shanties, converted factories, mansions, and slum tenements. Bowdoin Square
and the West End became a boardinghouse area for native in-migrants from rural areas. East Boston changed from a pleasant upper-
class suburb into a middle-class area inhabited by the skilled workers
of the shipyards; and then the introduction of steam ferry shuttles
charging $.02 fares converted it into a workingmen's district.[10]

Pemberton Square gave way to business pressures. Tremont
Street and Temple Place, including the famed "Colonnade Row"
built up between 1833 and 1840, were directly in the path of the
expanding retail center moving down Hanover, Washington, and
Tremont streets. Fort Hill's upper-class residents steadily departed
from the area as the business tide advanced and as the Irish immigrants entered the area. A little later the leveling of Fort Hill was
undertaken as a "health improvement project" and to facilitate business expansion, particularly of wholesale establishments, warehouses, hardware stores, and so on. Tenant resistance, however,
reached a high pitch. It was with great difficulty, one report observed,

that the residents in these streets could be made to comprehend that they
must leave their old homes and seek new ones elsewhere. This was no
easy task to accomplish. The fact that the Boston Gas and Light Company had developed a large territory at the North End, the extreme
scarcity of houses for the poorer classes and the exorbitant prices de-
manded for the poorest tenements disheartened all in their attempts; and
they besieged the Committee with petitions to delay the work till the
winter had passed. The common instincts of humanity caused us all to
feel a deep sympathy for these poor people; but it was necessary that the
work should go on and they were gradually compelled to leave their
houses. Some clung to their old homes till the roofs were taken off and
their homes laid open to the sky.[11]

For a time it appeared that South Boston might become the
new upper-class residential suburb. However, the successful widening of "the Neck" by the South Cove Corporation and the city of
Boston, coupled with the extension of the metropolitan horse-rail-
road line from Scollay Square to the South End and Roxbury
(1856), finally established the South End as the "exclusive" residential area of the city. Many former residents of the West End
and Fort Hill area moved to the new district (Map 3). But around
1875 the South End, too, started to decline. The immediate causes

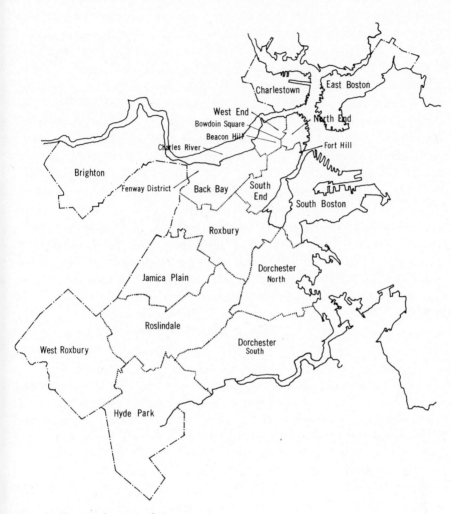

Map 3. Principal areas of Boston

were the commercial expansion at the northern and eastern boundaries; the foreclosures and conversions to rooming houses and tenements following the depression of 1873; the construction of cheaper dwellings along Columbus Avenue; and the competition of the newly established and highly fashionable Back Bay area. By 1890 the South End was the chief lodginghouse district of the city and a secondary immigration center. Even Beacon Hill, which till then had been spared the fate of the other upper-class districts because of its hills and lack of north-south traffic, began to slip as shops and offices moved into the buildings and many of its prominent families drifted to Back Bay.[12]

Meanwhile, sunless, crowded, and unsanitary tenements mushroomed in the West, North, and South ends, in parts of Roxbury, and elsewhere to house the poorer population. The new three-, four-, and five-family structures built in the period from 1872 to 1894 were a consequence of the building restrictions following the holocaust of 1872,[13] the constricted land area of central Boston, the high land values, the new influx of immigrants from Russia, Poland, and Southern Europe, and the profitable returns.[14] The remaining older houses with larger lots lost their spacious surroundings as new buildings crowded the land. Many wooden structures were demolished. Conversions transformed other buildings into cheap apartments. The subsequent outcry against tenements led to further restrictions, including height limits, lot coverage controls, and even more stringent fireproof and sanitary requirements.[15] The restrictions, however, plus higher costs, produced unanticipated effects. Construction for these income groups ended.[16]

Throughout this period, suburban expansion also occurred, causing considerable concern to the city fathers. Already in 1850 about 15,000 to 20,000 people employed in Boston, out of a total population for the city of 137,000, resided outside its boundaries.[17] Improvement of central areas by providing fountains, public squares, schools, and other public benefits was recommended as a means of arresting the trend. Another proposal was to sell at low prices, with liberal credit and little or no down payments, the remaining land "reclaimed" by the city from the "flats." The expressed purpose was to counteract the departure of "skilled mechanics." Though the city originally preferred to promote "high-class" residential development and high taxable values and to use the revenues to pay the city debt, the failure to sell land promptly and the fitful returns, plus the loss of many native Bostonians, prompted a reversal of policy.[18] The new tactics did not alter the trend. Large numbers of the population continued to leave Boston; by 1890 almost all available public land was gone, and the few remaining pieces were placed in the hands of the Board of Street Commissioners for disposal.[19]

The crowding and deterioration of the central residential districts intensified the tendency of the population to spread outward, even to areas formerly used for summer or country homes. East Boston, South Boston, Chelsea, East Cambridge, Somerville, Watertown, and Arlington received the first dispersal in the period from 1850 to 1875. Later Roxbury, Brighton, Dorchester, and other towns were "invaded." The pace of settlement accelerated with transportation improvements, particularly following the steam railroads after 1840, the omnibus, the horse cars, and then the electric cars and the railway system. By 1890 more than eight steam railroad trunk lines connecting Boston with outside areas in all directions had their terminal in the heart of Boston, only one half mile from the State House.[20] This cheapened and speedy transportation, plus the development of special commuting fares for workingmen,[21] kept channeling the flow of natives and second-generation immigrants into the surrounding communities.

With the development of the surrounding suburbs, a movement for annexation began. It was based on Boston's size, expanding taxable resources, and more efficient and unified municipal services, and on the desire to adjust municipal boundaries to the actual cluster of Boston's urban activities. Adjoining communities such as Brighton, West Roxbury, Dorchester, and Charlestown likewise favored the change. The fact that landowners and speculators in these communities hoped to tap the superior fiscal resources of the parent community for immediate road, transportation, and other projects was of vital importance in gaining support. Also, despite Boston's higher tax rate, its local government maintained until about the last quarter of the nineteenth century a rather enviable reputation for an efficient, if somewhat conservative, government, which did not offend neighboring sensibilities. Roxbury was, therefore, annexed in 1867; Dorchester in 1869; Charlestown, West Roxbury, and Brighton in 1873. Brookline, however, by a very close vote in 1873, refused; and since then the town has found more and more reasons for maintaining its independence, although its boundaries reach into the heart of the Boston corporate area. For all practical purposes, the annexation movement, which increased Boston's area by approximately thirty-eight square miles, ended during the 1870's. Minor adjustments were made here and there, but the only major exception was the admission of Hyde Park in 1910.

New building naturally occurred in the comparatively spacious annexed areas of Roxbury, Dorchester, Brighton, Charlestown, and West Roxbury. Between 1875 and 1880 the population of the annexed territory increased twice as fast as the city proper; from 1880 to 1885 the growth continued, with the annexed areas accounting for approximately 63 per cent of the increase; and similarly from 1885 to 1895, by far the highest percentage of increases in population took place in these wards. Towns outside of Boston had similar experiences. Malden, Brookline, and even Brighton, because they had no direct mass transportation connections, avoided much of the deluge; but the immediately adjacent and annexed communities, especially those boasting expanding economic activities, changed either in part or entirely into workingmen's or middle-class centers in spirit and appearance.[22]

1890–1960

The immigration tide had regained force during the 1880's. Many Russian and Polish Jews, fleeing the pogroms and the restrictive May Laws then introduced in Russia, emigrated to this country. The movement acquired further momentum in the next two decades. During the same period a great Italian influx began. Other national groups also came, including Poles, Greeks, Syrians, and Armenians. As a consequence, congestion in Boston's older areas increased despite the outflow of population.[23]

Almost 59,000 people lived in the North and West ends in 1900, that is, more than one tenth of the total population in less than one fiftieth of the city's area. By 1910 there was an increase of 10,825 in these two wards, or an increase in population of approximately 18 per cent. Between 1905 and 1910 density in terms of persons per gross acre increased in the North End from 209 to 231; in the West End it rose from 275 to 395. Some of the immigrant population, particularly the Polish and Italian groups, lived in incredible numbers within the same room or dwelling unit as lodgers. Partly a result of poverty, partly a desire to save money to send to relatives abroad or to get some initial capital, and partly a consequence of depressed foreign living standards, the practices created intensified problems of sanitation, morality, and housing conditions which strict room occupancy standards, inspection, and harsh penalties alone could not cure.[24]

Dispersal and regrouping came sooner and differently than the reform organizations had anticipated.[25] As noted earlier, between 1890 and 1914 there was a great boom in three-decker and, to a lesser extent, two-decker development in the city of Boston. Large sections of Dorchester, Brighton, Charlestown, and parts of East Boston were covered with these wooden structures. Many families living in central areas sought to improve their living conditions by a shift to these houses. From 1885 to 1895 population losses occurred in wards of South Boston, Roxbury, and the South End (Map 4A). But with the heavy immigration during the decade before World War I, the population in these areas rose once again, save for an outflow from certain wards of South and East Boston (Map 4B). During World War I and the following years there was a massive resumption of the outward movements. Between 1915 and 1920, Ward 5, the most congested ward (which included the North, West, and South ends), lost about 14,000 residents.[26] From 1915 to 1940, Charlestown, Roxbury, the North, South, and West ends, Back Bay, South and East Boston, and parts of Dorchester showed a significant drop in population (Maps 4C and 4D). The decline in these areas occurred because of the higher income generated during World War I, the search for better quarters, and the restrictive immigration legislation of the 1920's which ended the policy of relatively free entry.

The postwar construction boom during the 1920's resulted in the construction of high-priced apartments and one-family houses both outside Boston and in the few remaining open or low-density areas in Boston, such as along the Fenway, in Brighton and Allston, and in the outlying wards of Dorchester, Jamaica Plain, Roslindale, West Roxbury, and Hyde Park. Meanwhile, Back Bay, the most fashionable residential district of the city, reached its heyday during the 1920's and thereafter began to fade. Its famed precincts were invaded by the upper-class retail district, by "respectable" rooming houses for better-paid white-collar employees, and by professional offices, particularly of medical men. The tide in fashion away from town houses in favor of suburban dwellings dealt the area an almost fatal blow. Already in 1935, it was dubbed a "potential slum."[27] By 1940 and afterwards the suburban trend was the dom-

inant land-use phenomenon of Boston, despite some population increases in Charlestown, Back Bay, and parts of Roxbury, which were
partly a result of the housing shortage and probably only temporary
(Map 4E). And as it became clear that immigration[28] and business
expansion were no longer balancing the losses of both population
and industry to the surrounding areas,[29] interest in the rebuilding of
central areas mounted.

Chart 13 (based on census data in Table 17) provides an over-
all summary of the changes in the growth and location of population in Boston and its satellite areas for a half century, by decades.
Despite occasional exceptions, the chart generally depicts a slowing
down in the rate of population growth. Thus, the city of Boston
experienced a fairly steady decline for each decade following 1910.
Population increased by 19.6 per cent from 1900 to 1910; by 4.4
per cent from 1920 to 1930; and there was a loss of 1.3 per cent
from 1930 to 1940. Then the prospects seemed to change. From
1940 to 1950 there was a gain of 4 per cent; but it was short-lived,
since by 1955 the Commonwealth Census recorded a population
loss of 9.5 per cent. Although the surrounding ring also grew at a
slower rate, it increased close to 100 per cent for the period from
1900 to 1950, and almost two and a third times Boston City's rate
of increase for the same period. Data are not yet available for the
standard metropolitan area for the period from 1950 to 1960, but it
is likely that the substantial growth is continuing in the outer ring.[30]

THE EFFECT OF RISING INCOME ON RESIDENTIAL PATTERNS

Several factors conditioned Boston's land-use changes, including population "invasions," transportation improvements, industrial
and commercial "decentralization," prestige, and dissatisfaction with
the existing environment; but of these factors, perhaps the most
important in explaining the sustained movement from central to
peripheral areas, particularly for low- and middle-income families,
was the search for better shelter and a more satisfactory environment. The rising level of income made this shift possible. Cheaper
and more efficient transportation, coupled with industrial decentralization, in large measure reinforced the trend by enhancing the pull
of the suburbs while permitting contact with the varied job and
other opportunities of the metropolis.

Although total employment in downtown Boston between 1947
and 1957 decreased by about 14,000 jobs in manufacturing, whole-
saling, retailing, and in primary production, there was an increase

Percent
population change

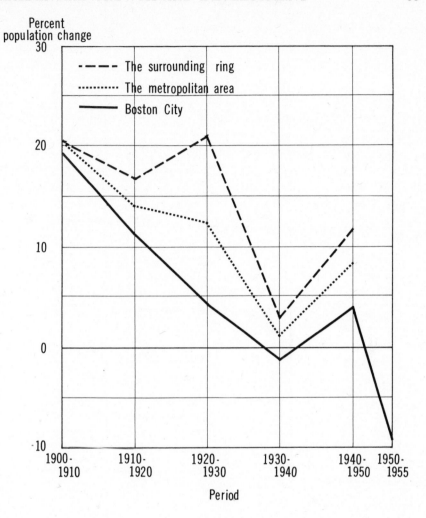

Chart 13. Per cent change in population of the Boston Standard Metropolitan Area, Boston City, and the surrounding ring, rural and urban, by
decades, 1900–1950
Source: Table 17

of about 70,000 jobs in the Boston Standard Metropolitan Area.[31]
Even if the jobs had not shifted, however, the family migration
would have occurred: this is because the influx of immigrants (Irish,
Jewish, Italian, and others) and native in-migrants into Boston's
"inner cordon" during the past century was but a prelude to their
eventual relocation in outer areas as their economic conditions improved.

TABLE 17. *Population and per cent change in population in the Boston Standard Metropolitan Area, Boston City, Lawrence, and Lowell, and the surrounding ring, rural and urban, by decades, 1900–1950*

Areas	Population 1900	% of change 1900–1910	Population 1910	% of change 1910–1920	Population 1920	% of change 1920–1930	Population 1930	% of change 1930–1940	Population 1940	% of change 1940–1950	Population 1950	% of change 1900–1950
Boston, Lawrence, and Lowell standard metropolitan areas	1,685,682	+ 20.1	2,025,286	+ 14.3	2,315,111	+ 12.8	2,611,926	+ 1.7	2,656,131	+ 8.3	2,875,876	+ 70.6
Central cities:	718,420	+ 20.1	862,771	+ 10.7	955,089	+ 1.2	966,490	− 1.0	956,528	+ 2.4	979,229	+ 36.3
Boston	560,892	+ 19.6	670,585	+ 11.6	748,060	+ 4.4	781,188	− 1.3	770,816	+ 4.0	801,444	+ 42.9
Lawrence	62,559	+ 37.3	85,892	+ 9.8	94,270	− 9.8	85,068	− 0.9	84,323	− 4.5	80,536	+ 28.7
Lowell	94,969	+ 11.9	106,294	+ 6.1	112,759	− 11.1	100,234	+ 1.2	101,389	− 4.1	97,249	+ 2.4
Ring:	967,262	+ 20.2	1,162,515	+ 17.0	1,360,022	+ 21.0	1,645,436	+ 3.3	1,699,603	+ 11.6	1,896,647	+ 96.1
Urban	844,826	+ 24.5	1,052,201	+ 18.7	1,249,042	+ 20.9	1,510,490	+ 2.4	1,546,344	+ 9.9	1,700,197	+ 101.2
Rural	122,436	− 9.9	110,314	+ 0.6	110,980	+ 21.6	134,946	+ 13.6	153,259	+ 28.2	196,450	+ 60.4

Source: D. J. Bogue, *Population Growth in Standard Metropolitan Areas 1900–1950*, Housing and Home Finance Agency, Washington, D.C., 1953, Appendix, Table 1, p. 62.

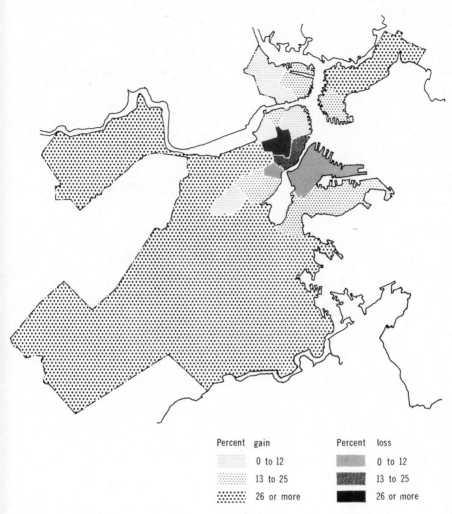

Percent	gain	Percent	loss
	0 to 12		0 to 12
	13 to 25		13 to 25
	26 or more		26 or more

Map 4A. Per cent of population changes in Boston City, 1885–1895
Source: Appendix D

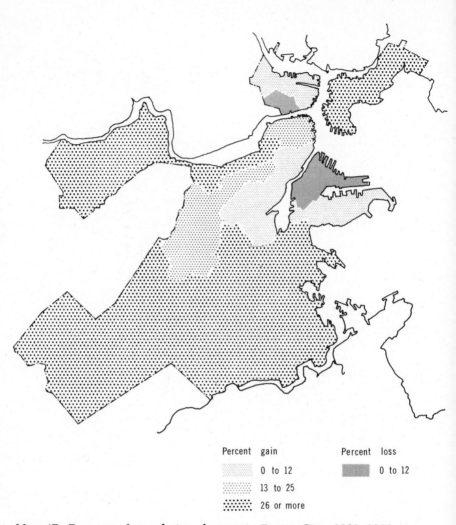

Percent gain

0 to 12

13 to 25

26 or more

Percent loss

0 to 12

Map 4B. Per cent of population changes in Boston City, 1900–1910
Source: Appendix D

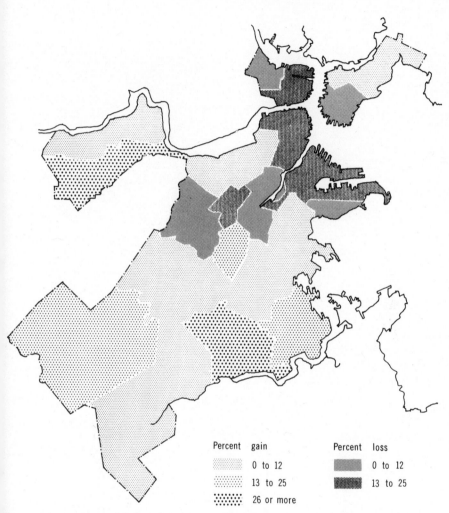

Percent gain

0 to 12

13 to 25

26 or more

Percent loss

0 to 12

13 to 25

Map 4C. Per cent of population changes in Boston City, 1915–1920
Source: Appendix D

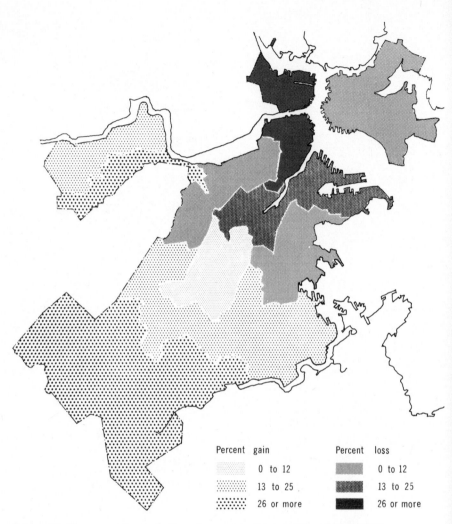

Percent gain

     0 to 12

     13 to 25

     26 or more

Percent loss

     0 to 12

     13 to 25

     26 or more

Map 4D. Per cent of population changes in Boston City, 1925–1939
Source: Appendix D

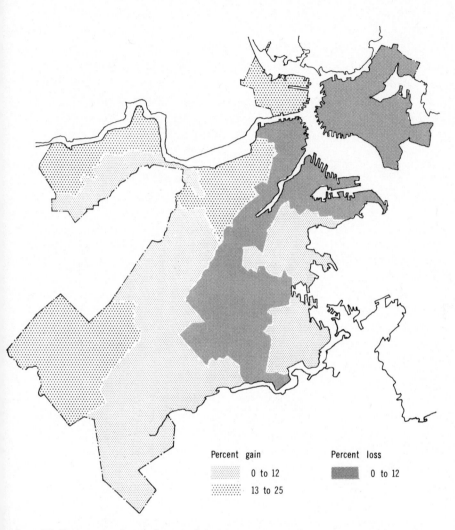

Map 4E. Per cent of population changes in Boston City, 1940–1950
Source: Appendix D

The important neighborhood changes accompanying the growth of foreign and native in-migrant population sometimes obscured the movements induced by economic progress and rising standards. But the effort to stem the drift of native mechanics from central Boston during 1850 and the following decades indicates that such trends were already under way a century ago, albeit less rapidly. Also, in the two decades before the Jewish immigration of the 1890's, many Irish workers moved to the South End, East Boston, Cambridge, and South Boston. As Professor Handlin observes,

> Primarily, this centrifugal movement winnowed the well-to-do from the impoverished, and consequently segregated the great mass of Irish within the narrow limits of old Boston. . . . Several towns convenient to these two primary Irish settlements [Fort Hill and the North End] . . . experienced approximately the same evolution. At first penetrated only by the very rich, and then by other natives and English, Scots, and Germans, they gradually attracted some of the more affluent Irishmen after 1845.[32]

The later migration of higher-income Jewish groups to Dorchester, Brighton, and Brookline likewise exhibits this tendency to seek better living conditions as income increases. Italians, too, began a relocation process, shifting from the North End to Roxbury, Allston, Brighton, East Boston, Revere, Quincy, Somerville, Everett, Medford, and Newton. This movement took place with few of the additional immigrant pressures that previous groups experienced. From these trends it is evident that the foreign influx simply accelerated a process already under way.[33]

The effect of rising income on residential relocation suggests an important modification of the "family cycle" thesis. According to this view, single persons and married couples without children tend to live in central areas, then move to the suburbs as the family grows, and return again when the children leave.[34] To the extent that it happens, this phenomenon applies primarily to middle- and upper-income groups. It is certainly not an accurate description of the experience of the immigrant population. There must be adequate transportation, plus sufficient income, job continuity, and immersal in middle-class ideals, to permit this suburban relocation.[35] The steady departure of population from the central area, in Boston and most other metropolitan communities, must be distinguished from the circular flow presumably characteristic of the family cycle. In contrast to this cycle, the relatively permanent losses of population in the "inner cordon" area of Boston indicate a deep-seated movement evidencing a fundamental dissatisfaction with the environment. In another sense, the trend may be interpreted as the participation of new middle-income families in the family cycle pattern, a fact which heretofore was impossible.[36]

Finally, the movement of many of these groups, particularly the first two or three generations of the foreign population, occurred within relatively defined areas and not simply by random diffusion of population throughout the community. Families from these foreign groups may be found, of course, in most parts of the metropolitan area; and there is evidence that the density of ethnic and nationality groupings declines at varying rates with the passage of time. Nonetheless, the bulk of the population shifted to relatively specific locations identifiable by the major ethnic and nationality, as well as rent, characteristics[37] (see Maps 5A–5D). Thus, most low-income Russian Jews are in the West and South ends, and Chelsea, Everett, and Lynn; those in the middle-income category, in Dorchester, Roxbury, Revere, Malden, and Lynn; and the higher-income groups, in Brighton, Brookline, and Newton. Low-income Italians occupy the North End, East Boston, South Boston, Chelsea, Revere, Lynn, and parts of Cambridge and Somerville; the middle-income families generally shifted to better areas in all of these communities and also to Dorchester, Quincy, Cambridge, and Waltham;[38] the highest prestige areas are in Watertown, Medford, Malden, and Winchester. Even the Irish, who have lived here longest and who are the most assimilated, show lowest-income grouping in the older areas of the South End, Charlestown, South Boston, and Roxbury; the middle-income families are in Fields Corner, Southeast Dorchester, Allston, Cambridge, and Somerville; and the highest, in areas such as Jamaica Plain, Roslindale West Roxbury, and Brookline. Perhaps the most poignant expression or lack of expression of these tendencies may be seen in the residential patterns of the most disadvantaged group, the Negroes. Their low-income families, which comprise the largest proportion of their group, are concentrated in the South End and Roxbury. Middle-income Negro families are for the most part in the latter areas but also in Cambridge and Medford; and those in higher brackets are in the same areas and in Dorchester and Newton.

Map 5A. Residence of Italian-born persons and median monthly ients in Boston City and in the inner metropolitan area, 1950
Source: Bureau of the Census, Boston, Massachusetts. Census Tracts, Census of Population, 1950. Bulletin P-D6, Department of Commerce, Table 1, pp. 7–33; Table 3, pp. 86–113

Medium contract monthly rent

☐ Less than $30
▨ $30 to $40
▧ $40 or more

Number of persons

· 100
• 500
● 1000

Map 5B. Residence of Russian-born persons and median monthly rents in
Boston City and in the inner metropolitan area, 1950
Source: Bureau of the Census, Boston, Massachusetts. Census Tracts, Census
of Population, 1950. Bulletin P-D6, Department of Commerce, Table 1, pp.
7–33; Table 3, pp. 86–113

Map 5C. Residence of Irish-born persons and median monthly rents in Boston City and in the inner metropolitan area, 1950
Source: Bureau of the Census, Boston, Massachusetts. Census Tracts, Census of Population, 1950. Bulletin P-D6, Department of Commerce, Table 1, pp. 7–33; Table 3, pp. 86–113

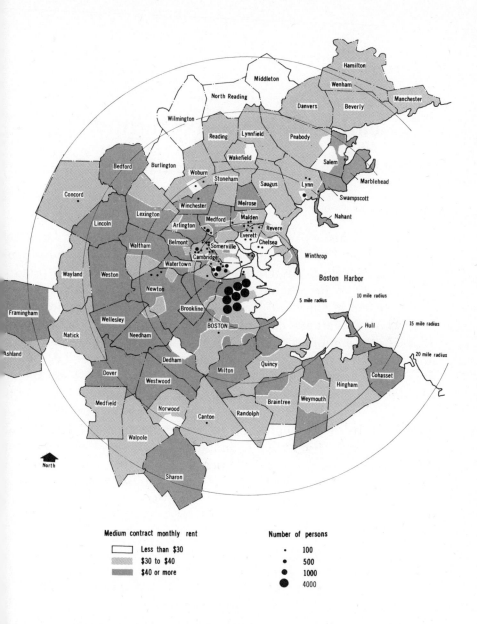

Medium contract monthly rent

☐ Less than $30
▨ $30 to $40
▧ $40 or more

Number of persons

· 100
• 500
● 1000
⬤ 4000

Map 5D. Residence of Negroes and median monthly rents in Boston City and
in the inner metropolitan area, 1950
Source: Bureau of the Census, Boston, Massachusetts. Census Tracts, Census
of Population, 1950. Bulletin P-D6, Department of Commerce, Table 1, pp.
7–33; Table 3, pp. 86–113

CHAPTER 6

....

Residential Growth and Structure:
Hypotheses and Generalizations

Boston's history can provide insights on still another aspect of residential land use.[1] A number of hypotheses and generalizations have been developed by Dr. Homer Hoyt in his study *The Structure and Growth of Residential Neighborhoods*. This was a pioneering effort. It had a considerable impact on certain mortgage insurance aspects of our national housing policy, and it still exercises influence on real estate appraisers and mortgage financing institutions. Were these ideas adequate, they should illumine, or at least find confirmation in, the pattern and history of Boston's land uses. They should also provide clues to the strategic factors which our policies need to take into account in dealing with current housing issues, such as the problems of the central city, the prospects for urban renewal and the growth of one-class communities in our suburbs. Judged or these terms, however, Hoyt's generalizations leave much to be desired. Perhaps we can better gauge their limitations and some of the ways in which the ideas need to be recast by examining them on the basis of the knowledge gleaned from our focus on Boston's residential development.[*]

CONCENTRIC AND SECTOR HYPOTHESES

We will have a better understanding of Hoyt's ideas if we glance first at E. W. Burgess' idealized view of urban land uses.[2] In effect, Homer Hoyt's studies gave the *coup de grâce* to this alternative thesis. Based on his investigations of Chicago, Burgess suggested that urban land uses tend to form a series of concentric circles. The

[*] For an evaluation of Walter Firey's critique of Hoyt's thesis and of Firey proposed alternative, see Appendix C.

successive rings of major land uses have the business and retail district in the center, with the financial district on the most valuable land. A transition zone follows, made up of hobohemia, slums, ghettos, Latin Quarters, and settlement houses. In the next area are the workingmen's residences and the dwellings of the second-generation immigrants, which, in turn, are surrounded by the better residential districts and then by the commuter's zone. Suggestive as this idealization has been in encouraging research on urban and residential growth and structure, its abandonment is well-nigh general because of the numerous land uses which it either fails to explain or directly contradicts. Zones are not of uniform or determinate lengths; retail shopping areas rather than financial districts tend to dominate the city's center; heavy manufacturing plants and retail subcenters have grown up on the periphery; and a number of studies of urban land structure, notably Hoyt's block data for 142 cities, show no evidence of typical residential areas surrounding a city.[3]

Hoyt, therefore, ventured the view that the pattern of residential land uses occurs largely in the form of sectors along the lines of transportation. High-rent districts presumably shape the trend by pulling "the growth of the entire city in the same direction."[4] Expansion tends toward the periphery, largely because the development of "intermediate rental areas" adjacent to "the leaders of society" prevents expansion in other directions. The point of origin for the most fashionable area, Hoyt found, is the retail and office center. Many higher-income groups work there, and it represents "the point farthest removed from the side of the city that has industries and warehouses."[5] Though not explicitly discussed, Hoyt took for granted that all of these adjustments would occur through the normal operation of market forces.

THE SECTOR THESIS AND BOSTON'S HOUSING PATTERNS

Because Hoyt's generalizations are pragmatic and express empirical tendencies, it is possible for individual cities to reflect divergences without invalidating the central tendency. Noting such discrepancies in the case of Boston would not necessarily invalidate Hoyt's thesis. However, these deviations may indicate certain weaknesses and furnish clues for the formulation of a more adequate hypothesis. They may also help to qualify some of Hoyt's narrow interpretations of the data, which tend to distort applications of the thesis.

Hoyt suggests that several general tendencies were characteristic of the pattern and movement of strategic high-rent areas. Let us review them and consider their applicability to Boston.

1. "High-grade residential growth tends to proceed from the given point of origin along established lines of travel or toward another existing nucleus of building or trading areas."[6]

Such patterns prevailed in Boston in the westward movement from the Beacon Hill–Back Bay area to the Fenway and Brookline districts by way of Beacon Street or Commonwealth and Brookline avenues; in the southwest movement to Dedham through Massachusetts Avenue and Columbus Avenue, and then along Washington Street; in the northwest movement to the Cambridge–Brattle Street section, using Massachusetts Avenue, and on to Belmont through Concord Avenue; and in the westward movement to Newton along Commonwealth Avenue and Cambridge and Beacon streets.

2. "The zone of high rent tends toward high ground which is free from risk of floods and to spread along lake, bay, river and ocean ports, where such water fronts are not used for industry."[7]

Boston's experiences have not been altogether consistent with this trend. South Boston, in competing with the South End for upper-class residential hegemony, lost despite the fact that it occupied a high bluff overlooking the ocean, whereas the South End, as well as Back Bay, was largely filled land. Better transportation routes were an important factor in the successful subdivisions on the peninsula, plus the continuity which the South End offered with former and existing areas of high prestige. Subdivisions in suburban areas, however, such as Belmont, Newton, and Dedham, seem to be in line with this trend, partly as a result of the increased importance of the automobile.

3. "High-rent residential districts tend to grow toward the section of the city which has free open country beyond the edges and away from 'dead end' sections which are limited by natural or artificial barriers to expansion."[8]

In the case of the North End and Beacon Hill, this generalization does not quite hold. Barriers surrounded both developments: the ocean, Charles River, and the Back Bay in the case of Beacon Hill, despite its suburban location when originally developed; and Boston's natural water boundaries and settled areas in the case of the North End during the period when it was the "court" district of town. The general tendencies may also not be consistent. For example, the movement toward high ground and the proximity to the new State House, which influenced the Beacon Hill subdivision, were more important than prospects of expansion. Hoyt, however, qualified these generalizations by indicating that the pattern would be set "by some combination"[9] of these factors, thereby imparting both flexibility and inconclusiveness to his observations.

4. "The higher-price residential neighborhood tends to grow toward the homes of the leaders of the community."[10]

Bowdoin and Beacon Hill, the South End, and then the Back Bay development seem to be evidence in favor of this proposition. High-priced homes have emerged elsewhere, however: in East Boston, for example, from 1840 to 1860; in Dorchester, Jamaica Plain, and West Roxbury, especially before 1890; and in suburban areas like Belmont, Milton, Melrose, and Dedham. This generalization is a key element in the sector thesis, but the evidence for it in Boston is equivocal, and doubts emerge even concerning the meaning of the statement.

5. "Trends of movement of office buildings, banks and stores (sometimes) pull the higher-priced residential neighborhoods in the same direction."[11]

A movement of office buildings and commercial activities toward the high-rent residential area was the dominant pattern reported by Hoyt. This trend is most apparent in the turn of Washington and Tremont Streets into Boylston Street and toward Copley Square. The reverse trend, formulated in (5) as an occasionally important exception, does not seem to be occurring in Boston.

6. "High-grade residential areas tend to develop along the fastest existing transportation lines."[12]

The South End's development along Huntington Avenue and Tremont Street, and the Back Bay's munificent Commonwealth Avenue are evidence in favor of this pattern. South Boston lost certain advantages in competition with the South End partly because of its limited transportation services and the opening of a more efficient omnibus service to Roxbury.[13] Beacon Hill, however, is an obvious exception, being deliberately designed to avoid north-south traffic. Hoyt also notes that the new trend is in favor of secluded suburbs, though the roads to these districts usually run through the old "axial high-grade areas."[14] This penchant for privacy explains at least in part why Beacon Hill has been susceptible to revival.

7. "The growth of high-rent neighborhoods continues in the same direction for a long period of time."[15]

Two possible meanings might be ascribed to this statement: that the general area maintains its character for a long time, or that the growth continues in that geographical direction for a long time. The first interpretation, if intended, is not confirmed by Boston's experience. One upper-class neighborhood after another has collapsed, sometimes with considerable financial loss. Bowdoin Square, Fort Hill, and Colonnade Row were soon absorbed by the rising tide of business. None of these areas survived more than a generation. The South End, initiated about 1840 to 1850, moved downhill rapidly after 1870–1873. South Boston had an even shorter period of glory, lasting approximately from 1845 to 1855. Beacon Hill, after the completion of the development, stayed in favor less than two generations and then started to decline. Even Back Bay has not been the top residential area for much more than half a century. Though it still retains a slightly frayed distinction, shops have invaded its precincts, and fashionable homes have been turned into "high-class" rooming houses and professional offices.[16]

On the other hand, there is some evidence in favor of the second interpretation, namely, that growth continues in the same direction a long time. Though there was a shift from the North End westward to Beacon Hill and then southward to Fort Hill, geographical limitations partly account for these seemingly erratic movements. The shift, however, from the South End to Back Bay cannot be explained so simply. Even though the general direction was the same, there was a decided change in the locus of fashionable areas. If, however, the movement from Fort Hill, Colonnade Row, and the South End is considered a relatively continuous line of development, and likewise for the Beacon Hill–Back Bay area, Boston's experience then supports the second generalization.

8. "De luxe apartment areas tend to be established near the business center in old residential areas."[17]

The observation is inaccurate for Boston, at least to the extent that this "reversal" refers only to de luxe apartment areas. Beacon Hill's rejuvenation into single-family homes occurred without substantial physical transformation, because of the quality of the buildings. Similar remodeling might occur in the future for other conveniently located and well-built areas of Boston, such as the South End.

9. "Real estate promoters may bend the direction of high-grade residential growth."[18]

Beacon Hill, the South End, and Back Bay were all speculative enterprises. All three required extraordinary exertions, the first in reducing the hills, and the other two in filling in the mud flats. Development on alternative sites could easily have occurred were it not for real estate promotion coupled with government assistance and subsidy for these areas. Not always do these schemes succeed, as is evident in the frantic and unsuccessful efforts at bridge and road building in South Boston. Significantly enough, Hoyt completely overlooks or slights the role of government and public policy in shaping residential patterns. In Boston at least, in reference to land and transportation policy, this influence was far from negligible.

Several other observations made by Hoyt ought to be noted and checked. They are summarized and commented upon in paragraph 10.[19]

10. "The high-rent neighborhoods do not skip about at random in the process of movement—they follow a definite path in one or more sectors of the city."[20] Moreover, movement by the wealthy is seldom reversed because: "On each side of them is usually an intermediate rental area, so they cannot move sideways. As they represent the highest income group, there are no houses above them abandoned by another group. They must build new houses on vacant land."[21] Hoyt also suggests that: "Intermediate rental areas on the periphery of other sectors of the city besides the ones in which the highest rental areas are located are found in certain cities."[22]

Though the general trends are in line with these observations, particularly the formation of nuclei and definite patterns, there are three interesting and possibly significant deviations in Boston's experience. First, as pointed out in many studies, the north slope adjoining Beacon Hill was occupied throughout most of its history by low-income and even socially disreputable groups. In other words, there is evidence of abrupt changes in adjacent land use,[23] at least as an exception to the general pattern. Second, the movement back to Beacon Hill following 1900 indicates the possibility of a special kind of secondhand housing for the wealthy,[24] a pattern which could assume more importance in the future. Finally, numerous and extremely broad intermediate areas may be found throughout Boston and its suburbs, notably in Dorchester, Brighton, Jamaica Plain, Malden, Medford, Arlington, and elsewhere, with no *close* relationship to upper-class developments. Absence of a close association raises important issues concerning the nature of intermediate areas which need to be explored.

To summarize the observed discrepancies: (1) upper-income residential developments in the past did not always move toward high ground or open country; (2) upper- and middle-income residential movements also occur in directions other than toward the homes of leaders of society; (3) upper-class districts often did not last for long periods, and though the trend was generally in the same direction, there were on occasion shifts in direction; (4) wealthy families returned to the city's center for well-built, second-hand town houses as well as de luxe apartment houses; (5) fashionable areas may be bounded by low-income as well as by "intermediate" areas; (6) government policy as well as real estate promoters may influence residential patterns; and (7) housing of the intermediate groups covers such a wide swathe that a locational description only on the basis of relationship to the upper-class district is probably inadequate.

The question arises whether these variations are peculiar to Boston or whether they evidence difficulties with the hypothesis itself. One or two items may be exceptional, such as the coexistence of high- and low-rent areas, or the relatively short life of fashionable areas in Boston. There is reason to suspect, however, that even if these cases are exceptional, they are important exceptions which an adequate theory must take into account.[25] Other items might still be fitted into the generalizations by slight modifications in formulation. For example, the return to the city's center can take place in older rehabilitated houses as well as de luxe apartments. Most of the other items, however, seem to be attributable to certain ambiguities, oversimplifications, and questionable assumptions which deserve careful, critical attention.

PROBLEMS AND ASSUMPTIONS OF THE SECTOR THESIS

In re-examining the sector thesis,[26] three basic terms and two assumptions require scrutiny: *i.e.*, "sector"; "leaders of society"; "intermediate income classes"; public policy; and the market mechanism.

Many of the issues raised by Hoyt's analysis can be ascribed to problems surrounding their meaning or use.

Sector

What is a sector? Would, for instance, Beacon Hill and Back Bay alone qualify? Or must it include the whole western and northwestern zone of well-to-do communities extending from Beacon Hill, Back Bay, and Brattle Street to Newton, Needham, and Dover or to Belmont, Lincoln, and Concord? If the broader areas were intended, then a critic might be justified in calling attention to the slums, industrial areas, and other land uses lying between these districts and communities. Clearly, in most cases, smaller boundaries would allow more homogeneous areas, and broader boundaries would tend to blur their character.

Perhaps we can clarify the issue by stating the minimum elements that the concept intended, or ought, to include. The sectors outlined on Hoyt's maps were based on rent classes. These classes ranged from less than $10, $10 to $19, $20 to $29, $30 to $49, and $50 and more. Variations in rent areas within the corporate boundaries of cities were mapped. Each rent area represented the rent average within the district, and block deviations within this district were ignored.[27] The maps indicated that the highest rental areas ($50 and more) were generally concentrated in one or several parts of the city. With these data Hoyt was able to test the concentric circle hypothesis and demonstrate its inadequacy by the fact that high-rent areas appeared only along one or several sides of the city rather than in the form of a ring pattern. He was also able to establish that various kinds of housing, particularly high-rent areas, were not scattered throughout the city in random fashion; and that upper-income families lived in relatively homogeneous groups, thus creating a neighborhood with sufficient similarity of living conditions to become an identifiable social and physical environment. Often, but not always, such an area had room for expansion, usually along or near an important transportation route. This characteristic is understandable, since a new development usually begins with small numbers, with other groups tending to follow. Few areas were or are completely built at the same time. These elements form the basis for Hoyt's sector, especially as it pertains to the upper-income group.

The sector, then, may be formally defined as a radial residential grouping, usually capable of expansion along or close to an avenue of transportation, and comprising enough families able to afford a comparable type of housing to establish a pattern. For purposes of measurement, one might add that the differences within the sector for key variables such as rent, consumption patterns, and social status, are less than the differences between the sector and outside areas.[28] If this interpretation is correct, then it is probably appropriate to consider areas such as Beacon Hill, Back Bay, and the South End as independent sectors. Within these areas, a fairly homogeneous pattern is observable and measurable, though not necessarily a complete exclusion of other uses adjacent to and even within the sector.[29] The broader pattern, i.e., the southwestern, western, or northwestern suburban trends, really reflects only a general direction of expansion, not sectors, though several clusters and higher average rents will also be found in the area.

Leaders of Society

The notion of "fashionable" residential areas is more troublesome. Hoyt's references vary from "leaders of society" and "most fashionable areas" to "high-grade districts" and "highest-rental areas." Contrary to Hoyt's supposition, these terms are not always synonymous.[30] Dealing with 142 cities made it necessary for Hoyt to find some relatively common denominator of several factors. Rent classes were used. Implicit in Hoyt's approach, however, is an oversimplification of class structure. In one sense this is curious. Though he deals with the composition of both urban inhabitants and minority groups in at least two separate portions of his study, he bypasses the relationship of class and ethnic patterns.[31] Society is divided into three classes: the upper classes who pay the highest rentals, the lower classes with the lowest rentals, and the "intermediate class" somewhere between the two. So gross an assumption of class structure in turn yields equally gross cartographical interpretations. His simplification is partly the explanation of the many limitations and discrepancies which might otherwise be blamed on such interpretations.

It is impossible to detail here the complicated class groupings and their ramifications which one encounters in most communities. A few minimum observations, however, are necessary. For most larger cities with significant population mixtures, complex and multiple class relationships prevail. These intricate patterns apply particularly to ethnic, religious, and nationality groups not yet diffused throughout the urban area. In Negro, Italian, Jewish, and other neighborhoods, strata will be found with upper, middle, and lower classes running on economic and sometimes other lines.[32] There is limited interest on the part of members of these distinct ethnic, nationality, and religious groups in moving in a direction other than toward their own leaders. For this reason, we can trace the locational shifts of such groups in metropolitan areas as we did in Chapter 5.

When a move starts and new nuclei form, the direction may tend toward upper-income areas, but it is not necessarily toward the highest social class[33] of the community. Because of this fact it is quite misleading to confine the analysis to three simple categories. Quite different theoretical and practical implications follow from these distinctions, as we shall soon indicate. Hoyt's thesis, it therefore appears, is really more directly applicable to small, relatively homogeneous communities than to larger metropolitan areas. If it is contended that possibly the whole pattern was really summarized in his simplified approach, the reply must be that not only is there no evidence of such an intention but also that allowance for the type or range of errors that would ensue was not made, assuming that it was at all possible. Moreover, it would often be injudicious to base policy in the immediate present and future on the basis of Hoyt's formulation and conclusions.[34]

Intermediate Income Groups

Uncertainty concerning the nature of intermediate groups likewise obscures the analysis. Whom do the intermediate groups represent? If the leaders of society are those in the Social Register or are arbitrarily defined as the highest-rental groups, then many fairly well-to-do groups will still live outside their sector(s). A considerable number in the latter category probably serve as leaders within different class groupings and reside in excellently "groomed" neighborhoods, not necessarily close to the "leaders of society."

The "intermediate class" is also a catch-all for other groups as well. For example, in Boston it presumably should include the broad middle-income group who lived in or owned three-deckers. The scope of the category is therefore significant: it forces a reconsideration of the notion of physical contiguity. Only a small portion of the intermediate- or even top-income groups can live adjacent to the "leaders of society."[35] Sheer numbers would soon force many to live in closer association with other "intermediate" income groups.

Under the circumstances, a considerable physical area of choice is possible. If it is impossible to live next to the nabobs, other alternatives may and probably will be explored. For example, moderately wealthy and middle-income groups in Boston occupy wide areas which are not at all close either physically or socially to the fashionable areas of Back Bay and Beacon Hill or those of Newton, Belmont, Lincoln, and the other upper-class communities outside of Boston. If we eliminate the North, West, and South ends plus East Boston, Charlestown, South Boston, and parts of Roxbury and Hyde Park as low-income areas, there is still a wide physical range within Dorchester, Brighton, and Jamaica Plain; and this range increases still further if we consider other communities such as Malden, Medford, Arlington, Waltham, Watertown, Cambridge, and Quincy. To explain the patterns in these areas on the monistic principle of upper-class polarity is to ignore the fact that leadership within groups, and other factors, may also create powerful attractions.

A simple explanation is still possible of the apparent "surrounding" of the "leaders of society." Having very high (if not the highest) rentals, their cluster is conspicuous, not only cartographically but visually as well, since the environs, both physically and socially, are as a rule very satisfying. Lesser socialites and income groups will undoubtedly move to the area. Unless special factors intervene, a gradual shading off of high- to moderate-income neighborhoods will occur.[36] Allowing for this pattern still does not eliminate the need to explain the locational pattern of the overwhelming majority of the remaining intermediate groups, in short, to gauge other influences which may affect their spatial distribution.

Public Policy and the Market Mechanism

Before we consider possible changes in the sector thesis, two assumptions require notice. First is the somewhat narrow perspective and problem which guided the inquiry. The Federal Housing Administration, which insured loans of financial institutions on residential properties, financed this study to obtain guidance for its policy decisions. The immediate aim was to protect the value of the properties underlying its insurance. There was negligible concern with general housing conditions or with the protection of the property values and public investments of the community as a whole, although these factors, too, were of importance even for the limited objectives Hoyt envisioned.

Second, Hoyt studied the residential patterns produced in a relatively free economy. However, his conclusions were intended to be used for practical decisions in the future; and they could be misleading if the constraints within which the market economy functioned changed significantly. Thus, real estate promoters, new inventions, and technological achievements influence city patterns; and they came within Hoyt's line of vision. But men's ideas on what the city should be like were not noticed at all. To an increasing extent, however, these ideas play a decisive role because of the expanding sphere of government and the recognized inadequacies of present urban and residential patterns. Objective and scholarly, therefore, as the sector analysis is, it is important to remember that its generalizations lean on past conditions, attitudes, and ideals, and that its bias is in the direction of the past. Undiscriminating reliance upon its conclusions may produce negative attitudes toward policies or changes not examined in Hoyt's study.

REFORMULATING THE THEORY OF RESIDENTIAL GROWTH AND
    STRUCTURE

Elimination of the defects in the sector theory requires a far more comprehensive and rigorous treatment of the relevant variables, as well as less parochial terms of reference. For example, we need to know more about the factors that influence the decisions of families on where to live. Undoubtedly the upper-class attractions which Hoyt emphasized are a vital force; but the problem is much more complex. There are subtle patterns of selective differentiation for various groups in the community. A variety of upper-class residential sectors exists, probably with some tendencies of gradation toward higher income and higher "class" locations. The study of these variant class relationships within and between social systems, their ecological characteristics and their possible variations, is still in the pioneer stage, and should yield fruitful insights.

It is also important to know what other factors may determine where low- and middle-income families might want to live. One basic influence is the role of a functionally adequate physical environment. The characteristics of such an environment will vary, of course, for different social and economic groups and for different historical periods and stages of technology. Among the diverse conditions sought today are adequate access to employment centers for the principal and secondary wage earners; convenient location to schools and shopping centers; and physical settings providing adequate and attractive housing, open space, traffic safety, and recreation areas. We do not know enough about the range and relative significance of these preferences for different groups, the forces that shape them, the patterns they may assume in the future. But we can be certain that significant readjustments would be necessary in the sector thesis if this desire for a functionally adequate environment proved to be as important a locational determinant as attractions to upper-class groups. Indeed, at the risk of some distortion and lack of refinement in analysis, it might be useful to explore the implications of such an additional assumption or hypothesis.[37]

Boston's Residential Location Patterns

To begin with, is this assumption concerning the physical environment useful in interpreting the history of Boston's residential uses? Let us consider first the negative evidence, i.e., the cases where apparently the factor of adequate environment was not the decisive element. South Boston, because of its superior physical location, might have proved to be a more satisfactory fashionable residential district than the South End or Back Bay, and yet it was unsuccessful. Inferior transportation was an important reason for its failure, plus the lack of continuity with an already existing fashionable area. The migration to Back Bay from the South End provides another example. Insufficient land sales, industrial and commercial infiltration from the north, plus the depression of 1873, resulted in forced liquidations and conversion to intensive and "inferior" uses. Prestige and status, however, were also important. They channeled the move to Back Bay and hastened the departure of many South End residents following the reduction of land prices and the building of relatively cheaper houses along Columbus Avenue. The shift at the same time from Beacon Hill to Back Bay was perhaps more a reflection of status than of superior environment. In short, despite the other elements involved, for these fashionable districts the role of prestige was undoubtedly of considerable importance.

On the other hand, the flight from Fort Hill to Colonnade Row and the South End resulted from commercial invasion and the profitable conversions of many of the houses into cheap slum quarters for Irish immigrants. Similarly, the departure from Back Bay illustrated the dissatisfaction with the old town houses. Throughout Boston's history, the movements of upper-income groups, except for the southwesterly trends toward the Beacon Hill, South End, and Back Bay areas, are better accounted for when the touchstone of environmental adequacy is added. Such was the case for the migrations to East Boston between 1845 and 1860, to Dorchester before 1890, and to Belmont, Lexington, and Newton today.

This assumption also provides a better basis for interpreting certain locational patterns in areas where the influence of physical or social proximity to upper-class districts was clearly minimized, namely, the developments in Dorchester, Somerville, Watertown, Medford, Malden, and other areas. Another way of putting it is that the assumption is helpful in explaining movements of the middle- and low-income groups. We have already discussed the tendency of these families to improve their housing as real income rose by seeking more rooms and services and by escaping from the overcrowded "inner cordon." The shifts of these same groups to suburban three-deckers are likewise more satisfactorily explained by taking environmental as well as class attractions into account.

Policy and Normative Issues

Financial institutions and zoning agencies were expected to apply the conclusions of the sector thesis. Presumably "good" expanding areas were to be identified for investment and other "good" areas in which investments were made were to be guarded. Perhaps Hoyt may not have had such an intention, but there is a strong emphasis in the study in favor of preserving the better neighborhoods rather than improving the poor ones. Certainly at least until 1954 the Federal Housing Administration, which financed the study, acted on this basis and resisted attempts to change this approach.

Avoidance of areas on the downgrade was understandable. It reflected in part the natural disinclination to tamper with the market mechanism. The jungle of properties in various stages of blight and obsolescence in such areas created a situation which market adjustments alone could scarcely cure within any reasonable period. Unfortunately, the end result of limiting investments to good areas was to accelerate the problems of blight and obsolescence, not to solve them. Since communities, however, have a strong interest in reversing or slowing down these unfavorable trends, they began to look with more favor on some form of government intervention and subsidy. A variety of measures, otherwise impossible, could be tapped through government action, including subsidized housing for low-income groups, more and better distributed parks and open spaces, and reclamation of wasted or misused areas.

The sector thesis, as formulated and applied, also tends to encourage the exclusion of certain groups from the better neighborhoods because of their alleged "inharmonious" characteristics. That they want to "get in" is generally taken for granted by the simple assumption of upper-class attraction. The exaggerated emphasis on this desire could be corrected, however, by recognizing their equally important interest in decent housing and salutary neighborhoods.

The housing problems of minorities provide an illustration. Negroes, for example, are denied decent quarters in many areas and cooped up in noisome slums; but there is often panic among whites lest these Negroes burst into a "good" area, change the character of a neighborhood, and deflate property values. Hoyt's analysis of the substandard conditions characteristic of Negro neighborhoods, his comments about the effect on rents of the presence of Negroes in twilight zones, plus the assumption of upper-class attraction and the investment attitude perpetually wary of "racial mixtures" or "inharmonious groups," add fuel to this hysteria.[38] The basic and inescapable policy conclusion is to "keep 'em out." One gets no inkling from his analysis that the desire of Negroes with rising income, as of other groups, is to find a decent home and neighborhood, and that frustration in this direction would push them with even greater pressure toward "good" white areas when openings develop. Aside from the ethical issues, a policy of exclusion is likely to prove self-defeating. Negroes and other minorities will not remain hemmed in ghettoes. As income and standards of demand rise, they seek the same improved housing standards sought by other middle-income families; and given contemporary attitudes, public policy is apt to provide increasing aid for them in this objective. The results of such efforts may well lead to bitterness and losses in some neighborhoods, but the ultimate results augur greater stability and sounder investments. For as these conditions are achieved, the moving of a few Negroes into white areas is less likely to arouse the specter of mass entry, white migrations, and financial losses. Racial prejudice will not disappear, but surely a greater possibility for accommodation and mutual understanding might then be encouraged.

PART THREE:

....

CONCLUDING OBSERVATIONS

CHAPTER 7

....

Housing and Economic Progress

In the previous chapters, we have seen how economic progress led to better housing, yet generated novel housing issues. As income increased and was better distributed among the population, there was evidence of higher standards of demand. Lower- and middle-income groups spent more for housing, obtained more rooms and space, purchased more utilities and services, and moved to better neighborhoods, usually to the suburbs.

A number of problems, however, accompanied this progress. Among the more important were the inflationary costs, the dangers in the intricate financial devices stimulating home ownership, and the impact of housing shortages and rent controls. There were also the issues posed by the expanding suburbs, the decline of central cities, the effects of invasion and cheaper developments on good neighborhoods, and the general character and pattern of residential development. The conviction grew that in the field of housing, as in some other areas, the free market was not responding adequately to social requirements. This feeling explains in part why the housing problem is no longer identified simply with the "lower classes" or the "deserving poor." The new image of the housing problem held by the public is one of tricky hurdles confronting practically the entire community and requiring local and national government action. Despite, or perhaps even because of, the solutions, issues of housing had apparently reached a new threshold of complexity; and in coping with some of them one is reminded of the aphorism of Freud that the problems of adolescence may be solved by marriage, but that does not thereby resolve the problems of marriage.

The changing issues are indicative of the gradual, subtle transformation in the nature of the housing problem and of some of the new directions in which future efforts may be necessary. Theoretically, some have argued, there is no housing problem: there is only a problem of allocating scarce resources; and since all resources are scarce, more or less, we should rely on our market economy which is the mechanism for making these allocational decisions. But there appears to be a discrepancy between the decisions made by the market mechanism and solutions which are socially acceptable or feasible. What we call our housing problem today grows out of this difference between what we want in the way of housing and other goods and services, what we may think is feasible with available technology and resources for consumption and investment, and what we actually get. Given the present climate of opinion, some form of public intervention occurs for better or worse if the discrepancy becomes too serious.

Whatever the theoretical merits of a competitive economy may be, a pattern of public intervention in market decisions has emerged in housing, particularly in relation to such matters as volume, costs, tenure, standards, rent controls, decentralization, and suburban development. This intervention takes several forms. New rules have been set up within which the market mechanism operates, the aim being to ensure certain minimum standards. Certain efforts have been made to influence consumer values in the direction of greater expenditure for housing, especially for home ownership. Public assistance or subsidy has been provided to help certain groups to bid more effectively for housing or to encourage the reorganization of land uses in central areas. Still other measures have sought to perfect the institutional mechanism serving private interests, to foster significant innovations, or to improve the basic information for decision-making, public and private.

These public policies evidence a profound dissatisfaction with the way the market mechanism functions when operating "independently"; and they reflect a pragmatic response based on the assumption that a vigorous market economy subject to controls and encouraged and restrained on appropriate occasions by a "steering mechanism" is preferable to any of the proposed alternatives. But something basic—what perhaps might be characterized as an effective strategy or a clear sense of direction—is still missing. The chief approaches in the last two decades have been to isolate a specific problem and to devise countermeasures; or later, as a growing number of problems were identified, to appeal for a "comprehensive" attack on all fronts. Both approaches appear to have little prospect of exerting disproportionate effects because the former is too limited in range, the latter too weak in terms of available resources. The desired effects, however, might possibly be obtained by intermediate measures. By concentrating on a few strategic areas, a successful attack may prove more feasible and might produce repercussions over a wide field. Focusing on the housing problems of families of middle income is an example.

The middle-income families are the "transitionals," those that are improving their circumstances and leaving low-income and low middle-income status. They are in the twilight zone between renting and ownership, and between the families who need no assistance and those who require very special assistance. They comprise the bulk of the families who live in or are leaving the "gray" areas, the miles of dingy neighborhoods meeting minimum standards, but not sufficiently adequate or attractive for their residents as standards of demand rise. The housing abandoned by these middle-income families can serve many low-income families as their income rises; and the new homes for these "transitional" families need not be built at minimum standards subject to the premature obsolescence which endangers most public housing as standards rise. Perhaps most important of all, this market constitutes the largest potential demand; and therefore it might offer effective leverage for influencing the larger builders who are interested in a mass market, likely to introduce innovations in methods, and sensitive to signals from a central government steering mechanism. Finally, serving the needs of these families more explicitly ought to enjoy vast political appeal.

Such a strategy would not be a substitute for existing policies; but it might serve either as a means of helping to extend the present programs, or of more effectively deploying existing housing tools for middle-income families. That at any rate is the premise; but we may avoid surprise and bewilderment if we remember that, as we come to grips with our housing problems, they are more likely to be transformed than solved. In part, this is because they are side effects of economic progress. Only in a stationary society is it likely that there will be no significant discrepancies between rates of change of family income, standards of demand, and achievable conditions of housing; only in a very wealthy society are these discrepancies unlikely to be matters of genuine concern; and only in utopias can we be sure that our ingenious solutions will not occasionally boomerang and frustrate our purposes.

APPENDICES

APPENDIX A

....

Derivation of Data on Income
and Housing Costs: 1846–1959

This appendix discusses the derivation of the estimates, for selected periods, of the following: (1) the ranges of income for middle-income families of Boston, and the rents for Boston's existing stock of housing; (2) the rents for minimum-standard new construction. We assume that the reader is familiar with the summary, in the first section of Chapter 2, of the general assumptions and procedures for deriving these estimates. If not, he should scan that section before continuing.

INCOME RANGES OF MIDDLE-INCOME FAMILIES, AND RENTS FOR EXISTING STOCK OF HOUSING IN BOSTON

1846

The Bureau of Statistics of Labor published in 1885 a study of wages and prices in Massachusetts from 1752 to 1860. Wages for skilled workers ranged from $1.25 to $1.75 per day in 1846, with special trades receiving as much as $2.00.[1] If we assume a work year of 300 days, plus additional income for supplementary wage earners equal to one third the income of the principal wage earner,[2] and an additional 16.7 per cent[3] higher wage level for the Boston community, annual family income would then range from $584 to $934. The rent-paying ability per annum would be $97 to $156, if one sixth of income were spent for shelter rent.[4] Adequate rent data for this period are unavailable. Rents for the worst slums in Boston in 1846, according to the Special Committee of the Common Council Relative to the Improvement of Tenement Districts of the City of Boston, ranged as high as $1 to $2 per week for a dark room or damp cellar. For dwellings having three to five rooms, a rent range of $1.75 to $3.00 a week, or about $91 to $156 a year, seems likely. "To-let" advertisements in the newspapers provide some evidence to support these estimates.[5] For the middle-income families, therefore, there was under optimum conditions only a normal problem of supplying housing in adequate volume and possibly a question of quality. But there was no serious rent problem except for the threat inherent in irregular or cyclical unemployment.

1875–1884

An 1875 study of wage and salary incomes in Massachusetts indicated that, despite the depression, the total family earnings of approximately 5000 "wage receivers" in Boston and 1600 salary receivers in Suffolk County averaged $1100[6] and $1715[7] respectively. Supplementary data reveal, as suspected, that both averages, and especially the latter, were too high. The schedule for salary receivers included many occupations not appropriately classified in the middle-income brackets.[8] On the other hand, the survey of the wage receivers included a very high proportion of skilled workers.[9] A survey in 1874 of earnings for skilled workers in Massachusetts yielded an average total family income of $817.[10] If we add 16.7 per cent to adjust for higher wage rates in Boston, the total earnings would be $953.

Another approach might be to examine prevailing rates of pay. For example, the average hourly and weekly wage rates in Massachusetts ranged from $0.17 to $0.23 an hour, or $10 to $14 a week.[11] With adjustments of one third for supplementary wage earners, plus 16.7 per cent for the Boston area, the range of total annual earnings would be from $809 to $1133. On the basis of these data, it appears appropriate to regard $950 as the approximate average middle income. It is necessary, however, to establish the range as well as the median for the middle-income bracket. One may start with the minimum average income of $600 for Massachusetts, below which figure dissavings or debt occurred.[12] A 16.7 per cent adjustment for the Boston area yields $700 as the probable lower limit of the middle-income group. The upper limit would then be $1200. For this income range, rent-paying capacity at one sixth of income would be $117 to $200.

If we make the same proportionate adjustments in the average rents, obtained from the Bureau of Statistics of Labor 1874 survey for Boston and Suffolk County, as we made for income, the result is adjusted average rents of $140 to $162. Newspaper advertisements indicate that the range of rents probably varied from $100 to $215. This range of rents is in line with budget studies of Massachusetts and Boston wage earners, as well as with other estimates made by contemporaries during this period.[13] Apparently there were fairly satisfactory dwellings available. Comments and statistics on the quality of workingmen's apartments in the 1874 survey show a fairly small proportion of units listed as *poor*, according to the standards then prevailing.[14]

1885–1899

Table 18 presents wage distribution data for Boston for 1885 and 1895. Economic depression during this period lowered income. Approximately one third of the families were in the weekly wage range from $9 to $14. However, this range is low, since no salaried workers were included in the census on which Table 18 is based. Robert Woods confirms this impression. He observed that most of the residents of the South End receiving wages below $12 a week

TABLE 18. *Number and per cent of wage earners in Boston, 1885 and 1895, by weekly wages*

Weekly wages	1885		1895	
	Number of wage earners	% of total	Number of wage earners	% of total
Under $5	3,530	10.8	7,300	10.2
$5–6	1,875	5.8	4,129	5.8
$6–7	2,200	6.8	5,047	7.0
$7–8	1,679	5.2	3,677	5.2
$8–9	1,925	5.9	3,966	5.6
$9–10	2,376	7.3	5,822	8.2
$10–12	4,245	13.0	7,609	10.7
$12–15	6,293	19.3	13,330	18.8
$15–20	6,503	20.1	15,771	22.1
$20 and over	1,976	6.1	4,688	6.6
Total[a]	32,602	100	71,339	100

[a] The total refers to the number of people reporting.

Source: The Census of Massachusetts, 1885, vol. 2, pp. 254–255; The Census of the Commonwealth of Massachusetts, 1895, vol. 5, p. 283.

were unskilled workers.[15] It is probably more reasonable to regard as the middle-income bracket those earning between $10 and $16 a week, or a total family income per annum of $693–$1109.[16] Their rent-paying capacity would be $116–$185 per annum.

Rents of the highest-grade tenement houses, apartments, and flats, according to Robert Woods, ranged from $20 to $35 and upwards a month,[17] or about $240–$420 a year. If this were the case, few, if any, of even the highest-paid workers could afford such accommodations. This would be true even if we included the supplementary earnings of members of the family[18] and made no deductions for earnings lost due to irregularity of employment or other reasons. The less expensive of these apartments would, however, come within the reach of some white-collar and professional families, since their average salary was $1151,[19] and probably closer to $1500 if we include supplementary earnings. This average is inflated and probably represents the penumbral zone between the middle- and upper-income brackets.

Our analysis hinges to some extent on the accuracy of Robert Woods' estimate of $20–$35 a month for good dwellings. This estimate probably referred to those in the higher income brackets. A later study of the South End just after the Spanish-American War indicated that well-paid operatives earning $20 and $30 a week paid $4 and $5 a week (or $18.00–$22.50 a month) for apartments in the South End.[20] There were dwelling units at least $1 a week cheaper ($13.50–$18.00 a month) in the suburbs. Rents in the worst tenements of Boston, however, ranged from $5 to $14 a month and averaged approximately $8.50.[21] It seems reasonable to assume that there were probably minimum-standard dwellings available somewhere between $8 and $14 per month. We can, therefore, estimate the rent range for middle-income housing at $11 to $17 per month, or $132 to $204 per annum. Newspaper advertisements for three- to five-room tenements, and the data on the distribution of families by rent classes in the Tenement House Census (Table 19), support this judgment. But though the prevailing rents were within the range of the middle-income groups, the data indicate that the lower middle-income families were hard pressed.[22]

1900–1915
Unfortunately we found neither wage nor rent distribution data for Boston for the period 1900–1915. However, some con-

temporary studies containing rent and income estimates enable us to reconstruct the major groupings with substantial accuracy. Thus, Estabrook's report for the 1915 Housing Committee of Boston indicates typical rents in the North End and West End slums approximating $11.50 a month and room rents averaging $0.90 a week.[23] Probably most slum housing continued to fall below $12 per month. Almost all of the general pronouncements during the period on meeting the needs of the unskilled wage earner refer to the necessity of achieving rents ranging from $8 to $14 a month. As a matter

TABLE 19. *Number and per cent of families living in tenements in Boston, 1892, by monthly rent*

Monthly rent	Number of families	% of total families
Under $10	18,108	25.3
$10–19	36,174	50.5
$20–29	9,116	12.7
$30–49	5,291	7.4
$50 and over	2,976	4.2
Total	71,665	100

Source: Wadlin, *A Tenement House Census of Boston,* 1892, pp. 490–491.

TABLE 20. *Predominant weekly rents of working-class dwelling units in Boston, 1909, by number of rooms per dwelling unit*

Number of rooms per dwelling unit	Predominant weekly rents
Two	$1.60–$2.10
Three	1.85– 2.55
Four	2.30– 3.25
Five	3.25– 3.90
Six	3.70– 5.30

Source: Bureau of Statistics of Labor, *Forty-First Annual Report,* 1910, Table 24, p. 251.

of fact, a careful survey during 1909 revealed the predominant working-class rents shown in Table 20.[24]

Yet Mr. P. F. Hall, Chairman, Town Improvement Committee, Brookline Civic Society, arguing against the three-decker type of construction declared that cheap, suitable, and relatively non-combustible housing was available for $25–$45 per month, with typical examples generally cited at a rent of $31.[25] This range appears a little high compared to Robert Woods' estimate for the previous period. At rents equal to one sixth of income, families would require incomes of $1800–$3240 to secure these units. Yet it is not unfair to assume that Mr. Hall cited the lowest possible rent in order to make his point. Also, the prices of dwelling units bringing $20 a month or more rose about 20 per cent during this period.[26] It would seem conservative, therefore, to estimate that monthly middle-income rents were approximately $12 to $31.

Since income distributions are not available, we must determine the middle-income range from wage schedules for semiskilled and skilled labor. Typical wage rates, available in several studies and official sources, vary from $14 to $26 per week.[27] Assuming continuous employment, annual family income probably ranged from $874 to $1622. This estimate provides for a one-fifth increase over the income of the family head, because of supplementary wage earners. The upward adjustment represents a compromise between the 10 per cent to 12 per cent increase recommended by E. E. Wood[28] and the higher proportions used for the three previous periods based on other studies.

The rent-paying ability of this group ranged from $146 to $270 per annum, or $12 to $25 per month. Even if there had been completely satisfactory housing at $20 a month, which is much lower than the $25 or $31 cited by P. F. Hall, it is clear that most of this group would have been inadequately served were it not for the extraordinary boom in three-decker houses. Usually ranging in price from $12 to $31, although sometimes as high as $45, per month,[29] they served mainly the middle-income families and the fringes on top and bottom. Below par in some respects, superior in others, the three-decker was a telling example of one kind of middle-income housing solution.

1920–1929
War and postwar prosperity improved the economic position

of many, but the housing shortage and inflation between 1915 and 1930 erased much of the gains. Unfortunately, there are no data on the distribution of families by income for the period. We must, therefore, determine the income range for middle-income families from wage schedules for semiskilled workers and salaried employees. These rates ranged mainly between $25 to $43 a week.[30] If we assume once again continuous employment, plus an upward adjustment of one-fifth for supplementary wage earners, then annual income ranged from $1560 to $2683. Rent-paying capacity, likewise, varied from $260 to $447 per annum. This distribution seems reasonable and possibly somewhat generous, especially if compared with other strands of evidence. Thus, in August 1924 the Massachusetts Department of Labor and Industries indicated that the average wage for male employees in Massachusetts was about $27 a week. Boston's average for skilled and semi-skilled workers was doubtless higher. Edith Elmer Wood made a relatively comparable estimate, namely, $1600–$2500 for New York City's middle-income families during the 1920's.[31]

However, it was the families earning between $28 and $42 per week who experienced the greatest pinch of rent inflation during the 1920's. The Special Commission on the Necessaries of Life reported that, following 1922, "most of the complaints and requests for advice and assistance . . . received by the Commission were in regard to property renting for less than $40 a month."[32] They made repeated references to the need for construction that would rent between $26 and $40. Rents for existing apartments, it was claimed, rose almost to a level with rents for new construction.[33] Judging from newspaper advertisements, as well as the somewhat deflated 1930 rent distribution (Table 21),[34] modal rents for middle-income families probably ranged from $29 to $48 per month.

No adequate record exists for the second half of the decade, since the life of the commission was ended, despite pleas for continuance. Between December 1926 and December 1929, however, the situation appeared slightly eased, since the Bureau of Labor Statistics rent index dropped from 117.4 to 114.1.[35] Income, however, was also declining. If we examine the 1930 census rent distribution for Boston (Table 21), it is possible to estimate the extent of the rent squeeze even at the tail end of the shortage. Approximately 18 per cent of the families paid monthly rents below $22;[36] 34 per cent paid between $22 and $37; and approximately 48 per cent paid

Table 21. *Per cent of families in Boston, 1930, by monthly rents*

Monthly rent	% of families paying rent
Under $10	0.6
$10–14	3.8
$15–19	8.5
$20–29	22.6
$30–49	40.9
$50–74	16.9
$75–99	3.3
$100–149	1.1
$150–199	0.3
$200 and over	0.4
Not reported	1.7
Total	100

Source: Computed from the Fifteenth Census, U.S., 1930, *Population*, vol. 6, pp. 601–602.

rents over $37.[37] Assuming that two thirds of the population could afford a rent of only $37 per month or less, we find that 15 per cent of the families in the lower and middle brackets paid rents beyond their means.

1930–1939

There is no income distribution for Boston for the mid-1930's, but the National Resources Committee's analysis of family income indicates that 55 per cent of the families had incomes below $1,250 and 79 per cent below $2,000.[38] Boston's income was undoubtedly higher than the national average, and it seems reasonable (possibly generous) to assume that the income of Boston's middle third income group probably ranged between $1,300 and $2,100.[39] Actually, if we examine the family income distribution available for 1939, a period of higher income due to economic recovery and the beginning of defense preparations, we find that 41 per cent of the families fall below $1,300 and 31 per cent between $1,300 and $2,100, a total of 72 per cent.[40] But since this distribution is based on families reporting no other income, it is probably skewed somewhat towards the lower-income classes. There is also other evidence supporting a higher estimate. First, the Boston region has a more stable economic base than most cities.[41] Second, the cost-of-living study for Boston as prepared by the Works Progress Administration in 1935, using the budgetary requirements at maintenance level of a four-person manual worker's family, indicated a minimum income of $1,353.[42] Also, data available in the National Resources Committee report suggest that the average middle-income third for cities having a population of 100,000–1,500,000 lies between $1,200 and $2,000,[43] and Boston, Baltimore, Philadelphia, and other cities probably were higher than the average. Moreover, $1,150–$1,300 was about the average income maximum set then for eligibility in Boston's public housing projects.[44]

There was practically no minimum-standard housing, however, at rents below $20–$25 a month. In the years following 1920, it will be recalled, complaints multiplied because of the shortages and rent increases that occurred in apartments renting below $40. Rent maxima in Boston's public housing projects reached $26 per month.[45] Also approximately 50 per cent of all dwelling units renting between $25–$29 were built before 1900; and more than 40 per cent were three-family structures, probably the cheaper three-deckers.[46] Finally, the Real Property Inventory in Boston listed as "good" dwelling units only 23 per cent of the dwelling units renting between $25 and $30; and only 43 per cent between $30 and $39.[47] Since our derived middle-income group ($1300–$2100) required housing priced somewhere from $18 to $29 a month, it appears that a large proportion of this group (possibly more than half) was not too well housed. And despite doubling-up and shifts to inferior quarters, the proportion of rent to income was fairly high. According to the data of the Boston Real Property Inventory, 22 per cent of Boston's families paid monthly rents below $18; 32 per cent paid rents between $18 and $29; and 46 per cent paid over $29.[48] Table 22, based on census data obtained at the end of the decade, indicates that more than half the families of Boston were paying shelter rents of $30 and more.

1940–1947

Economic recovery, defense preparations, and then war and postwar prosperity again inflated incomes. Protests against rent and price rises largely ended in 1942 with the establishment of price and rent controls. They started again with the lifting of price regulations on new housing at the end of the war. Rents of existing housing, however, were kept under control until 1956.

A carefully prepared extrapolation of the income distribution in 1946 for the Boston metropolitan area[49] indicates that 34 per cent of the families had incomes below $2500, 30 per cent between $2500 and $4000, and 36 per cent over $4000.[50] Because of the price inflation (which, incidentally, pushed up to $2500 the maximum income limit set for eligibility for Boston's public housing projects), we may consider the families earning between $2500 and $4000 as the middle-income group.[51] Though they could pay rents ranging from $35 to $56 a month,[52] an April 1947 sample census survey indicated that much lower rents were in effect. Actually, 57 per cent of those reporting paid less than $35, 31 per cent between $35 and $50, and 11 per cent paid $50 or more.[53] These data do not show the effects of the relaxation of controls in July 1947, or the curtailed services and the extensive use of "bonuses" and other illegal stratagems.[54] Nonetheless, the data do indicate the prevailing trends, and it is clear that because of the relatively low rents the middle- and low-income groups reaped considerable cost-of-living benefits. It is not altogether certain in what form the improvement came. Rent controls and increased income created three major possibilities: higher real income because of reduced relative rent; or better housing by paying a higher price or rent; or some combination of the two.

1956–1959
The postwar shortage had eased considerably by the late 1950's. Rents of existing housing were still quite moderate, probably due to the residual effects of rent control, which had ended completely on December 31, 1956. A survey of the characteristics of the 1956 housing inventory of the Boston Standard Metropolitan Area showed that approximately 32 per cent of the reporting families had incomes of approximately $4000–$6000.[55] The families in this income range represent the middle-income brackets, though strictly speaking a slightly lower range would probably be more accurate. The bulk of the middle-income families paid gross rents of $50–$99.[56] Assuming that utilities averaged about 6.5 per cent of the gross rent, prevailing shelter rents then probably ranged from $47 to $94 per dwelling unit, or an average annual rental of $564 to $1128. The average estimated rent was approximately 17 per cent of average

TABLE 22. *Number and per cent of tenant-occupied and total dwelling units for Boston City and Boston metropolitan area, 1940, by monthly shelter rent*

Monthly shelter rent[a]	Boston City				Boston Metropolitan Area			
	All dwelling units[b]		Tenant-occupied units		All dwelling units[b]		Tenant-occupied units	
	Number	% of total	Number	% of total	Number	% of total	Number	% of total
$17 and under	33,468	16.2	26,542	17.1	75,168	11.9	55,365	14.4
$18–29	68,138	32.8	56,423	36.3	197,227	31.2	144,897	37.7
$30 and over	105,763	51.0	72,491	46.5	359,727	57.0	183,767	47.8
Total	207,369	100	155,456	100	632,122	100	384,029	100

[a] The figures for each rent class were derived by interpolation. Equal distribution within the census rent classes was assumed.
[b] These data refer to the reported contract rent of tenant-occupied nonfarm dwelling units and the reported estimated rental value of all other dwelling units, except the owner-occupied farm homes.

Source: Computed from the Sixteenth Census, U.S., 1940, *Housing*, vol. 3, part 2, Tables B-1, B-3, C-1, C-3, pp. 13, 15, 18, and 20.

income during this period; and this estimate of the rent–income ratio is roughly in line with corresponding ratios found for these middle-income families in the 1956 survey of the characteristics of Boston's housing inventory.[57]

RENTS AND PRICE RANGES FOR NEW CONSTRUCTION OF
MINIMUM-STANDARD

Up to this point, we have made comparisons primarily between the derived income of the middle-income families and the prevailing rents for existing minimum-standard housing of the period. Rents for new construction would indicate whether builders served the middle-income families directly. The price levels at which new units enter the market and the volume of units produced will determine the adequacy of the filtration process in making second-hand housing available at a lower price to families of modest income.[58]

For this analysis, we need rent estimates for dwellings in newly built low-cost construction. Since our purpose is only to determine the rents for such housing, we can ignore the complexities growing out of variations in type and quality. The paragraphs below review typical examples of low-priced construction for each period and make summary estimates of the probable rent ranges for such construction, based primarily on the studies and data already discussed.

Judging by the newspaper advertisements, the yearly rent per room for new minimum-standard housing in 1846 ranged from $25 to $35. Accordingly, newly built three- to five-room tenements for middle-income families probably rented annually for between $90 and $175.

During the 1870's the Boston Cooperative Company built model housing. Rents in the East Canton Houses, containing 125 tenements, ranged from $156 to $247 per annum for three- and four-room units.[59] It is probable that these rates were characteristic of rents for minimum-standard new construction.[60]

Robert Paine reported that in the 1890's, prior to the enactment of the law of 1897 requiring fireproof construction for all tenement buildings, builders could put up tenements renting for $16 a month or less.[61] A range of $180–$264 per annum results, if we take a rent of $15 a month as the low point and if we accept R. F. Phelps' estimate of $22 as the prevalent high rent for skilled workers in the center of the city.[62]

During the three-decker period (1900–1914), rents for new houses in Boston, according to the comprehensive British Board of Trade survey, generally ranged from $14 to $35 per month.[63]

During the decade following World War I, rents for new minimum-standard apartments varied from $40 to $60 a month.[64] Between 1930 and 1945 relatively few units were built, and most of these were for higher-income groups. It is doubtful whether the builders supplied middle-income housing at rents lower than $35–$45 a month.[65]

Following World War II, builders of low-priced housing erected dwelling units at rents ranging from $75 to $100 per month.[66]

By 1956 to 1959, specialists of the Boston Real Estate Board and other local real estate experts estimated that inexpensive new one- to three-bedroom units rented at a monthly rate of $100 to $150.

Finally, the Boeckh building cost index numbers, as indicated in Chapter 2, provide independent confirmation. They show the same relative increase in construction costs compared to the relative changes in rent levels for new minimum standard housing over the past four periods and between each of the past four periods as are disclosed by the data assembled in Table 1.

APPENDIX B

....

Rent Control and Housing

Despite the controversy surrounding the policy of rent control, there are practically no serious studies of the effects of different controls on the housing market.[1] This gap is almost matched by the gap in adequate studies of housing market behavior. Our appendix will not fill these gaps. Its aims are far more limited, namely to indicate the complexity of the issues and to suggest some possible explanations to account for the empirical findings of Chapter 4.

SOME ASPECTS OF HOUSING MARKET BEHAVIOR IN THE
SHORT RUN

To trace the effects in which we are interested, it would be helpful to know more about the behavior of certain housing submarkets in the short run. For example, there is the submarket for the existing stock of housing and the submarkets for conversions and for new construction; and these in turn can be divided into categories such as single-family owner occupancy, single-family leasing, multifamily leasing, etc.[2] These submarkets are interrelated on both the supply and the demand side. For example, rental and sales housing are to some extent substitutes; and the rent–sale price ratio will often influence whether individual families choose to buy or rent. But this choice will also depend on levels of income, the availability of rental and sales housing, the amount of liquid assets, terms of financing, tax considerations, expectations, the prospects of land speculation, migration trends, prices of substitutes, and household formation and composition. In general, rental housing in this country is a good example of the "poor man's good" in economic literature: for as the income of families increase, they prefer as a rule to own rather than rent.[3]

There are also interrelationships on the supply side. Thus, the intensity of use of housing will depend on the size of the family and on the availability of dwelling units of different size,[4] as well as on consumer attitudes and expectations and the relative levels of sale prices and rents. Similarly, the type of housing built will depend not only on the relative costs of different housing types, the existing sale prices, the rents of the existing stock of such housing, and consumer preferences: it will also be influenced by vacancies, the prospects for land value appreciation, tax policy, relative risks, the production period, ease of entry and egress of productive factors, expectations, capitalization of the typical builder, government policy, and the terms of financing, such as the availability of credit for different types of housing.

The fact that our knowledge is quite limited on most of these matters does not seem to have inhibited some writers from developing cavalier prescriptions for policy in a period of housing shortage.[5] Rent control, they suggest, is a naïve expedient seriously espoused only by the economically illiterate. Higher prices, they maintain, provide the signals for fresh additions to the stock of housing to be made by the builder, and the higher prices will also allocate existing housing more objectively and economically than is possible under controls. In their view, housing shortage and increased income add no basically new elements to the problems faced by the price mechanism: these two factors only intensify the scarcity of housing resources which it is the job of the market mechanism to allocate. Rent control, they suggest, only worsens the situation: for it interferes with normal market adjustments, deflects the rationing role of the price mechanism, increases the effective demand in a period of shortage, and tends to dampen expectations and discourage new production; and, if rent control occurs without sales price control, as is likely to be the case in our society, because of the resentment and resistance such an effort would entail, the net effect, it is argued, would be to distort the price–income ratio in the direction of selling rather than leasing of rental properties.

Perhaps it is because the effects seem so clear cut that there has scarcely been any closer scrutiny of this position. And yet, as is the case with many controversial issues, reality is often not nearly so simple or so obedient to our doctrines. To show why this may be so, we must peer a little more closely at some of the probable patterns of housing market behavior in a period of shortage and increased income, both when the market is free and when there are rent controls.

Housing Market Behavior in a Free Market

Tenure Shifts

First let us examine tenure shifts on the demand side. Assuming that a housing shortage exists in a free market, in what direction are these shifts likely to occur? There are several possibilities. Families preferring to rent may be forced to buy a house. Others interested in owning may rent instead, because of high sale prices. Still others desiring to rent or to own may buy rental housing (one-, two-, three-, or more family units) in order to reduce their own monthly payments or to find an adequate home relatively well suited to their requirements. Many families will double up or accept inferior accommodations if prices are too high, or, in any case, beyond their means. Others will remain in existing accommodations, so that the pinch of the shortage will be felt most acutely by newcomers to the market, such as veterans, in-migrants, and newly formed families, and by those who for some reason or other were dispossessed of their home. All of these forces are eventually reflected in price changes and in the net changes in the per cent of owner-occupied and tenant-occupied dwellings. Is it possible, however, to judge the probable direction of tenure shifts without reference to these component decisions, the data for which do not exist?

What, for example, are likely to be the effects of increased demand that may result from a numerical increase of households, from increased income, or from the two combined? A numerical increase of housholds tends to exert pressure on rental housing. Newly formed families, in-migrants, and returning veterans are largely in the low- and middle-income groups requiring rental housing. The first two categories tend to increase substantially in periods of prosperity. If rental housing does not increase proportionately, rents rise. Many families may then be forced into ownership, either because of the urgent need for quarters or because rents have risen to the point where equal or lower monthly outlays plus a small down payment will buy an equity in a house. A large proportion of middle-income families, however, remain tenants because of lack of cash for down payments, inability to make monthly payments higher than their rent, or unwillingness to become tied to a house. Their alternatives are to pay increased rents and reduce other expenditures, to seek smaller and less desirable accommodations, or to double up. If enough suitable accommodations are made available—for example, through conversions—a percentage increase of tenancy may result. For numerical increase of households, therefore, we can venture no determinate answer concerning the shifts in tenure unless there is information on the number of families who might choose to own. How many families make this choice depends on several factors, including the number of families close to the income category where ownership predominates, the savings of these families, terms of financing, and the cost of new and old owner-occupied units.[6]

The size, distribution, and permanence of increased real income will also determine the impact on tenure. In ordinary circumstances, increased income draws families into ownership status.[7] The impact, of course, would vary for different communities, depending largely on the number and distribution of families close to the margin of ownership status. The increase would also be partially arrested by the resulting price hike for housing. As a rule, however, the larger the rise in real income, the greater the trend to ownership. The result of both increased income and an increased number of families would probably be strong pressure on both rental and sales prices. Some families would be able to buy homes; still others would prefer to own rather than pay higher rents; and some, lacking accommodations, might distort their expenditure budgets and purchase a house. In short, both forced and voluntary increases in ownership would occur.

Two further points, however, require notice. First, the increase in income may be an increase in dollar income rather than real income. And second, income increases may be temporary, while ownership commitments are generally for long periods. Optimism concerning the future, and miscalculations based on an apparent increase of income would tend to push still more families who have enough savings or the prospects of steady income into ownership status.

On the supply side, the pressure toward ownership may be somewhat tempered by the reluctance of landlords to sell if they have a prospect of high rental returns. Both possibilities being available, much would depend on the attitudes and financial policies of the landlords in handling their properties and their judgments concerning the strength and duration of the sellers' market. In the absence of relevant data or previous analysis of these factors, perhaps it would be useful to assume for short-term periods a principle of inertia—that is, that the homes which are owner-occupied will stay owner-occupied and the houses which are rented will stay rented, except when other important forces come into play. During a housing shortage and period of rising income and price inflation, the predominant "other forces" in a free market encourage the trend toward ownership. Persons or firms owning rental properties that are questionable investments are eager to sell as the market rises. Then, at or toward the peak of the market, many may perhaps prefer to hold their properties for rental. As confidence in the duration of the shortage or the sellers' market ebbs, the tendency to sell reasserts itself. In the movement toward and away from the inflationary peaks, many rental properties change tenure.

Though these observations apply primarily to one- and two-family houses, sales of other types, including individual units in apartment houses, are not impossible and may often occur. True, countervailing tendencies exist, such as the dividing of large houses in an effort to cut costs, the creation of kitchenette apartments in private homes for the duration of the shortage to gain income, and possibly even the renting of homes that would ordinarily be sold in the market. Though such two-way shifts of tenure do occur, nonetheless, because of the larger number of rental units, the urge to get rid of dubious investments, and the lure of a "quick killing," at least an even balance is achieved, with the probability of ownership pressures dominating.

New Construction and Tenure

Builders today tend to produce primarily one-family dwellings for sale. A variety of circumstances has led to this situation. First and most obvious, the average builder with limited capital, who flits in and out of business, wants to risk as little as possible and wants to get even that little bit back very quickly, so that it can be used in other operations. This tendency applies also to larger builders who wish to get the most turnover with whatever capital is available. Construction of small houses for sale is therefore the favored practice. Second, the most profitable market is found among the higher-income groups, who have increasingly turned toward suburban one-family developments. Third, the breakdown of the traditional faith in the appreciation of land values has largely removed one of the chief incentives for rental investments. Clearly, ease of business entry and egress, limited capital, desire for quick turnover, plus higher profit, induces building for sale.

Familiar deterrents also exist for many firms that might otherwise be interested in building rental housing. Inflexible physical developments, involving huge and relatively nonliquid financial investments, must withstand the dangers of tax disadvantages, new fashions in housing design, neighborhood changes, rigid fixed costs, and extreme competition in periods of overbuilding or deflation. For these reasons, most new residential construction is built for sale.[8]

After a downturn of construction activity, building for sale generally starts earlier than building for rent. At first this seems surprising, since some savings are necessary to meet the down payment required for ownership. But in a "normal" building cycle, such building generally occurs first because the supply of owned homes probably came close to rock bottom[9] in the preceding period of deflation and foreclosure, and some equities are built up in the period of recovery. Owing to the same forces, the rental market is swamped on the downswing.[10] New rental investments do not get under way until vacancies are low and rents point upward. A war economy accelerates this process. Income and savings rise, building is curtailed, and vacancies vanish. Nonetheless, rental investments may still not be made. Cost trends are crucial. If these trends are uncertain or seem unduly high, compared with existing rents and values, or because of the fear of deflation, long-term commitments will be eschewed or made warily. When this fact is coupled with pressures in the direction of producing housing for sale, with its fewer risks and surer profit prospects, it becomes apparent that unusual circumstances must prevail to create an early rental building boom.

However, the tendencies noted above require some qualification. First, special governmental inducements can stimulate the building of additional housing for rent. A recent example was the extension of mortgage insurance for rental housing, which opened intriguing prospects for profiteering and financial legerdemain under the liberal appraisals and supervision of the Federal Housing Administration.[11] Even with this assistance, the proportion of rental housing produced was significantly below the requirements for the nation.[12] Second, a tendency to build two- and three-family units may emerge in inflationary periods. There is a market for such homes because rental returns can help cut the high costs. But this tendency is partially circumscribed by the limited number of purchasers able to meet the initial financial requirements which higher capital costs presuppose. Finally, the patterns described above are characteristic of the *whole* housing market area. Within the central core of large cities, the proportion of rental housing built will tend to be higher because of limited space and higher land values.

Efficiency and Economy

A favorite contention in behalf of the free-market economy is that it achieves relatively efficient solutions. According to Friedman and Stigler, the free market approximates such solutions even in a period of shortage: they believe that as the shortage increases and prices are bid up, the relative value of housing for individual families is presumably expressed by what they are willing to pay for their quarters. Those who cannot or will not pay higher rents must economize on space by moving to smaller houses or doubling-up. In the process, space is made available for other families. If this situation tends to favor some groups and discriminate against others, because of varying ability to pay, the fault, if any, lies with the distribution of income, not with the price system. To change that distribution, it is contended, poses serious problems which should be tackled directly and not implicitly through the medium of rent controls.[13]

This line of argument raises at least two issues: the efficiency of the price solution, and the economical use of housing space. There is reason to question whether the price mechanism alone will necessarily result in efficient exchange relationships. It is extremely doubtful whether the assumptions of a competitive model are appropriate for a very imperfect housing market, and especially in a period of severe housing shortage. The commodity is "lumpy" and not homogeneous; utility is not measurable; prices are not parameters more or less set by the market; there are restrictions to the entry of labor into the industry and of housing into the community; and the supply of rental housing is comparatively inelastic because of the excessive risks and high capital requirements. Exchange is often transformed into duress, and rents easily become extortionate. A pure monopoly does not exist, but it is clear that substantial monopolistic elements are present. Agreements reached under such conditions do not result in efficient distribution and exchange.[14] The situation is serious, moreover, in the same sense that monopolies are: namely, high prices do not attract, quickly or directly, new competitive resources. This is true partly because of the long period of time required to build an adequate supply of new housing, partly because the building of new housing is principally for sale rather than for rent, partly because builders may be waiting for construction costs to stabilize or decline, and partly because of the deterrents to rental investments already noted. An important consequence of this situation is that, because of the absence of real alternatives, families may rarely be in a position to economize on space; instead there may be a redistribution of income in favor of those who are able to take advantage of it.

From the viewpoint of economic theory, therefore, we cannot justify the market allocation of residential space in time of shortages on the grounds of efficiency. Other criteria may be required, such as comparative inefficiency, production incentives, or social objectives. But we are not able in this case to measure comparative inefficiency; and our analysis has already indicated that the production of rental housing in a free market tends to be retarded, especially in a period of inflated costs.

As for the impact on social objectives, that depends on what effects are valued. Avoidance of rent controls is more compatible with the nation's general preference for a market economy; but in a period of housing shortage it is probable that the main brunt of the redistribution of income or space economies are likely to be shouldered by the renters. Relief in the form of new construction would also come last to the lower-income groups, because builders serve the upper-income market first. In particular, the families of in-migrants, evictees, and veterans, the groups who (as will be indicated shortly) are in the most disadvantageous position under rent controls, would be in an even less enviable position, because the shortage still exists and the prices are higher for inferior accommodations. Contrary to the conclusions reached by Professors Friedman and Stigler,[15] "less desirable" tenants, such as those with children, might still be subject to discrimination. Since real income is reduced, inflationary pressures for wage increases may also develop or be intensified. The potential sustained market for home ownership too might be considerably curtailed, because of the reduction or wiping out of possible savings or cash equities.

HOUSING MARKET BEHAVIOR UNDER RENT CONTROLS

A variety of rent or price control procedures is possible. Controls may be imposed on rents below a certain level, on the size of rent increases, on sale prices as well as rents, on certain types of buildings, on new construction as well as existing housing, and they may be designed for short or long periods of time. The system of controls may be isolated, or it may be linked to controls of materials, wage rates, and to incentive programs geared to stimulate certain types of production. Obviously, all of these alternatives cannot be explored here. This analysis deals with the probable effects of one type of control evolved in the postwar period, namely, control of rents in existing houses.[16] Except where otherwise stated we assume that reasonable enforcement measures are applied, and that controls permit reasonable adjustments for rising costs and for new improvements. To avoid duplication, the rest of the analysis will concentrate on the points where differences might arise as a result of this type of control as opposed to free-market patterns.

Tenure Shifts

New families, in-migrants, veterans, and evictees are still at a disadvantage under rent controls, but less so than without controls. In a free market, there would be difficulty in finding quarters, since rents would be raised, and few, if any, reasonably priced vacancies would be available because of the housing shortage. Under controls, while all newcomers to the market find accommodations with difficulty, rents for existing housing are less expensive for those lucky enough to have or to obtain such units.[17]

Increased incomes intensify the search for better accommodations. Ownership pressures, particularly from the top middle- and upper-income groups, are generated. A countervailing force, however, might largely, if not entirely, negate this tendency. Many families who would otherwise purchase might choose to rent instead, because of the more favorable situation in existing housing compared with prices for new construction.

Forced ownership under controls may still develop, of course, because of the need for many families to find homes. This pressure, however, might be reduced to the extent that other families would not be forced to join the search, since there would be fewer abrupt rent increases.[18] Moreover, additional income, available to tenants as a result of lower rents, may contribute to savings as well as to increased consumption by families of other items. The improved financial position of some of these families would help to build up equities for home purchases; and, therefore, ownership may eventually be possible for many families on a more reasonable basis because of rent controls.

A tendency to sell will also develop. Higher sale prices may in many cases prove more attractive to landlords than controlled rents. However, larger rental properties are generally not involved, except where "cooperatives" may be established; and, in some cases, higher returns from reduced repairs and services, and few or no vacancies, may make renting desirable.[19] The transfer of smaller properties would depend on their financial and housing status. If properties are bad risks or yield low returns, they will probably be sold, which is approximately the situation without controls.

Probably a larger number of conversions would occur under controls, if they were reasonably administered. Tight limitations on allowable rents would simply dry up this source of rental units. But if the initial rents are set by owners and accepted by the control agency as a base line for rents, many units will be temporarily brought into the market by owners wishing to profit from, as well as those anxious to help alleviate, the shortage. Many owners will resort to conversions as a means of circumventing existing rent ceilings on their properties.[20] If the rent ceilings are too low, not only will conversions cease, but existing properties will probably suffer from inadequate maintenance and repairs, and their deterioration will be accelerated. Evasions of controls can be anticipated, but the incidence will be a function of the fairness of the base date, the adequacy of the legislation, and the reasonableness of the administrative and enforcement measures.

For tenants the chief beneficial effects of controls are increased real income and the reduction (not elimination) of forced purchases. A tendency toward more and sounder ownership as a result of increased real income would also occur, especially if sale prices remained within reach. Single-, two-, and to a much smaller extent, three-family homes in *tenancy status* would probably be the most important classes of property influencing the over-all percentage of tenure shifts. Their importance would vary with the number of such units in the community, and the financial plans and prospects for these properties. Though increased ownership may be anticipated, it seems doubtful whether the increase in ownership would greatly exceed, if at all, the shifts that would occur without controls.

New Construction and Tenure

If rents of new construction were controlled, there would be a deterrent influence on the quantity and type of new construction. Overly strict requirements, especially in the face of rising costs, might discourage or put an end to new construction. High or flexible ceilings would allow some latitude for reasonable and even substantial profit; but some curtailment in building might result from uncertainty as to possible shifts in policy. Such flexible controls, however, might have special importance in cases where high priority needs exist and where materials and labor shortages make it mandatory that new construction be channeled in these directions. Though many builders might drop out, others would continue, some even if returns reached only a break-even point, in order to maintain the continuity of their building operations. Additional incentives—for example, subsidies—might be required to secure construction in less profitable areas, such as rental housing for moderate- and low-income groups.

The case in which we are particularly interested, however, concerns rent controls on existing housing, with new construction remaining free of restrictions. Building under these conditions would not vary significantly from the characteristic patterns developed under the free market. Most new construction would be for owner occupancy. Building of rental housing would serve the top-income market because of high construction costs, and then somewhat tardily because of the numerous handicaps confronting such investments.

Two factors may, nonetheless, serve further to limit new rental construction. Fear of expanded controls might create an additional obstacle for venture capital, though it is difficult to determine the effects of this influence. It could be important or negligible, depending on the confidence of the builder in the existence of limited controls and the strength of the market for housing. The second limiting factor may be fear of competition. If construction costs are high and rising, rentals in new construction will greatly exceed those charged for existing houses under controls. In these circumstances, many tenants would rather stay where they are than switch to new houses; and this possibility may worry new investors. Though the fear may be justified eventually, particularly if controls continue indefinitely, it is often premature. New residences offer certain improvements over existing housing. Even more important is the fact that in periods of shortage a large market exists, comprised of those families inadequately housed. This market will increase if the building of rental housing gets off to its characteristically slow start.[21]

Removal of controls on existing housing might temporarily expand the immediate market and create additional incentives. But it is doubtful whether this policy would significantly offset the general impediments to building for rent. In any case, building following a downswing in construction activity would not commence earlier or in greater volume than in the free market, where the process is already clearly retarded.

Efficiency and Economy

Under rent controls, the economist's criterion of efficiency is not achieved any more effectively than it is in a free market. If the control program is administered fairly, the result is primarily to limit exploitation by the landlord of his favored position. But despite controls, monopolistic elements still survive. Tenants have almost no real alternatives. Often by cutting services and sometimes even basic maintenance and repairs, the landlord can further augment his immediate income. This practice may occur to a considerable extent even without controls. If, however, rent increases by the control agency are contingent upon improvements, a considerable improvement of housing quality may actually develop.

Ordinarily, with high income, short supply, and imposition of price controls, some form of unit rationing of goods is required. Otherwise some families will not be served. Commodity rationing, however, is administratively inapplicable to housing, which unlike sugar or butter, is not a homogeneous product that can be fairly apportioned in small units.[22] Doubling-up and resort to slums, therefore, will take place just as under the free market.

With increased income, more space is likely to be purchased. A housing shortage coupled with rent control will freeze the situation. Use of more space will occur more often than not *prior* to the imposition of rent controls. The lack of alternative accommodations forces families to cling to their existing quarters, and rent control tends to make this possible.

Important variations, however, may occur between owners and tenants in the use of space. With steep sale prices, a tendency will exist to buy smaller houses or apartments. Many families, however, may rent even more space than they need just as others may buy homes to secure shelter. Owners, however, who constitute the over-whelming majority of those who have space to spare, will be far less affected.[23] Without controls, the economical use of space, when it does occur, is imposed on all tenants in existing houses, prospective tenants, and prospective purchasers of houses. Under controls, the onus is confined to prospective tenants and owners and to some extent to existing tenants who may cooperate in the doubling-up process.

In judging economy in the use of space produced by higher prices, other criteria must also be taken into account. Two already considered in the above discussion are the freeing of space for others and the nature of the groups upon whom the burden of space economy will fall. Housing standards are a third factor of impor-tance. Rent rises tend to strike with regressive effects, especially since the greatest pressure exists on housing for low- and middle-income groups. The effect of rent controls is to protect higher stand-ards, particularly for the segments of the population which the na-tion believes require such aid.

SUMMARY

If the previous account is correct, a severe housing inflation and crisis may be expected if there are no controls. For many years, no adequate relief in the form of new construction will come, despite high rents. The building of high-priced houses for sale would be stimulated, but rental housing construction will be small in propor-tion and relatively slow in starting. Forced shifts to ownership will occur, possibly in an intensified form. Housing resources will not be priced efficiently, and the demand, both effective and social, will not be adequately met. The principal effect of higher prices may be to redistribute income rather than to get families to relinquish space; and, to the extent that space is relinquished, the greatest pressure will fall on tenants living in the most crowded dwellings rather than on owners, who have more available space and whose tenure rights insulate them from some of the pressures.

Rent control, in the form described, does nothing to solve the housing shortage, but under controls real income for most tenants will remain higher. Better space standards will also prevail. Comparable or somewhat greater shifts of tenure will probably take place, particularly for one- and two-family houses previously rented. Forced ownership will likewise occur, but perhaps to a lesser extent. A sounder potential market of home purchasers may be created. More rental units are also likely to develop through conversions, induced in part by controls. After the building program has continued for some time, the prevalence of lower rents in existing housing may curtail further construction. There would be a tendency, especially under unfair administration, real or imaginary, for housing production to slow down; but new rental housing would be only slightly affected since in any case it would be retarded and small.

Notes on Walter Firey's Critique

of the Sector Thesis

Walter Firey has sharply challenged Homer Hoyt's sector thesis and has formulated an alternative theory.[1] Firey's ideas are of interest, partly because of the attention we devoted to this subject in Chapter 6 and partly because Firey leans on the experience of land use in central Boston to buttress his views.

In his analysis, Firey lays great stress on the role of cultural and social systems in conditioning land use.[2] Properties of space and the ends of the social system using the space, he explains, derive from the cultural system. In some cases like Beacon Hill, the Boston Common, and even the North End, the society–space relationships may be "nonintrinsic," i.e., the area assumes certain symbolic qualities related to the cultural system. Activities come to such space because of the significance of the symbol.[3] The values or ends of the cultural system thus directly and actively determine the locational pattern. In other cases, space is not endowed with such qualities. Activities adapt themselves to the space on the basis of their "interests," as, for example, land used for business purposes. But here too, the relationship is indirectly but culturally conditioned: this is because the use of the space reflects the rational adjustments of these activities to the requirements of a particular cultural and social system, such as the historically contingent "contractualistic" or market economy as contrasted with possible alternatives to such an economy. Where conflict may occur between two types of systems, the older system may wield a selective influence shaping the priority, types, and patterns of new uses, as for example the better boardinghouses or shopping facilities in the declining but still fashionable Back Bay area.[4] It is Firey's belief that this socio-cultural approach will clear away the discrepancies implicit in the prevailing economic or "determin-istic" analyses and offer a more logically consistent and empirically satisfactory ecological theory.[5]

Firey's study is a curious anomaly. It is a model of correct methodology, thoughtful formulation of hypotheses, imaginative ap-plication of sociological theory, painstaking scholarship, and keen criticism—all of which is marred by misunderstanding or distortions of the theories he criticizes, incorrect interpretations of the data, lack of appreciation of the role of economic analysis, and a some-what superficial and inadequate ecological "theory" of proportion-ality borrowed from the economists. It is nonetheless a sufficiently impressive contribution, as Hoyt himself observed,[6] to warrant close examination.

Firey's initial insistence on the mechanism and determinism of Hoyt's thesis is inaccurate.[7] Hoyt recognizes the role of noneco-nomic values. In fact, his principal thesis depends upon such a force, i.e., the prestige of "leaders of society" to explain the cluster and development of housing in the direction of upper-class environs.[8] Hoyt, moreover, is obviously describing and interpreting past loca-tion tendencies and makes no claim for inevitability. Firey, also, seems to overlook the fact that for certain problems cultural phe-nomena can be treated as parameters.[9] Economists have frequently taken tastes, values, and technology for granted. The simplification is useful and desirable. It does not mean that these factors cannot be treated differently for other inquiries.[10] The result of Firey's misinterpretation of Hoyt's position is that he has failed to attack its strongest features, and his argument as a consequence is ineffec-tual.

Existence of a significant sector pattern either in Boston's past history or current housing patterns is likewise denied by Firey. De-spite his detailed documentation, however, Firey's position may be questioned. He forgets that Hoyt indicated the possibility of several sectors. Hence, when Firey finds several sectors in the early period he seems to argue that their existence contradicts the theory.[11] The North End, Beacon Hill, and Fort Hill–Pearl Street districts at the time of the Revolution could be regarded as sectors in Hoyt's sense. But Firey contends that the movement of these upper-class districts was "from North to West, then from West to South following no consistent sector outward. . . ."[12] He overlooks the role of topog-raphy, however. Expansion to the north was impossible, and Beacon

Hill's growth was cut off by the still-unfilled Back Bay. Thus it was logical that the southern Fort Hill–Pearl Street area should be developed. Afterwards the line of growth continued in a southerly direction down Colonnade Row (Tremont Street) and later toward the South End.[13] Only after Back Bay was filled in did the Beacon Hill–Bowdoin Square neighborhoods have an area for expansion, and many families shifted from the South End to be closer to that neighborhood. True, scattered upper-class families lived elsewhere, and the sector is not entirely homogeneous; but it is astonishing even on the basis of Firey's own data and information to see him conclude that "The discovery of any sector of upper-class residential distribution from such an arrangement appears to be quite impossible."[14]

When Firey finally discovers something that resembles a sector in 1865, he immediately reinterprets his conclusions. He calls attention to the fact that the Beacon Hill and Colonnade Row–South End neighborhoods comprised two distinct noncontiguous concentrations, which is true but perfectly consistent with Hoyt's thesis. As for the "direct linear succession outward from Colonnade Row to the South End which might confirm the dynamic aspects of Hoyt's theory,"[15] Firey dismisses the pattern as an improper validation due to the peculiar, topographical configuration which forced development southward. Firey detects here the role of topography, whereas its importance for the earlier period in forcing a reversal of development in the North End and Beacon Hill completely escaped his attention. In any case, expansion of the upper-income neighborhood need not have proceeded inexorably toward the "Neck" and South End as Firey maintains. An upper-class residential district might have and almost did spring up in South Boston, something which many people anticipated and which Firey himself points out elsewhere.[16]

Later Firey scrutinizes the Back Bay development from a variety of aspects, all designed to show that it was not inevitable. Granting that this is true, it was clearly a possibility that materialized. Nowhere, however, is there any mention of the obvious and undeniable sector appearance of Back Bay and its marked continuity with the Beacon Hill area. Firey's analysis of the role of prestige, precedent, and values does help to explain why the rich live together in neighborhoods, factors that Hoyt in a sense took for granted. Little in Firey's approach, however, accounts for the location, shape, or direction of growth of areas such as Boston's Back Bay.

Contemporary trends, Firey discovers, indicate a clear-cut southwesterly high-rental or upper-class "band" extending outward from Beacon Hill, which again would seem to confirm the sector hypothesis. This cartographic misapprehension Firey immediately attributes to the existence of many upper-class towns or summer resorts where the rich had country homes. Their existence presumably antedated the radial development, and thus are not accepted as evidence for Hoyt's thesis.[17] Quite the contrary could be argued, however. Hoyt specifically contends that "high-grade residential growth tends to proceed from the given point of origin along established lines of travel or toward another existing nucleus of building or trading centers."[18] It is perfectly reasonable, or at any rate not inconsistent, to find that the direction of growth was toward areas where the upper class had their summer homes or friends. However, Firey suggests that within these broad sectors considerable heterogeneity occurs, so that the sector is really more apparent than real. As an example, he cites the working-class and commercial areas lying between the Beacon Hill–Back Bay area and the fashionable Brattle Street residential section of Cambridge. Though the point has some merit, Hoyt could easily side-step the charge by considering these areas as two separate sectors, as well they might be, since Brattle Street is some distance from the Beacon Hill–Back Bay area and not at all directly in the line of development from this area. The same argument holds for the Back Bay–Fens–Brookline development and the Dedham district to which Firey refers. Depending therefore on the period and the interpretation of a sector,[19] Beacon Hill, Colonnade Row, South End, Back Bay, Brattle Street, and still other areas might be regarded as upper-class residential sectors from Hoyt's point of view.

Firey finally proposes that the community must serve as a "social system" with functional requirements set by the larger society, and that the allocation of space for the various ends is to be achieved according to a criterion which he calls the "proportionalization of ends," i.e., a point of maximum satisfaction or attainment of the various ends of the community. This theory of "proportionality" does Firey a disservice in several respects. It is a close parallel to indifference curve analysis of economists, and a comparison will quickly reveal its weaknesses. Specifically the proportionality "theory" suggests that ends must be so served spatially as to minimize "end-deprivation."[20] Firey explicitly indicates that it refers to more than costs, thus indicating he is thinking in economists' terms but wishes to broaden the elements included in the analysis. But his "theory" stops at that point. Economists, however, go much further. Refined assumptions, marginal analysis, use of the substitution principle, plus price ratios are required to arrive at relatively significant and determinate conclusions rigorously deduced. In the absence of these or comparable elements Firey's proposition is an empty, even if well-intentioned, exhortation. The fact that he wants to extend the scope of noneconomic activities would further complicate the analysis, as Firey would learn if he consulted the welfare economists who have been exploring social costs and who have become increasingly discouraged by the difficulties of making interpersonal and intergroup comparisons.

Firey's conclusions, which are intended to serve as implications of a cultural ecology, reflect all of these limitations. He favors redevelopment of central areas, long-range planning, broadened urban boundaries, slum clearance, subsidized low-rent housing, and more parks, all presumably as deductions from the theory of proportionality. One may or may not share these conclusions, but it would be easy to come to just the opposite conclusions if one so desired and if so amenable an instrument served as a guide. If, to cite some examples, a realtor claimed that in the long run the community would be better off with no public housing, or if a "houser" favored redevelopment of peripheral rather than central areas, Firey would be assuming the proof if he argued that on the contrary these proposals increased "end deprivation." At best his conclusions may be consistent with his principle, but they are not in any way derived therefrom. Firey himself reflects uneasiness on this score in his last paragraph, declaring that these conclusions "may not all be sound or feasible and they may not all have been properly deduced from our theoretical construct, though every effort has been exerted to make them so."[21] His conclusions likewise indicate that Firey missed or dismissed part of the aim of Hoyt's analysis, namely, to search for possible *locational* generalizations describing the contemporary structure and growth of urban land use. The explanation is simple enough: Firey does not believe that such generalizations are possible.[22]

The purpose of this analysis is not to defend Hoyt's sector thesis, as the discussion in Chapter 6 indicates. But it must be clear that Firey's ideas hardly graze Hoyt's generalizations on residential structure and growth. A satisfactory alternative must be able to introduce issues of public policy and social values without pulling solutions out of the air or abandoning usable methodology, and without ignoring either actual empirical tendencies or valid elements in existing hypotheses, however crudely they may be formulated. Subject to these reservations, Firey undoubtedly provides a more thorough and theoretically sophisticated appraisal of social structure and relationships than Hoyt's simple explanation. In particular, Firey's study sheds light on

1. The historically contingent character of all our urban land uses;

2. How values, purposes, and community sentiments, as in the case of the Boston Common and Beacon Hill, may significantly influence land use;

3. The role of social systems and cultural values in shaping adaptive behavior and use patterns within defined areas, such as Back Bay and the North and South ends.

Per cent of Population Changes in Boston by Wards for Selected Periods, 1885–1950

Wards	1885–1895	1900–1910	1915–1920	1925–1939	1940–1950
1	52.1	30.0	4.0	−10.3	−10.7
2	19.1	25.7	− 8.6	−32.5	22.5
3	13.1	5.3	−11.7	−27.7	− 4.8
4	6.8	0.3	−15.5	−10.1	16.4
5	1.2	− 0.3	−18.4	− 8.7	20.4
6	5.4	17.1	− 6.0	−21.3	− 2.6
7	7.7	0.9	8.6	− 5.1	3.8
8	16.7	12.5	2.1	−16.4	− 1.4
9	5.5	7.5	−14.8	−22.2	13.7
10	−39.6	14.3	− 0.1	−11.7	11.9
11	44.0	42.4	2.4	1.3	1.7
12	−22.4	2.8	− 4.8	11.0	− 2.0
13	− 9.0	− 5.6	−13.6	− 2.3	4.2
14	22.7	9.9	− 6.5	17.0	− 3.2
15	20.1	7.7	− 1.0	− 0.4	− 3.9
16	− 0.7	28.1	15.6	23.9	1.4
17	13.3	5.5	5.5	21.7	− 0.2
18	25.3	1.5	10.3	35.1	11.7
19	10.0	16.7	9.1	17.7	4.0
20	44.1	71.1	15.6	51.0	12.9
21	81.5	27.8	28.1	31.3	12.5
22	64.2	17.0	9.1	25.8	3.3
23	88.0	29.7	16.1	—	—
24	90.4	39.2	5.5	—	—
25	76.1	37.8	35.6	—	—
26	—	—	8.9	—	—

Source: Computed from federal and state census reports for the years indicated above. (For exact citations, see the Bibliography.)

APPENDIX E

Ward Boundaries of Boston

Map 6A. Ward boundaries of Boston: 1846
Source: L. Shattuck, Report to the Committee of the Council to obtain the census of Boston, for the year 1845, Boston, 1846

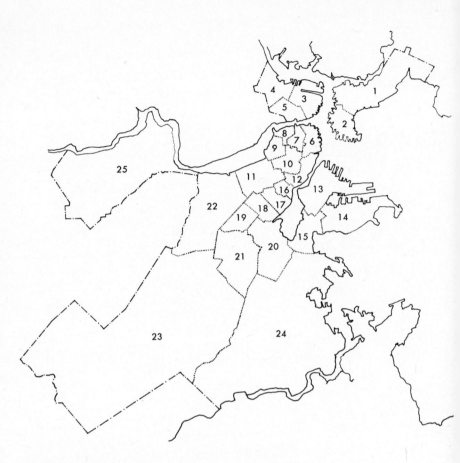

Map 6B. Ward boundaries of Boston: 1875–1895
Source: Municipal Register of Boston, 1894

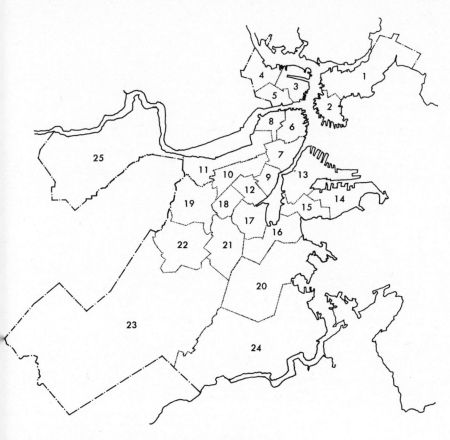

Map 6C. Ward boundaries of Boston: 1896–1913
Source: Municipal Register of Boston, 1903

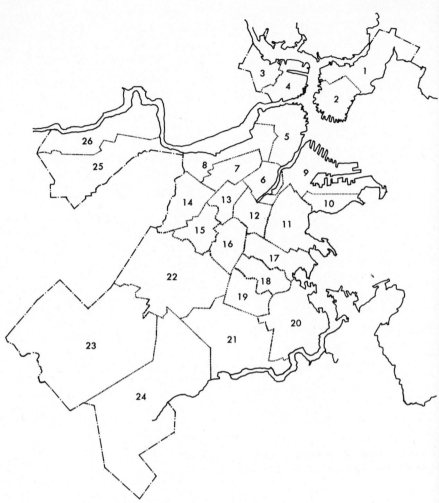

Map 6D. Ward boundaries of Boston: 1914–1923
Source: Municipal Register of Boston, 1920

Map 6E. Ward boundaries of Boston: 1924–1960
Source: Municipal Register of Boston, 1925

List of References

A. Books, Monographs and Articles

Abrams, C. *The Future of Housing*. New York: Harper and Bros., 1946.

Adams, J. T. "The Historical Background" in J. T. Adams, H. S. Graves, E. A. Filene, *et al.*, *New England's Prospect*, American Geographical Society Special Publication 16. New York, 1933.

Address of the Mayor (Josiah Quincy) to the City Council of Boston, Jan. 4, 1847. *Boston City Documents*, 1847, no. 1.

"As the 'Little Transcript' Knew Its Boston," *Boston Transcript Centenary*, July 24, 1930.

Ascher, C. S. "The Suburb" in Leon Carnovsky and Lowell Martin, eds., *The Library in the Community*. Chicago: University of Chicago Press, 1943.

Ballard, W. H. *Proposals for Downtown Boston: A Survey in Respect to the Decentralization of the Boston Central Business District*. Boston: Urban Land Institute, 1940.

Bauer, C. "We Face a Housing Shortage" in *Housing Yearbook*. Chicago: National Association of Housing Officials, 1937.

Blank, D. M., and L. Winnick. "The Structure of the Housing Market," *Quarterly Journal of Economics*, vol. 67, no. 2 (May 1953).

Bloomberg, L. N. "Rent Control and the Housing Shortage," *Journal of Land and Public Utility Economics*, vol. 23, no. 2 (May 1947).

Blumenfeld, H. "Correlation between Value of Dwelling Units and Altitude," *Land Economics*, vol. 24, no. 4 (November 1948).

Bodfish, M. *History of Building and Loan in the United States*. Chicago: United States Building and Loan League, 1931.

Bodfish, M., and A. D. Theobald. *Savings and Loan Principles*. New York: Prentice Hall, Inc., 1938.

Boeckh, E. H., and Associates, Inc. *A Study in Relative Construction Costs, Boston, Mass.* (1406 17 Street, N.W., Washington 5, D.C., and Times Star Building, Cincinnati 2, Ohio.) Issued monthly. No page listing.

Bogue, D. J. *The Population of the United States*. Glencoe: The Free Press, 1959.

———. *Population Growth in Standard Metropolitan Areas, 1900–1950*. Housing and Home Finance Agency, Washington, D.C., 1953.

Boston Building Department, Commonwealth of Massachusetts. "Annual Statistical Reports" (unpublished). On file in Building Department, City of Boston.

———. "Report on the Housing Situation in Boston," *Boston City Record*, vol. 12, July 17, 1920.

———. *Zoning for Boston: A Survey and a Comprehensive Plan*. Boston, 1924.

———. "Report on Real Property Inventory for the City of Boston," vol. 1, 1935.

Boston City Planning Board. *Building a Better Boston: A General Statement on Rehabilitation and an Analysis of Existing Conditions in the South End.* Boston, October 1941.

Boston Cooperative Building Company. *Fourth Annual Report,* 1875. *Fifth Annual Report,* 1876. *Twenty-Ninth Annual Report,* 1900.

Boston Elevated Railway Company. *Fifty Years of Unified Transportation in Metropolitan Boston.* Boston, 1938.

Boston Housing Authority. *Rehousing the Low Income Families of Boston: 1936–1940.* Boston, 1941.

Boston, Mass., Finance Commission. *A Study of Certain of the Effects of Decentralization on Boston and Some Neighboring Cities and Towns.* City of Boston Printing Department, 1941.

Boston Superintendent of Streets. "Annual Report," *Boston City Documents,* 1867, no. 6.

Boston Year Book. City of Boston Printing Department, 1924.

Bradford, Robert Fiske. *Special Message to the General Court,* Commonwealth of Massachusetts, Senate no. 561, Boston, 1947.

———. *Annual Message,* Commonwealth of Massachusetts, Senate no. 1, Boston, 1948.

Brogan, D. W. *The American Character.* New York: Alfred A. Knopf, Inc., 1944.

Bureau of Statistics of Labor, Commonwealth of Massachusetts. (The following reports, except the last, are on the year ending March 1 of the year in the title.)

[First Annual] *Report,* Senate no. 120, Boston, 1870.
[Second Annual] *Report,* Senate no. 150, Boston, 1871.
Sixth Annual Report, Public Document no. 31, Boston, 1875.
Seventh Annual Report, Public Document no. 31, 1876.
Tenth Annual Report, Public Document no. 31, 1879.
Fifteenth Annual Report, Public Document no. 15, 1884.
Sixteenth Annual Report, Public Document no. 15, 1885.
Seventeenth Annual Report, Public Document no. 15, 1886.
Twenty-Second Annual Report, Public Document no. 15, 1892.
Forty-First Annual Report [for the year 1910], Public Document no. 15, 1911. Part 3, "Living Conditions of the Wage-Earning Population in Certain Cities in Massachusetts."

Burgess, Ernest W. "The Growth of the City: An Introduction to a Research Project" in R. E. Park and E. W. Burgess, eds., *The City.* Chicago: University of Chicago Press, 1925.

Bushee, F. A. "Population" in R. A. Woods, ed., *The City Wilderness.* Boston and New York: Houghton Mifflin Co., 1898.

Chamberlain, Allen. *Beacon Hill: Its Ancient Pastures and Early Mansions.* Boston: Houghton Mifflin Co., 1925.

Chamberlin, Joseph E. *The Boston Transcript: A History of Its First Hundred Years.* Boston: Houghton Mifflin Co., 1930.

Chickering, Jesse. "A Comparative View of the Population of Boston in 1850 with the Births, Marriages, and Deaths in 1849 and 1850," *Boston City Documents,* 1851, no. 60.

Clark, Horace F., and Frank A. Chase. *Elements of the Modern Building and Loan Associations.* New York: The Macmillan Co., 1927.

Colean, M. L. *American Housing: Problems and Prospects.* New York: Twentieth Century Fund, 1944.

————. "The Rental Housing Mystery," *Architectural Record,* vol. 105, no. 2 (February 1947).

————. *The Impact of Government on Real Estate Finance in the United States.* New York: National Bureau of Economic Research, 1950.

Commission on the Cost of Living, Commonwealth of Massachusetts. *Report,* House no. 1750, May 1910.

Commission to Investigate Tenement House Conditions, Commonwealth of Massachusetts. "Report," *Boston City Documents,* 1904, vol. 3, no. 77.

Commissioner of Savings Banks, Commonwealth of Massachusetts. "Annual Reports," 1–10, 1866–1875, Public Document No. 8.

Committee Appointed by Mayor Peters on Housing. "Report," *Boston City Documents,* 1918, no. 121.

Committee on the Expediency of Providing Better Tenements for Relief of the Poor. *Report.* Boston: Eastburn's Press, 1846.

Committee on Tenement Districts, Commonwealth of Massachusetts. "Report," *Boston City Documents,* 1895, vol. 4, no. 224.

Davis, O. W. "Shall We Encourage or Discourage the Apartment House?" in *Housing Problems in America,* Proc. National Housing Association, vol. 5 (1916).

Dean, J. P. *Home Ownership: Is It Sound?* New York: Harper and Bros., 1945.

Dewey, D. R. *State Banking before the Civil War.* National Monetary Commission. Washington, D.C.: Government Printing Office, 1910.

Division on the Necessaries of Life, Department of Labor and Industries, Commonwealth of Massachusetts. *Report.* 1936. (Reprint from the *Annual Report,* Department of Labor and Industries.)

Douglas, P. H. *Real Wages in the United States.* Boston: Houghton Mifflin Co., 1930.

Eldredge, Daniel. *Massachusetts Cooperative Banks or Building Associations.* Boston: G. H. Ellis, 1893.

Engels, F. *The Housing Question.* New York: International Publishers, n.d.

Estabrook, Harold K. *Some Slums in Boston.* Boston: Twentieth Century Club, 1898. Pamphlet.

————. "Congestion in the North and West End" in Housing Committee of Boston—1915, *Report.*

"FHA's Impact on Financing and Designs in Apartments," *Architectural Forum,* vol. 92, no. 1 (January 1950).

Firey, Walter. *Land Use in Central Boston.* Cambridge, Mass.: Harvard University Press, 1947.

Ford, J. *Slums and Housing.* Cambridge, Mass.: Harvard University Press, 1936. 2 vols.

Friedman, Milton, and G. J. Stigler. *Roofs or Ceilings.* The Foundation for Economic Education, Inc. New York: Irvington-on-Hudson, 1947.

Gibbs, George Jr. "East Boston: A Survey and A Comprehensive Plan" in "Report of the City Planning Board," *Boston City Documents,* 1915, no. 116.

Greater Boston Economic Study Committee. *A Report for Downtown Boston.* May 1959. (Copies are available from the Committee, 200 Berkeley St., Boston, Mass.)

Grebler, L. *Housing Market Behavior in a Declining Area.* New York: Columbia University Press, 1952.

————. "Implications of Rent Control in the United States," *International Labour Review,* vol. 65, no. 4 (April 1952).

————. *The Role of Federal Credit Aids in Residential Construction,* Studies in Capital Formation and Financing, Occasional Paper 39. New York: National Bureau of Economic Research, 1953.

Grebler, Leo, D. M. Blank, and L. Winnick. *Capital Formation in Residential Real Estate*. Princeton: Princeton University Press, 1956.

Hale, E. A. "Massachusetts" in M. Bodfish, *History of Building and Loan in the United States*. Chicago: United States Building and Loan League, 1931.

Hall, P. F. "The Menace of the Three Decker" in *Housing Problems in America*, Proc. National Housing Association, vol. 5 (1916).

Handlin, Oscar. *Boston's Immigrants, 1790–1865*. Cambridge, Mass.: Harvard University Press, 1941.

Harris, M. L. *A Memorandum on the Population Trends in Metropolitan Boston*. Boston: New England Trust Company, 1942.

Haynes, F. E. "Historical" in R. A. Woods, ed., *The City Wilderness*. Boston and New York: Houghton Mifflin Co., 1898.

Herlihy, E. M. "The Housing Situation in Boston," *Housing Betterment*, vol. 10, no. 2 (June 1921).

Herndon, Richard. *Boston of To-Day*. Boston: Post Publishing Co., 1892.

Hibbard, B. H. *History of Public Land Policy*. New York: The Macmillan Co., 1924.

Homestead Commission, Commonwealth of Massachusetts. *First Annual Report*, House no. 2000, January 1913.

Horne, H. O. *A History of Savings Banks*. London and New York: Oxford University Press, 1947.

Housing Association of Metropolitan Boston. *Housing Action in Metropolitan Boston*, vol. 2, no. 1 (August 1948). Reprint.

Housing Committee of Boston—1915. *Report*. Presented to the Board of Directors and accepted by them, April 11, 1910.

Howard, G. "Filtering Down and the Elimination of Substandard Housing: A Reply," *Journal of Land and Public Utility Economics*, vol. 22 (August 1946).

Howie, D. H. "Family Budgets" in Commission on the Cost of Living, Commonwealth of Massachusetts, *Report*, House no. 1750, May 1910.

Hoyt, Homer. *The Structure and Growth of Residential Neighborhoods in American Cities*. Federal Housing Administration. Washington, D.C.: Government Printing Office, 1939.

———. Review of Walter Firey's *Land Use in Central Boston, Journal of the American Institute of Planners*, vol. 12, no. 1 (Winter 1947).

Huse, C. P. *The Financial History of Boston*. Cambridge, Mass.: Harvard University Press, 1919.

Insurance Commissioners of Massachusetts (Loan and Fund Associations). *Annual Reports*, 1–8, 1857–1864. Department of Banking and Insurance, Commonwealth of Massachusetts.

Jordan, I. "Room Overcrowding and the Lodger Evil Problem" in *Housing Problems in America*, Proc. National Housing Association, vol. 2 (1912).

Kelly, B., and Associates. *Design and the Production of Housing*. New York: McGraw-Hill Book Co., 1959.

Koren, John. *Boston: 1822 to 1922*. City of Boston Printing Department, Document 39, 1922.

Kristof, F. S. (Bureau of the Census). "Components of Change in the Nation's Housing Inventory in Relation to the 1960 Census." Paper presented at the Annual Meeting of the American Statistical Association, Dec. 28, 1959.

Land Committee. "Report on Petition of John S. Tyler and Others For Inducements to Build on Lands Purchased of the City," *Boston City Documents,* 1852, no. 11.

Leahy, William A. "A Compendium of Reports and Studies Relating to the Commerce and Industries of Boston," *Boston City Documents,* 1924, no. 81. The City Planning Board, Boston, Mass., 1924.

Lerner, A. P. *The Economics of Control.* New York: The Macmillan Co., 1944.

Lintner, J. *Mutual Savings Banks in the Savings and Mortgage Markets.* Cambridge, Mass.: Division of Research, Graduate School of Business Administration, Harvard University, 1948.

Maisel, S. J. "Have We Underestimated Increases in Rents and Shelter Expenditures?" *Journal of Political Economy,* vol. 57, no. 2 (April 1949).

Marble, E. H. "The Menace of the Three Decker" in *Housing Problems in America,* Proc. National Housing Association, vol. 5 (1916).

Massachusetts Civic League. *The Housing Law for Cities.* Boston, Mass., 1913. Pamphlet.

Massachusetts Department of Labor and Industries. *Time Rates of Wages and Hours of Labor in Massachusetts, 1935,* Labor Bulletin no. 173. (Part 2 of *Annual Report on the Statistics of Labor,* Public Document No. 15, Boston, 1936.)

Massachusetts State Board of Housing. *Special Report Relative to Procurement of Homes for War Veterans.* Commonwealth of Massachusetts, House no. 1240, 1945.

————. *Report of the Director to the Chairman.* Boston, Dec. 31, 1948.

McKeever, J. R. "Beacon Hill: A Thesis in Site Planning." Unpublished Master's Thesis, Rotch Library, Massachusetts Institute of Technology, 1936.

Miles, R. E. "The Boston Housing Situation," *Charities and the Commons,* vol. 12, no. 1 (Oct. 6, 1906).

Morton, J. E. *Urban Mortgage Lending: Comparative Markets and Experience.* Princeton: Princeton University Press, 1956.

Naigles, M. H. "Housing and the Increase in Population," *Monthly Labor Review,* vol. 54, no. 4 (April 1942).

Paine, Robert T. "Homes for the People" in *Contributions to the Science of Society, 1879–1903.* Boston: Tolman and White, Printers, 1882. Reprinted from the *Journal of Social Science,* vol. 15 (1881).

————. "The Housing Conditions in Boston," *Annals of the American Academy of Political and Social Science,* vol. 20, no. 345 (July 1902).

Peters, Mayor A. J. "The City's Obligation in Housing" in *Housing Problems in America,* Proc. National Housing Association, vol. 7 (1918).

Phelps, Roswell F. *South End Operatives, Employment and Residence.* Boston: South End House Association, 1903.

Phillipson, J. B. "Consumption Standards and Housing," *Annals of the American Academy of Political and Social Science,* vol. 190 (March 1937).

Pinanski, A. E. *The Street Railway System of Metropolitan Boston.* New York: McGraw Publishing Co., 1908.

Porter, Dwight. *Report upon a Sanitary Inspection of Certain Tenement-House Districts of Boston.* Boston: Press of Rockwell and Churchill, 1889.

Rapid Transit Commission, Commonwealth of Massachusetts. *Report to the Massachusetts Legislature,* April 5, 1892.

Rapkin, C., L. Winnick, and D. M. Blank. *Housing Market Analysis.* Housing and Home Finance Agency, Washington, D.C., 1953.

Ratcliff, R. U. "Filtering Down," *Journal of Land and Public Utility Economics,* vol. 21, no. 4 (November 1945).

Robbins, R. *Our Landed Heritage*. Princeton: Princeton University Press, 1942.

Rodwin, Lloyd. "Middle Income Housing Problems in Boston." Unpublished Ph.D. Thesis, Widener Library, Harvard University, Cambridge, Mass., 1949.

———. "The Theory of Residential Growth and Structure," *The Appraisal Journal*, vol. 27, no. 3 (July 1950).

———. "Rent Control and Housing," *Social Research*, vol. 17, no. 3 (September 1950).

———. "Income and Housing Cost Trends of Boston's Middle-Income Groups: 1846–1947," *Land Economics*, vol. 26, no. 4 (November 1950).

———. "Rent Control and Housing: A Cast Study," *Land Economics*, vol. 27, no. 4 (November 1951).

———. "Studies in Middle-Income Housing," *Social Forces*, vol. 30, no. 3 (March 1952).

Rosen, Ben. "The Trend of Jewish Population in Boston," in Boston Federated Jewish Charities, *Monographs*, vol. 1, no. 1, 1921.

Rossi, P. *Why Families Move*. Glencoe: The Free Press, 1955.

Roterus, V. "Stability of Annual Employment, Cincinnati and Selected Cities," *Economic Geography*, vol. 23, no. 2 (April 1947).

Rutan, E. Y. "Before the Invasion" in R. A. Woods, ed., *Americans in Process*. Boston: Houghton Mifflin Co., 1902.

Samuelson, P. A. *Economics: An Introductory Analysis*. New York: McGraw-Hill Book Co., 1948.

Shattuck, L. *Report to the Committee of the City Council Appointed to Obtain the Census of Boston. For the year 1845*. Boston, 1846.

Special Commission on the Necessaries of Life, Commonwealth of Massachusetts.
> *Report*, House No. 1500, February 1920.
> *Report*, House No. 1400, 1922.
> *Report*, House No. 1250, January 1923.
> *Report*, House No. 1210, January 1925.

Special Commission Relative to the Immediate Relief of Traffic, Housing, Street Lighting and Recreational Conditions of the City of Boston. *Partial and Preliminary Report*, Commonwealth of Massachusetts, House no. 1741, December 3, 1947.

Special Commission to Make a Survey and Study of Problems Relating to Veterans, Including Housing and Hospital Facilities. *Report*, part I, "Veterans' Housing," Commonwealth of Massachusetts, House No. 1740, December 1947.

Special Committee of the Common Council Relative to the Improvement of Tenement Districts of the City of Boston. "Report," *Boston City Documents*, 1895, no. 125.

———. "Report," *Boston City Documents*, 1896, vol. 3, no. 75.

Special Recess Commission on Housing. *Report*, Commonwealth of Massachusetts, House no. 1643, January 1947.

Stanwood, E. "Topography and Landmarks of the Last Hundred Years" in Justin Winsor, ed., *The Memorial History of Boston*, vol. 4, "The Last Hundred Years." Boston: J. R. Osgood and Co., 1881–82.

Topping, S. "Displaced Persons of '48 Fulfill Their Hopes in the United States," *The New York Times*, Oct. 12, 1959, pp. 1, 3.

Townsend, R. G. "Some Economic Aspects of Urban Housing with Special Reference to Metropolitan Boston." Unpublished Ph.D. Thesis, Widener Library, Harvard University, Cambridge, Mass., 1948.

Tucker, D. S. *The Evolution of People's Banks.* Studies in History, Economics and Public Law, vol. 102, no. 1. New York: Columbia University Press, 1922.

United States Commissioner of Labor. *Ninth Annual Report, 1893, Building and Loan Associations.* Washington, D.C., 1894.

United States Congress. House of Representatives. *Investigation of Real Estate Bondholders' Reorganizations.* Report no. 35, Preliminary Report, 74th Congress, 1st Session. Washington, D.C., 1935.

————. House of Representatives. *Investigation of Real Estate Bondholders' Reorganizations.* Report no. 35, Supplementary Report, part 2, 74th Congress, 2nd Session. Washington, D.C., June 1936.

————. House of Representatives. *Final Majority Report of the Joint Committee on Housing, Housing Study and Investigation,* part 2, "Statistics of Housing." Report no. 1564, 80th Congress, 2nd Session. Washington, D.C., 1948.

————. Senate. *Hearings before the Joint Committee on Housing,* part 3. 80th Congress, 1st Session, Washington, D.C., 1948.

————. Senate *High Cost of Housing* (Report of a Subcommittee of the Joint Committee on Housing) 80th Congress, 1st Session, Washington, D.C., 1948.

————. Senate. *Hearings before a Subcommittee of the Committee on Banking and Currency on Middle-Income Housing.* 81st Congress, 2nd Session, Washington, D.C., Jan. 10–Feb. 18, 1950.

————. Senate. *Report of the Senate Committee on Banking and Currency on the FHA Investigation.* Senate Report no. 1, 84th Congress, Jan. 6, 1955.

United States Department of Labor. Bureau of Labor Statistics. *Wholesale Price of Building Materials,* Annual Index, "Boston." Mimeographed.

————. Bureau of Labor Statistics. "Wholesale Prices and Price Indices." *Construction Volume and Costs 1915–1956* (monthly issues). Mimeographed.

————. Bureau of Labor Statistics. *Consumer's Price Index for Moderate Income Families: Boston, Massachusetts: 1914–1960,* "Rent." 1914 Forward Series D-4. Washington, D.C. Mimeographed.

————. Bureau of Labor Statistics. *Money Disbursements of Wage Earners and Clerical Workers in the North Atlantic Region, 1934–1936.* Bulletin no. 637, vol. 2. Washington, D.C., 1939.

————. Bureau of Labor Statistics (in cooperation with the Works Progress Administration). *Family Expenditures in Selected Cities, 1935–1936,* vol. 1, "Housing." Bulletin no. 648 (Study of Consumer Purchases), Washington, D.C., 1941.

————. Bureau of Labor Statistics. "Progress of Housing Program in Boston, Massachusetts Area." Press Release dated 2/10/48. Table attached.

————. Bureau of Labor Statistics. "Progress of Housing Program in Boston, Massachusetts Area." Press Release dated 1/30/49. Table attached.

United States Federal Housing Administration. *FHA Homes in Metropolitan Districts.* Washington, D.C., Government Printing Office, 1942.

United States Housing and Home Finance Agency. *Housing Statistics Handbook.* Washington, D.C., 1948.

————. *Fifth Annual Report, 1954.* Washington, D.C.; Government Printing Office, 1955.

United States National Resources Committee. *Consumer Incomes in the United States: Their Distribution in 1935–36.* Washington, D.C.: G.P.O., 1938.

United States Office of Price Administration. Rent Department, Cost Analysis

Branch. *Income and Expense under Rent Control: Boston Rental Housing 1939–1943*. Washington, D.C., December 1944.

Veiller, L. *Housing Conditions and Tenement Laws in Leading American Cities*, prepared for the Tenement House Commission. New York: The Evening Post job printing house, 1900.

———. "The Housing Problem in American Cities," *Annals of the American Academy of Political and Social Science*, 1905.

Vernon, R. *The Changing Economic Function of the Central City*, New York: The Committee for Economic Development, 1959.

Wadlin, H. G. *A Tenement House Census of Boston*. Part 1, sec. 2, "Sanitary Condition of Tenements" and part 2, sec. 3, "Place of Birth, Occupations, etc., of Residents in Tenement Houses" in Bureau of Statistics of Labor, *Twenty-Third Annual Report*, 1892 (published 1893), Public Document no. 15.

Walker, Francis. *Land and Its Rent*. Boston: Little, Brown and Co., 1883.

Wallace, E. S. "Survey of Federal Legislation Affecting Private Home Financing Since 1932," *Law and Contemporary Problems*, vol. 4, no. 4 (Autumn 1938).

Warner, B. S., and E. Sydenstridker. *Health Insurance: Its Relation to Public Health*. United States Treasury Department, 1916.

Warner, W. L., and P. S. Lunt. *The Social Life of a Modern Community*. New Haven: Yale University Press, 1941.

Whitehill, W. Muir. *Boston: A Topographical History*. Cambridge, Mass.: The Belknap Press of Harvard University Press, 1959.

Whitmore, H. "Real Estate Values in Boston," *Publications of the American Statistical Association*, vol. 5, no. 33 (March 1896).

Whyte, W. F. *Street Corner Society: The Social Structure of an Italian Slum*. Chicago: University of Chicago Press, 1947.

Winnick, L. "The Burden of the Residential Mortgage Debt," *The Journal of Finance*, vol. 11, no. 2 (May 1956).

———. *American Housing and Its Use*. New York: J. Wiley and Sons, 1957.

———. *Rental Housing: Opportunities for Private Investment*. New York: McGraw Hill Co., 1958.

Winsor, Justin, ed. *The Memorial History of Boston: 1630–1880*. Boston: J. R. Osgood and Co., 1881–82. 4 vols.

Winston, C., and M. A. Smith, "Sensitivity of State Income Payments to Nation's Total," *Survey of Current Business* (January 1946).

Wolfe, A. B. *The Lodging House Problem in Boston*. Boston: Houghton Mifflin Co., 1906.

Wood, E. E. "Government Housing" in *Housing Problems in America*, Proc. Seventh National Conference on Housing, Boston, 1918.

———. *The Housing of the Unskilled Wage Earner*. New York: The Macmillan Co., 1919.

———. *Recent Trends in American Housing*. New York: The Macmillan Co., 1931.

———. *Introduction to Housing: Facts and Principles*. Washington, D.C.: Federal Works Agency, United States Housing Authority, 1940.

Woods, R. A., ed. *The City Wilderness*. Boston and New York: Houghton Mifflin Co., 1898.

———, ed. *Americans in Process*. Boston: Houghton Mifflin Co., 1902.

Wright, C. D. *Comparative Wages and Prices: 1860–1883*, "Massachusetts and Great Britain." Included in Bureau of Statistics of Labor, *Sixteenth Annual Report*, Public Document no. 15, 1885.

Wright, C. D., and H. G. Wadlin. "The Industries of the Last Hundred Years" in Justin Winsor, ed., *The Memorial History of Boston: 1630–1880*, vol. 4. Boston: J. R. Osgood and Co., 1881–82.

Wyatt, W. W. Press Release of a 12-page summary of a statement made by him to the United States Congress on November 7, 1946.

B. Census Reports

1. Massachusetts and Boston Census Reports (in chronological order)

Shattuck, L. *Report to the Committee of the City Council Appointed to Obtain the Census of Boston. For the year 1845*. Boston, 1846.

"Report and Tabular Statement of the Censors Appointed by the Board of Mayor and Aldermen to Obtain the State Census of Boston, May 1, 1850 (Including Dr. Chickering's Report to the Committee on the State Census, for the City of Boston)," *Boston City Documents*, 1850, no. 42.

"Report to the Joint Special Committee of the City Government on the Census of Boston in 1855," *Boston City Documents*, 1855, vol. 2, no. 69.

Abstract of the Census of the Commonwealth of Massachusetts, 1855, 1860, and 1865.

The Census of Massachusetts: 1875.
   Vol. 1. *Population and Social Statistics*.
   Vol. 2. *Manufactures and Occupations*.
   Vol. 3. *Agricultural Products and Property*.

The Census of Massachusetts: 1885.
   Vol. 1. *Population and Social Statistics*. (2 parts.)
   Vol. 2. *Manufactures, the Fisheries and Commerce*.

The Census of the Commonwealth of Massachusetts: 1895.
   Vols. 1–4. *Population and Social Statistics*.
   Vol. 5. *Manufactures*.
   Vol. 7. *Social Statistics and General Summaries*.

The Census of the Commonwealth of Massachusetts: 1905.
   Vol. 1. *Population and Social Statistics*.
   Vol. 2. *Occupations and Defective Social and Physical Conditions*.

The Census of the Commonwealth of Massachusetts: 1915.

The Decennial Census of the Commonwealth of Massachusetts: 1925, 1935, 1945.

The Commonwealth of Massachusetts: *The Decennial Census, 1955, Population and Legal Voters of Massachusetts*.

2. United States Department of Commerce, Bureau of the Census, Reports and Surveys

Statistical Abstracts of the United States. Issued annually.

Seventh Census of the United States: 1850.

Eighth Census of the United States: 1860.
   Vol. 1. *Population of the United States in 1860*.

Ninth Census of the United States: 1870.
   Vol. 1. *Statistics of the Population of the United States*.

Tenth Census of the United States: 1880.
   Vol. 1. *Statistics of the Population of the United States*.

Eleventh Census of the United States: 1890.

Vol. 1. *Report on the Population of the United States.* (2 parts.)
Vol. 4. *Vital and Social Statistics in the United States.*
  Part 2. "Cities over 100,000 Population."
Vol. 6. *Report on Manufacturing Industries in the United States.*
  Part 2. "Statistics for Cities."
Vol. 12. *Report on Real Estate Mortages in the United States.*
Vol. 13. *Report on Farms and Homes: Proprietorship and Indebtedness in the United States.*
Vol. 15. *Report on Wealth, Debt and Taxation.*
  Part 2. "Valuation and Taxation."
Twelfth Census of the United States: 1900.
Vol. 1. *Population* (part 1).
Vol. 2. *Population* (part 2).
Thirteenth Census of the United States: 1910.
Vol. 1. *Population—General Report and Analysis.*
Vol. 2. *Population—Reports by States with Statistics for Counties, Cities, and Other Civil Subdivisions.*
Vol. 4. *Population—Occupation Statistics.*
Vol. 9. *Manufactures—Reports by States with Statistics for Principal Cities.*
Census of Manufactures: 1914.
Vol. 1. *Reports by States with Statistics for Principal Cities and Metropolitan Districts.*
Abstract of the Census of Manufactures: 1919.
Fourteenth Census of the United States: 1920.
Census Monograph II. *Mortgages on Homes.*
Manufactures: Vol. 8. *General Report and Analytical Tables.*
  Vol. 9. *Reports for States, with Statistics for Principal Cities.*
Population: Vol. 2. *General Report and Analytical Tables.*
  Vol. 3. *Composition and Characteristics of the Population by States.*
  Vol. 4. *Occupations.*
Fifteenth Census of the United States: 1930.
Construction Industry
Population: Vol. 1. *Number and Distribution of Inhabitants.*
  Vol. 2. *General Report, Statistics by States.*
  Vol. 3. Part 1, *Reports by States Showing the Composition and Characteristics of the Population for Counties, Cities and Townships or other Minor Civil Divisions.*
  Vol. 4. *Occupations, by States.*
  Vol. 6. *Families.*
Sixteenth Census of the United States: 1940.
Analytical Maps, Boston, Massachusetts Block Statistics.
Housing Supplement to the First Series, Housing Bulletin for Massachusetts. Boston, Block Statistics.
Vol. 3. *Reports for States and Outlying Areas.*
Housing: Vol. 1. *Data for Small Areas.*
  Part 1. "U.S. Summary and Alabama–Nebraska."
  Vol. 2. *General Characteristics* [Occupancy and Tenure Status. . . .]
  Part 3. "Iowa–Montana."

Vol. 3. *Characteristics by Monthly Rent or Value.*
Part 2. "Alabama–New Hampshire."
Vol. 4. *Mortgages on Owner Occupied Nonfarm Homes.*
Part 2. "Alabama–New York."
Population: Vol. 2. *Characteristics of the Population . . .*
Part 3. "Reports by States, Kansas to Michigan."
Vol. 3. *The Labor Force.*
Part 3. "Reports by States, Iowa–Montana."
Population: Special Reports
Comparative Statistics for the United States, 1870–1940.
Internal Migration: 1935–1940. Social Characteristics of Migrants.
Nativity and Percentage of the White Population, General Characteristics.
Population and Housing, Families, General Characteristics.
State of Birth of the Native Population.
Seventeenth Census of the United States: 1950.
Population: Vol. 1. *Number of Inhabitants.*
Survey of World War II Veterans and Dwelling Unit Vacancy and Occupancy in the Boston Area, Massachusetts. Population, H-Vet No. 19. Washington, D.C., October 30, 1946.
Housing Characteristics of the Boston, Massachusetts, Metropolitan District: April 1947.
Current Population Reports, Housing, Series P–71, No. 2. Washington, D.C., July 18, 1947.
Estimated Population of the United States, By Regions, Divisions, and States: July 1, 1946. Current Population Reports, Housing, Series P–25, No. 2. Washington, D.C., August 15, 1947.
Housing and Home Finance Agency. *Housing Characteristics in 108 Selected Areas.* Census Series H–Vet No. 115, H.H.F.A. Statistics Bulletin No. 1. Washington, D.C., December 1947.
The Growth of Metropolitan Districts in the United States: 1900–1940. Washington, D.C., 1948.
Income of Nonfarm Families and Individuals: 1946. Current Population Reports (Consumer Income), Series P–60, No. 1. Washington, D.C., January 28, 1948.
Internal Migration in the United States: April 1940 to April 1947. Current Population Reports, Series P–20, No. 14. Washington, D.C., April 15, 1948.
Vacancy, Occupancy and Tenure in Selected Areas: 1945 to 1947. Current Population Reports, Housing, Series P–72, No. 1. Washington, D.C., June 16, 1948.
Seventeenth Decennial Census of the United States: 1950.
Boston, Nonfarm Housing Characteristics. 1950 United States Census of Housing Bulletin, H–B26.
Housing: Vol. 1. *General Characteristics.*
Part 3. "Idaho–Massachusetts."
Vol. 2. *Nonfarm Housing Characteristics.*
Part 3. "Detroit–Memphis."
Vol. 4. *Residential Financing.*
Part 2. "Large Standard Metropolitan Areas."
Population: Vol. 2. *Characteristics of the Population.*
Part 21. "Massachusetts."

1956 National Housing Inventory, Washington, 1958.
    Vol. 1. *Components of Change, 1950 to 1956.*
        Part 3. "Boston."
    Vol. 3. *Characteristics of the 1956 Inventory.*
        Part 3. "Boston."
Preliminary Report. Series PC (P2)–21. Washington, D.C., August 1960.

Notes

The List of References on pp. 171–182 provides the complete citation for the books, monographs, articles, and census reports referred to in these notes.

Chapter 2. *Income, Rent Levels, Expenditure*

Patterns, and Standards: 1846–1959

1. This chapter is a thoroughly revised version of the paper "Income and Housing Cost Trends of Boston's Middle-Income Groups: 1846–1947," published in *Land Economics*, vol. 26, no. 4 (November 1950), pp. 368–382.

2. See Sixteenth Census, U.S., 1940, *Population, Comparative Statistics for the United States, 1870–1940*, p. 183; *Population*, vol. 3, part 3, Table 16, p. 546; Bogue, *The Population of the United States*, chap. xviii.

3. The closest equivalent to the rule that one week's salary should be paid for a month's rent is 23 per cent of annual income, assuming 52 weeks of employment. Also, cf. Samuelson, *Economics*, p. 202.

4. See Sixteenth Census, U.S., 1940, *Housing*, vol. 3, part 2, Table B-3, p. 15, and Table C-3, p. 20; Seventeenth Census, U.S., 1950, *Housing*, vol. 1, part 3, Table 21, pp. 21–33.

5. Cf. Abrams, *The Future of Housing*, p. 40, note 1.

6. C. L. L. Engle's conclusion that the proportion of income spent for rent, fuel, and light is generally invariable is questioned by H. Schwabe and others. (See Phillipson, "Consumption Standards and Housing," *Annals of the American Academy of Political and Social Science*, pp. 122–123.) Note also the careful criticism of Engle's thesis on the basis of Massachusetts budget studies in Bureau of Statistics of Labor, *Sixth Annual Report, 1875*, pp. 438–442. All the more recent expenditure studies of the Bureau of Labor Statistics show a decrease of the percentage spent for rent for higher-income classes. For example, see U.S. Dept. of Labor, Bureau of Labor Statistics, *Family Expenditures in Selected Cities, 1935–1936*, vol. 1, Table 8, p. 24; and cf. Townsend, "Some Economic Aspects of Urban Housing with Special Reference to Metropolitan Boston," Charts 1–6.

7. This experience of higher costs for new construction is confirmed by Paul Douglas' study, which indicates "that in the periods of rising prices, rents increase more slowly than either the general price level or the costs of building" (*Real Wages in the United States*, pp. 39–40).

8. Other barriers which may further block the process of filtration are geographical variations between demand and supply, tenure differences, group prejudices, and so on. Also, a new impediment may emerge if city planning ever becomes successful enough to stabilize property values. Cf. Howard, "Filtering Down and the Elimination of Substandard Housing," *Journal of Land and Public Utility Economics*, p. 294.

9. Bureau of Statistics of Labor, *Seventh Annual Report, 1876*, Tables 69

and 100. The trends are also supported by three budget and expenditure surveys of Massachusetts families prepared between 1874 and 1903. These studies disclose an increase in the average per cent expenditure for rent, namely, from 17 per cent to 20 per cent from 1874 to 1903. The averages for all income groups, however, are not too reliable, since they depend on the proportion of the total number of families that fall into the various income groups in the community. See Howie, "Family Budgets" in Commission on the Cost of Living, *Report*, Appendix B and pp. 574–576.

10. Sources for the statements in this paragraph are: Division on the Necessaries of Life, *Report*, Appendix I, pp. 17 and 36; Special Commission on the Necessaries of Life, *Report*, January 1925, p. 36; U.S. Dept. of Labor, Bureau of Labor Statistics, *Money Disbursements of Wage Earners and Clerical Workers in the North Atlantic Region, 1934–1936*, Table 6, p. 209.

11. Grebler, Blank, and Winnick, *Capital Formation in Residential Real Estate*, chaps. vii–ix. For a criticism of this thesis, see Kelly and Associates, *Design and the Production of Housing*, pp. 50–56.

12. Committee on the Expediency of Providing Better Tenements for Relief of the Poor, *Report*, p. 24.

13. R. A. Woods, ed., *The City Wilderness*, pp. 101–102.

14. Sixteenth Census, U.S., 1940, *Housing*, vol. 3, part 2, Table B-1, p. 13.

15. U.S. Bureau of the Census, *1956 National Housing Inventory*, vol. 3; *Characteristics of the 1956 Inventory*, part 3, "Boston," Table 1, p. 11.

16. *Ibid.*, Table 11, p. 20.

17. Dr. L. Winnick has shown in a comparison of American housing standards with other countries that "since real income is assumed to be an important factor in determining the per capita amount of space, the most striking feature that emerges from this quick survey of international differences is not that we are better off than everybody else, but rather that we are not as much better off as might be expected from observed differences in income and general housing standards" (*American Housing and Its Use*, p. 3).

Chapter 3. *Middle-Income Housing: Past and Present*

1. This chapter is a larger and substantially revised version of an article published in *Social Forces*, vol. 30, no. 3 (March 1952), under the title "Studies in Middle-Income Housing."

2. Success in activities, such as fishing and trade, supplied part of the funds. State currency and manufacture of funds through commercial and land banks provided other dubious sources. Europe also was an important creditor then, though not always a generous one and for understandable reasons. Incorrigible speculative tendencies in the States, plus frequent crises and repudiation of debts by states and other debtors, often created an unsavory reputation for American loans. One Boston representative who was sent abroad in 1846 to search for funds for underwriting a water project returned empty-handed. He was unable to secure a loan from leading European bankers, many of whom had complained that repudiated debts of states "had made it impossible to dispose of American bonds. During a part of 1847, the rate for money was 2% a month on the best paper." (Address of the Mayor, Josiah Quincy, to the City Council of Boston, Jan. 4, 1847, *Boston City Documents*, pp. 6–9.) Cf. Robbins, *Our Landed Heritage*, chap. iv; Dewey, *State Banking before the Civil War*, pp. 153–160; Lintner, *Mutual Savings Banks in the Savings and Mortgage Markets*, pp. 46–55.

3. The Bank Commissioner of New York pointed out that, under the guise of business paper, commercial banks supplied credit to those engaged in real estate speculation. The same charge applied to Cincinnati, where funds were made available to dealers in real estate and town lots and houses in cities "rather than to the discounting of real bills of exchange, which was but a minor branch of the business. The banks encouraged the renewal of notes and by taking mortgages on the property would finally come into possession of a large part at their own price. There were, indeed, two such sales of nearly the whole city by the United States Bank. In a settled population such a system could not last long, but in American towns where there was a continuous change, experience was lost and the practice could easily be repeated." (Dewey, *State Banking before the Civil War*, pp. 159–160.)

4. Boston pioneered with savings as well as building and loan banks: it had the first mutual savings bank and the first incorporated cooperative bank (building and loan association). The Provident Institution for Savings was chartered in the town of Boston in 1816 and is still in existence. The first building and loan association, known as the Loan and Fund Association, was organized in Boston as a voluntary terminating association. (Bodfish, *History of Building and Loan in the United States*, pp. 9, 14, and 425; Horne, *A History of Savings Banks*, chaps. ii–xiii.) The European building societies are also interesting. Unlike the American societies they first began to prosper about 1885, when they built tenements for rent to their members. While interest rates were high at first, amounting to approximately 15 per cent (although by 1900 they averaged 5 to 6 per cent), the banks were important because loans were made available for a purpose not previously served. (Tucker, *The Evolution of People's Banks*, pp. 149–155 and 178–179.) Savings banks, as the Insurance Commissioner pointed out, frequently loaned their money for mortgage loans only to higher-income groups. Cf. Insurance Commissioner of Massachusetts (Loan and Fund Associations), *Eighth Annual Report*, 1864, p. 7.

5. H. S. Rosenthal, "Building and Loan Literature" in Bodfish, *History of Building and Loan in the United States*, chap. xv, pp. 234–241.

6. Insurance Commissioners of Massachusetts (Loan and Fund Associations), *First Annual Report*, 1857, p. 3. Note that the commissioners made this statement to show only that the objective was laudable. Actual practices were sharply criticized.

7. Engels, *The Housing Question*, pp. 64–67. Engels' point is of interest, for his reference to the group served. He had in mind mainly the English and Continental societies, but his observations apply all the more to the United States. His barbs against speculation are particularly relevant to a later phase of the building and loan movement in this country. See Bodfish, *History of Building and Loan in the United States*, chap. xii.

8. Insurance Commissioners of Massachusetts (Loan and Fund Associations), *First to Eighth Annual Reports*, 1857–1864. See also Lintner, *Mutual Savings Banks*, p. 55; and Hale, "Massachusetts" in Bodfish, *History of Building and Loan in the United States*, p. 427. Many of the groups failed, and others (known as terminating associations) served a small group which participated in the plan and then wound up the enterprise (Insurance Commissioners of Massachusetts, Loan and Fund Associations, *Sixth Annual Report*, 1862, p. 6).

9. Hale, "Massachusetts," p. 429. A survey of building and loan associations in 1893 by the Commissioner of Labor indicated that most of the shareholders, at least according to their classified occupations, were largely in the

upper brackets of the middle-income groups. See United States Commissioner of Labor, *Ninth Annual Report,* 1894, Table 16, pp. 321 and 323.

10. Eldredge, *Massachusetts Cooperative Banks or Building Associations,* p. 6. The remarks are cited from an editorial of *The Boston Herald* in January 1877. Other papers favoring the legislation were *The Daily Advertiser,* and *The Boston Evening Transcript.*

11. Lintner, *Mutual Savings Banks,* p. 108, Chart 21; pp. 464–465, Table II-2. See also Hale, "Massachusetts," p. 434.

12. Wood, *The Housing of the Unskilled Wage Earner,* p. 234.

13. Lintner, *Mutual Savings Banks,* pp. 54 and 132–143.

14. See Eleventh Census, U.S., 1890, *Report on Farms and Homes: Proprietorship and Indebtedness in the United States.* This report found no correlation then between ownership and the number of building and loan associations in a community (p. 51). See also Sixteenth Census, U.S., 1940, *Housing,* vol. 4, part 2, Table D-3, p. 616.

15. Paine, "Homes for the People" in *Contributions to the Science of Society, 1879–1903,* pp. 15–17. It took considerable time and resources to accumulate the equity even in the form of investments in building and loan shares prior to the request for a loan.

16. See Clark and Chase, *Elements of the Modern Building and Loan Association,* p. 9 and Table 28, p. 442; and Bodfish and Theobald, who refer to 66⅔ per cent as the "traditional rate" (*Savings and Loan Principles,* pp. 202–203). Since the 1930's the maximum limit allowed is 80 per cent.

Conversations with officials of the State Commission on Banking and most of the larger building and loan associations in Boston indicated that 65 per cent was a reasonably conservative assumption, since the average real estate first-mortgage loan refers to the balance outstanding of all such loans. By and large the average tends to be an understatement because the total loans include reloans and many loans which were partly paid off. However, the understatement is probably offset by the fact that the loans apply to multifamily as well as single-family units. The estimates of approximate average value of new houses financed by building and loan associations appear to be roughly in line with what one might expect from other data. For example, R. T. Paine cites $1600 as the cost of a new home for families of modest income in Boston in 1880 ("Homes for the People"). Our figure for about the same time is $1760. As for a more recent period, the Sixteenth Census indicates that the average value of one- to four-family properties on which building and loan associations held mortgages in 1940 was $5375 in Boston City and $5144 for the Boston metropolitan area. These figures are roughly comparable with the estimate of $5145 for 1935 and $4739 for 1940 arrived at by the above assumption. (Sixteenth Census, U.S., 1940, vol. 4, part 2, Table E-3, p. 620.)

17. Wallace, "Survey of Federal Legislation Affecting Private Home Financing Since 1932" in *Law and Contemporary Problems,* p. 488. See also Colean, *The Impact of Government on Real Estate Finance in the United States,* chaps. iii–vi, x; and Morton, *Urban Mortgage Lending.*

18. See Grebler, *The Role of Federal Credit Aids In Residential Construction,* and Abrams, *The Future of Housing.*

19. The data may be obtained from the office of the Massachusetts Commissioner of Banks. They represent a weighted average showing first-mortgage real estate loans made by building and loan associations in Boston during the one-year period ending at the close of business, October 1948.

20. Seventeenth Census, U.S., 1950, *Housing*, vol. 4, part 2, Table 4, p. 205; and *Population*, vol. 2, part 21, Table 34, pp. 21–66.

21. Marble, "The Menace of the Three Decker" in *Housing Problems in America*, p. 321.

22. *Housing Betterment*, vol. 5, no. 2 (May 1916), p. 19. The 1846 *Report of the Committee on the Expediency of Providing Better Tenements for the Poor* was perhaps the first official pronouncement in Massachusetts against the slums. Subsequent surveys and investigations followed, including the reports of the Sanitary Commission; the 1855 Census of Boston, detailing conditions in the foreign tenements and cellar dwellings; the individual studies and reports of the Bureau of Statistics of Labor during the 1870's; the increasing data made available in the 1875 Decennial Census; the strenuous efforts of groups like the Associated Charities for stricter tenement laws and their enforcement; the sober study and revelations of Dwight Porter and his M.I.T. students, climaxed finally by the Tenement House Census of 1892. The campaign was continued until the beginning of World War I, as indicated in the Common Council Reports of 1895 and 1896; the Twentieth Century Club Tenement House Study of 1897; the public hearing of the Board of Health in 1898; the Tenement House Commission Report of 1903; the "alliance" during this decade of the Women's League of Boston with the housing committee of the Chamber of Commerce as well as labor groups; the work of the housing committee of the "Boston: 1915" movement; and the formation of the Homestead Commission in 1909 with labor support and the development of a tiny public housing program of $50,000 for 25 houses in 1910.

The changing attitudes could be seen in the pronouncements of men like General Francis Walker. He, who once dubbed himself "the Ricardian of Ricardians" (Walker, *Land and Its Rent*, p. 5), now contended he had "of late been coming rapidly to the conviction that ere long there will be a general consent of conservative citizens, in every enlightened state to regard as thoroughly good politics all interference by law which may be necessary to prevent any portion of the people from living in houses which are unfit for human habitation, residence in which is incompatible with health or with social or personal decency" (Porter, *Report upon a Sanitary Inspection of Certain Tenement-House Districts of Boston*, pp. v–vi). And even though intemperance was assigned by H. G. Wadlin in the 1892 *Tenement Census* as the major reason why people lived in slums, he still urged stricter health and sanitary enforcement measures, the condemnation of slums (with compensation to owners, of course), and the building of public baths, laundry facilities, and parks in the slum areas (Wadlin, *A Tenement House Census of Boston*, pp. 418–440).

23. Bureau of Statistics of Labor, *Forty-First Annual Report*, 1911, Part 3, pp. 249–250. The three-decker spread throughout the state and region to such an extent that it has been called "the Massachusetts type of tenement" (Massachusetts Civic League, *The Housing Law for Cities*, pp. 1–2). Actually its popularity stems from the fact that it was peculiarly adapted to serve many other needs, as is indicated later in the chapter. It also spread to other cities, such as Chicago, Jersey City, Newark, and San Francisco (Ford, *Slums and Housing*, vol. I, p. 272).

24. Mayor Peters, "The City's Obligation in Housing" in *Housing Problems in America*, p. 332.

25. Massachusetts Civic League, *The Housing Law for Cities*. Previously,

parts of the city had managed to block erection of the units, as, for example, East Boston. Various districts were established in 1916, and the law was apparently more severe for tenements inside the fire limits. Most of the units were built beyond the fire limits, i.e., beyond Trumbull Street on to Breed's Island. (Gibbs, "East Boston," in "Report of the City Planning Board," pp. 45–48.)

Brookline, Massachusetts, had quickly passed legislation against this type of building and managed to avoid the aftereffects, especially in terms of land values (Hall, "The Menace of the Three Decker" in *Housing Problems in America,* p. 147).

26. Hall, p. 142. See also Massachusetts Civic League, *The Housing Law for Cities,* pp. 1–2.

27. Hall, p. 145.

28. See Hall, pp. 147–150; see also Committee Appointed by Mayor Peters on Housing, "Report," p. 13; Gibbs, "East Boston," p. 49; Marble, "The Menace of the Three Decker," p. 326.

29. At least, the third floor had much light. If the houses were crowded together, the two lower floors were darkened. Other advantages cited were those often mentioned in discussions of the preference for an apartment rather than a home, i.e., common heating, group living, cheaper heating costs, and often the absence of responsibilities and chores that go with ownership. See, for instance, the observations of Marble, p. 323, and Hall, p. 135.

C. Bauer after reading this section observed in a letter to the author that: "Aside from fire hazard (and I wonder if they really did kill more people than the East Side tenements at that?) and ugliness (which was true of practically all building of that period) the free standing three-decker was probably the most economical dwelling form ever devised which provided some light and air on four sides for each family, a large private balcony, and private access to the ground, not to mention an opportunity for small ownership and investment and the economy of owner maintenance. I'd a lot rather live in one, if properly maintained, than in a new law tenement in New York or even a New York Housing Authority Project."

New York, in fact, witnessed a campaign to have the three-decker exempted from the provisions of the tenement law on the grounds that it was better housing, cost less, would appeal to the person of small means, and would create additional owners. The same apparently was true for Chicago, especially the ownership aspects. (*Housing Betterment,* vol. 5, no. 1, February 1915, pp. 17–18.)

30. Hall, "The Menace of the Three Decker," pp. 147–150; Marble, "The Menace of the Three Decker," p. 324; Bureau of Statistics of Labor, *Forty-First Annual Report,* 1910, part 3, pp. 243 and 249–250. Actually, some of these houses had sufficient services, such as steam heat, hot and cold water, and janitor services, to put them almost in the "business class" (Brighton), whereas others in Charlestown with dark rooms and no conveniences but cold water and a private water closet on the landing actually served the slum dweller (*ibid.,* pp. 243–244). See also Davis, "Shall We Encourage or Discourage the Apartment House?" in *Housing Problems in America,* discussion, p. 342.

31. The City Planning Board pointed out in 1924: "Despite the housing congestion in certain sections of the city, the greater part of the residential area of Boston is composed of one- and two-family houses which take up 18% of the city's area. Four per cent is in three-family houses, and only one per cent in apartments or tenement houses and hotels. Zoning sets aside 60% of the city for all residential purposes of which 55% is for general residential use,

including apartment houses and 5% is for single residences. . . ." (Boston City Planning Board, *Zoning for Boston*, p. 22.) Forty-foot districts, moreover, which allowed three-deckers covered large areas in Dorchester, Roxbury, Jamaica Plain, Brighton, Charlestown, South Boston, East Boston, and elsewhere (Leahy, "A Compendium of Reports and Studies Relating to the Commerce and Industries of Boston," p. 308).

32. The City Planning Board reports that a survey of employees in an industrial and mercantile plant during 1919 indicated a rent range of $14 to $40 and a preference for one- and two-family houses. The sample was limited and so the results are not too reliable—but even the low- and middle-income public on the basis of this evidence had lost interest in the three-decker. (Boston City Planning Board, "Report on the Housing Situation in Boston," pp. 699–700.)

33. Perhaps the zoning victory was significant in view of the fact that restoration was made more difficult if price deflation suddenly makes this kind of construction feasible. The point made in the text may also apply to tenement house legislation. Perhaps higher costs and standards of demand were more effective than enacted legislation in ending slum tenement construction; but, just as in the case of three-deckers, such legislation would still be necessary in situations where price deflation or shortages made such jerry-building profitable.

For more details on the cost data, see Special Commission on the Necessaries of Life, *Report*, February 1920, p. 101. See also Hall, "The Menace of the Three Decker," p. 148.

34. Brogan, *The American Character*.

35. These data contain some possibility of error. They are based on the number of existing dwellings in Boston for which age was reported. About 11 to 12 per cent did not report the year built for metropolitan Boston and Boston City. Most of these units were probably older units built before 1890. (Cf. Blumenfeld, "Correlation between Value of Dwelling Units and Attitudes," *Journal of Land and Public Utility Economics*, p. 396.) It is probable that the same or even higher proportions apply to the units not reporting.

Some units were also converted or destroyed. It is doubtful whether the number of conversions would significantly change the proportions for the two periods; moreover, this possibility applies to all periods. Also, accurate data on demolitions for this period are not available. Even though demolitions might tend to be greater for some types of structures, it is nevertheless doubtful whether demolitions, either by percentage or type of structure, significantly affected the proportion for the two periods.

The data by housing type for the period 1940–1956 are not available but can also be estimated. Between 1950 and 1956, 69,276 dwelling units were added in the Boston metropolitan area, of which 42,370, or 61 per cent, were one-dwelling units detached. If year-built data on a 4 per cent sample may be trusted, of approximately 46,000 units built between 1940 and 1950, 30,000, or 65 per cent, were one-dwelling units detached. See Seventeenth Census, U.S., 1950, *Boston, Nonfarm Housing Characteristics*, Table A-6, pp. 26–28; U.S. Bureau of the Census, *1956 National Housing Inventory*, vol. 3, *Characteristics of the 1956 Inventory*, part 3, "Boston," Table 1, p. 11. See also Chap. 4, note 39, above.

36. Shattuck, *Report to the Committee of the City Council . . .* , Appendix M, pp. 22–23; Sixteenth Census, U.S., 1940, *Housing*, vol. 2, part 3, pp. 446–447; Seventeenth Census, U.S., 1950, *Boston, Nonfarm Housing Characteristics*, Tables A-1, A-2, pp. 26:3, 26:4.

See also Sixteenth Census, U.S., 1940, *Housing*, vol. 3, part 2, Table B-1, p. 13; and U.S. Bureau of the Census, *1956 National Housing Inventory*, vol. 3, *Characteristics of the 1956 Inventory*, part 3, "Boston," Table 1, p. 11.

37. Tenure data for 1890 are not available for the Boston metropolitan area as now defined by the Bureau of the Census. Many of the present districts in fact were country suburbs or farms. Since information was available only for a small number of towns and cities that now comprise the census metropolitan district, percentages were secured instead for the basic counties now included in whole or in part in the present metropolitan area: Suffolk, Middlesex, Essex, Bristol, Plymouth, and Norfolk. These data do not show the full increase, since a higher percentage of tenancy probably prevailed in 1890 for the existing metropolitan area compared to the data by counties, which include many rural areas. The ownership percentages for these counties are 31.6 per cent for 1890, 33.1 per cent for 1920, 42.6 per cent for 1930, and 36.8 per cent for 1940. (Computed from Eleventh Census, U.S., 1890, *Report on Farms and Homes*, Table 98, p. 341; Fourteenth Census, U.S., 1920, *Population*, vol. 2, p. 1310; Fifteenth Census, U.S., 1930, *Population*, vol. 6, Table 19, p. 619; Sixteenth Census, U.S., 1940, *Housing*, vol. 2, part 3, Table 22, pp. 229–237. The percentages of families owning homes in metropolitan Boston whose homes were encumbered with mortgages were 58 in 1920, 66 in 1940, and 68 in 1950. See also Seventeenth Census, U.S., 1950, *Housing*, vol. 1, part 3, Table 17, p. 21:16; and U.S. Bureau of Census, *1956 National Housing Inventory*, vol. 3, *Characteristics of the 1956 Inventory*, part 3, "Boston," Table 1, p. 11.

38. Seventeenth Census, U.S., 1950, *Housing*, vol. 1, part 3, Table 21, pp. 21:33 and 21:35.

39. Winnick, "The Burden of the Residential Mortgage Debt," *The Journal of Finance*, p. 173.

40. Special Commission on the Necessaries of Life, *Report*, 1922, pp. 67–69.

41. Herlihy, "The Housing Situation in Boston" in *Housing Betterment*, p. 167. Nationally, the problem was reflected in the movement to establish the Home Loan Bank Credit Reserve. A bill to this effect was introduced by Senator Calder and failed. See also Fourteenth Census, U.S., 1920, *Mortgages on Homes*, pp. 172–173.

42. Herlihy, p. 167. The amendment read: "Article 47. The maintenance and distribution at reasonable rates, during the time of war, public exigency, emergency or distress of a sufficient supply of food and other common necessaries of life and the providing of shelter are public functions, and the commonwealth and the cities and towns therein may take and provide the same for their inhabitants."

43. Herlihy, p. 166. Specific individuals and organizations had favored ownership in the past, as for example J. Quincy, R. T. Paine, and the building and loan association officials, though not for these reasons. There was also a period when ownership was particularly deplored and feared, i.e., the three-decker period. See Special Commission on the Necessaries of Life, *Report*, January 1923, p. 83; and *Report*, January 1925, p. 37. See also *Housing Betterment*, vol. 8, no. 2 (June 1919), pp. 32–34, and Dean, *Home Ownership*, chap. ii.

44. Special Commission on the Necessaries of Life, *Report*, January 1925, p. 36. Whoever made this observation betrayed an ironical as well as pathetic ignorance of the housing experiences of Boston's foreign population.

45. In 1918, E. E. Wood sounded like a voice crying out in the wilderness

when she declared that "Building costs are such, not simply now but on a basis of prewar prices, as to make it an economic impossibility to build a home of acceptable standards and rent it at a price which the unskilled wage earner can pay and produce a commercial return on the capital market. It simply cannot be done. This has been proved over and over again at these conferences . . . the final inferences have not always been drawn from the facts presented. The only solution, therefore, is the elimination of commercial profit and this can only be done by the government." (E. E. Wood, "Government Housing" in *Housing Problems in America,* pp. 292–293.) E. E. Wood then advocated the "radical" policy of using postal savings to help finance housing.

46. Special Commission on the Necessaries of Life, *Report,* February 1920, p. 101 (italic supplied).

47. Special Commission on the Necessaries of Life, *Report,* January 1923, p. 83.

48. See Special Commission on the Necessaries of Life, *Report,* January 1925, pp. 36, 41–45; *Report,* 1922, pp. 66ff; and *Report,* January 1923, pp. 37–38.

49. Rental housing built later in the decade soon passed from the stage of a profitable investment or speculation skimming the cream of the market into a fleecing or promotional racket. Frequently houses were built, put on the market at exorbitant rentals, and then sold to the tenants at inflated valuations for cooperative ownership and management with the threat of eviction hanging over recalcitrant residents. Even more often, apartment houses were built and sold at swollen valuations because of profits inherent in the promotional possibilities. Numerous bond houses, established and otherwise, participated in these schemes in spite of obvious overbuilding and growing vacancies for higher-income groups. Bankruptcy followed the inevitable crisis and panic—but even in these proceedings, fantastic profits in fees, receiverships, and reorganizations were extracted by the same irresponsible groups. (Special Commission on the Necessaries of Life, *Report,* 1922, pp. 66ff; and *Report,* January 1925, p. 38. Cf. U. S. Congress, House of Representatives, *Investigation of Real Estate Bondholder's Reorganizations,* 1935 and 1936.)

50. A census housing survey of the Boston area in 1946 indicated that "two out of five married World War II veterans were doubling up with relatives or friends or living in rented rooms, trailers or tourist cabins." Approximately 75 per cent of the veterans in Boston City planning to rent indicated that they could pay no more than $49 a month, the median gross monthly rental for the group being $43. The figures for the metropolitan area were $49 and $44 respectively. Those intending to buy or build indicated a median price range of $7,100 and a median gross monthly rent of $66. These figures are quite high and already reflect the inflated price levels and realities of the period. Yet in 1947, "Representatives of builders and housing construction companies stated the cost for rooms in the Boston area ranged from $2,000 to $2,400." (U.S. Bureau of the Census, *Survey of World War II Veterans and Dwelling Unit Vacancy and Occupancy in the Boston Area, Massachusetts,* p. 1 and Table 4, p. 6; Special Commission to Make a Survey and Study of Problems Relating to Veterans, Including Hospitals and Hospital Facilities, *Report,* part 1, "Veterans' Housing," p. 7.) Phillip Nicholls, prominent lawyer who was then Massachusetts State Housing Board Chairman, urged local communities and the General Court to take decisive steps to meet the needs of an estimated 60,000 veterans who needed homes. Authority to act, he contended, existed in the 1917 amendment to the constitution permitting the state to build in

time of emergency, public exigency or distress—an interpretation which it should be noted completely reversed the position taken by the Boston Attorney General during the 1920's. Recommended as lines of action for communities were surveys of housing needs, purchase of land and sale with or without houses, use of ships in coastal areas, resort to eminent domain to acquire houses from which veterans were evicted, use of tax delinquent and foreclosed land, relaxation of building, zoning, and fire regulations for five years for temporary housing, municipal building of temporary or permanent housing, and cooperation with the federal government. (Mass. State Board of Housing, *Special Report Relative to the Procurement of Homes for War Veterans*, pp. 7–13.)

See also Bradford, *Special Message to the General Court;* and the Special Commission to Make a Survey and Study of Problems Relating to Veterans, *Report*, part 1, "Veterans' Housing." This report recommended public housing, state rent control if federal controls were eliminated, and legislation to extend the courts' power to stop evictions for a period of four months. The Special Recess Commission on Housing declared that "The need for low rental dwelling by veterans is paramount. This fact was established by various surveys taken in widely scattered congested areas of the Commonwealth. The majority of veterans expressed a desire to rent under their present economic status." (*Report*, p. 13.) A year later in his *Annual Message* of 1948 Governor Bradford declared that "In 1947 approximately 11,500 apartments and homes were completed in Massachusetts. But the greatest of our housing needs remains unmet: the creation of low-cost multifamily rental units. Rising costs have so discouraged new building for low-income rental, and evictions have reached such an acute state that we must do more than we have done in the past if we are to cope at all effectively with the emergency" (p. 7). The public housing program of 20,000 low-rental units was subsequently endorsed.

51. For example, in 1946 Wilson W. Wyatt, then Housing Expediter and Administrator of the National Housing Agency, emphasized in a statement to Congress that with the "present tools, we can't get enough rental housing produced, and many veterans find it necessary to rent rather than buy. In fact, under current conditions only about 53 per cent of the veterans want to buy housing while fully 47 per cent want to rent. . . . The need for additional rental housing clearly emphasizes the need for additional tools which the Wagner-Ellender-Taft bill would provide for stimulating the production of an adequate volume of such housing, especially the plans for yield insurance, and for extending FHA mortgage insurance on more satisfactory terms for mutual ownership and cooperative housing, and for low rent public housing." (Wyatt, Press Release of a 12-page summary of a statement made by him to the U.S. Congress on November 7, 1946.

52. In 1946, for example, Massachusetts enacted legislation authorizing communities to borrow money outside of statutory debt limits up to a maximum of 2 per cent, with which to build housing for low-income veterans at rents they could afford (Chapter 372 of the Acts of 1946). However, the maximum subsidy could be no more than 10 per cent of total cost. The law, since amended by Chapter 479 of the Acts of 1947, relieved municipalities of liability for interest and bond retirement costs that would be reflected in local tax rates. A 2 per cent state subsidy for five years was substituted, and after this period the homes were subject to sale. The original legislation only provided for one- and two-family houses, and this was changed in Chapter 479 to include multifamily construction. This legislation also empowered cities to

acquire sites and provide utilities for surplus temporary housing, which, if these conditions were fulfilled, the federal government made available at no other cost to local communities. Incidentally, this statutory power was first made available in Chapter 13, Acts of 1946. See P. Nicholls in Mass. State Board of Housing, *Special Report,* pp. 1–5; and Mass. State Board of Housing, *Report of the Director to the Chairman,* Appendix E, pp. 5–6.

To catalyze local action the state later agreed to share half the losses sustained under the program. After five years, the tenant could purchase the home, credit being allowed in the final purchase price for rent paid during the first five years of occupancy. Boston's city council accordingly approved a twenty million dollar loan fund for one-, two-, and multiple-family houses under this program.

State legislation was also enacted creating an Emergency Housing Commission to expedite building construction and also to grant, where necessary, variances from local housing codes refused by local boards of appeal (Chapter 592, Acts of 1946). A later act provided for the development of alternative and statewide standards of performance, which might be substituted for requirements established in local building codes (Chapter 631, Acts of 1947). This was a pioneering legislative enactment. (See also the Special Recess Commission on Housing, *Report,* pp. 15–17.) To mobilize complete use of community resources, establishment of nonprofit corporations to build housing with tax privileges on municipal land was urged. Efforts were also made to stimulate investment in housing by savings banks and insurance companies. Finally, as these activities proved inadequate, a $200 million veterans' housing program, with a potential of 20,000 rental units and modeled on the federal public housing legislation, was passed. (Chapter 200, Acts of 1948 and Mass. State Board of Housing, *Report of the Director to the Chairman,* p. 14.) Management and construction of the homes for veterans was handled through local housing authorities with state supervision and a guarantee of local bonds and notes. A maximum subsidy of $5 million annually (i.e., 2½ per cent of development costs) or a total of $125 million of subsidies over a period of twenty-five years was also provided. Boston promptly applied for $8 million in state credit to build 4,800 housing units.

Chapter 4. *Boston's Experience With and Without Rent Controls*

1. This chapter is based on a substantial revision of the article "Rent Control and Housing: A Case Study," which was published in *Land Economics,* vol. 27, no. 4 (November 1951).

2. See Appendix B, notes 2 and 3.

3. U.S. Dept. of Labor, Bureau of Labor Statistics, *Consumer's Price Index for Moderate Income Families: Boston, Massachusetts: 1914–1960,* "Rent," 1914-Forward Series D-4, p. 1. The Consumer's Price Index, formerly calculated on the base period 1935–39 = 100 has been converted to the new base 1947–49 = 100, in compliance with the United States Bureau of the Budget, Office of Statistical Standards. The changes cited use the new base. This estimate may be low. Cf. Maisel, "Have We Underestimated Increases in Rents and Shelter Expenditures?" *Journal of Political Economy,* pp. 106–117.

4. The percentages are based on the Boeckh Index for frame and brick residences. See U.S. Housing and Home Finance Agency, *Housing Statistics Handbook,* Tables 29 and 30, pp. 34–35. See also Chart 2 and Table 2, above.

5. Fourteenth Census, U.S., 1920, *Mortgages on Homes,* p. 192; and Fif-

teenth Census, U.S., 1930, *Population*, vol. 6, p. 60. The Consumer's Price Index for all items for Boston was 89.1 in 1920, 76.5 in 1928, 76.6 in 1929, and 74.8 in 1930. The index for Wholesale Prices of Building Materials for the nation was 78.2 in 1920, 49.0 in 1928, 49.7 in 1929, and 46.8 in 1930. See U.S. Department of Labor, Bureau of Labor Statistics, *Consumer's Price Index for Moderate Income Families*, 1914-Forward Series A-4, and "Wholesale Prices and Price Indices," *Construction Volume and Costs, 1915–1956* (monthly issues). The Special Commission on the Necessaries of Life also recognized these trends. They observed that "the great increase in the cost of construction and speculation in old property have resulted in increasing rents for old property to substantially as high a level as that which must be charged for new property. . . . Rent reductions will be slow as much property has changed hands in the speculative period, and the apparent speculative investment in the old property now equals the investment in newly constructed housing." (*Report*, January 1925, p. 36.)

6. *Ibid.*, pp. 34 and 37. See also *Report*, January 1920, pp. 96–98. For further data on the rise of rents and high rent income ratios, see U.S. Dept. of Labor, Bureau of Labor Statistics, *Consumer's Price Index;* and Chap. 3.

7. Special Commission on the Necessaries of Life, *Report*, January 1923, p. 71; and *Report*, January 1925, p. 37.

8. Special Commission on the Necessaries of Life, *Reports*—February 1920, pp. 96–97; 1922, pp. 69–70.

9. Special Commission on the Necessaries of Life, *Report*, January 1925, p. 47.

10. Lintner, *Mutual Savings Banks in the Savings and Mortgage Markets*, pp. 270–271 and Chart 38.

11. A larger number of transfers to ownership probably occur, but they are offset by shifts of units from ownership to tenancy.

12. Fifteenth Census, U.S., 1930, *Population*, vol. 6, p. 57.

13. Special Commission on the Necessaries of Life, *Report*, January 1923, p. 71.

14. Sixteenth Census, U.S., 1940, *Housing, Characteristics by Type of Structure*, "Regions, States, Cities of 10,000 or More and Principal Metropolitan Districts," Table B-1, p. 160. The number of four-family dwelling units is too small to be of significance. Note that a discrepancy exists between the Census data and the Building Department data. The figures of the Building Department may be inflated because the permit data may exceed the actual number of units built by approximately 3 to 5 per cent. The Census data are based on the number of dwelling units (by year built) which were enumerated in 1940. The Census data may vary from the Building Department data because of demolitions and conversions, and also because approximately 26,547 units did not report the year built. Most of the nonreporting units were probably in the older categories, however. The Census data were used primarily because comparable information was also available for the metropolitan area.

15. *Ibid.*, Table C-1, p. 161. The figures in Table 3 indicate the amount and types of housing in Boston by the year built. Since a considerable number were converted to two or more dwelling units during the 1930's, the per cent of one-family units indicated in the table understates the number actually built. The proportion of one-family units built in the 1920's and still standing is approximately 41 per cent.

16. M. H. Naigles, describing the chief building patterns in the United States during this period, concluded that "the position of the single-family

house as the preferred type of American nonfarm home was at no time challenged between 1920 and 1940. It regularly accounted for more than half of
the annual construction of new housekeeping units." ("Housing and the Increase in Population," *Monthly Labor Review,* p. 6.)

17. Special Commission on the Necessaries of Life, *Report,* January 1925,
p. 37.

18. *Ibid.,* pp. 35–37.

19. Special Commission on the Necessaries of Life, *Report,* February 1920,
pp. 34–37.

20. Special Commission on the Necessaries of Life, *Report,* January 1923.
The commission observed that these groups have "suffered most severely. . . . When living conditions were rapidly rising because of the high
wages they were the center of most of the trouble. In many cases their income
did not increase in the same proportion as those who had formerly lived in less
desirable quarters. Now when the readjustments are downward, the most
trouble again is in this class of apartments as many of those who formerly
lived in the high price type of apartment with special services are obliged to
get something at a lower price" (p. 73). See also *Report,* January 1925, p. 36.

21. *Ibid.,* pp. 34 and 36. Mayor Curley indicated in his "Annual Address to
the City Council" in February 1924 that "many apartment blocks are being
erected but nothing is being done to meet the needs of those with children"
(*Boston Year Book,* 1924, p. 51).

22. Some of the landlords may have represented middle-income families,
but tenants are more numerous and poorer in the Boston metropolitan area. In
1950, 43.2 per cent of the families in owner-occupied units had incomes of
$4000 or less, compared to 62 per cent for renter-occupied units. Seventeenth
Census, U.S., 1950, *Housing,* vol. 2, part 3, Table A-8, p. 26–10.

23. Special Commission on the Necessaries of Life, *Report,* 1920, pp. 96–
97; Bauer, "We Face a Housing Shortage" in *Housing Yearbook,* pp. 61–72;
and Division on the Necessaries of Life, *Report,* 1936, p. 9. The division urged
that "building on a large scale should be started now in order to prevent a
recurrence of the conditions which existed for several years after the war."

24. See Chap. 2, Tables 1 and 2.

25. Townsend, "Some Economic Aspects of Urban Housing," p. 231, note 1.
Mr. Loring, Executive Director of the Housing Association of Metropolitan
Boston indicated that "the least expensive, up to standard, used dwelling units
are selling at $3,000 per unit in three-deckers in poor neighborhoods." (U.S.
Congress, Senate, *Hearings before the Joint Committee on Housing,* part 3,
p. 2592).

26. Cf. Chap. 1, Chart 1 and Table 1. The Consumer Price Index for Boston
indicates a rise of less than 50 per cent. But it probably underestimated the
rise. See U.S. Dept. of Labor, Bureau of Labor Statistics, *Consumer's Price
Index for Moderate Income Families: Boston, Massachusetts: 1914–1960;* and
Maisel, "Have We Underestimated Increases in Rents and Shelter Expenditures?" *op. cit.* pp. 106–118.

27. U.S. Office of Price Administration, Rent Dept., Cost Analysis Branch,
Income and Expense under Rent Control: Boston Rental Housing. 1939–1943,
pp. 1–18. Though no further studies were published, accountancy surveys were
made through the year 1947. Mr. H. E. Berquist, Acting Deputy Housing Director, indicated to this writer in a letter dated September 29, 1948, that the
survey for the Fiscal Year ending June 30, 1947, showed the following indexes
based upon 1939 equals 100:

	Apartment houses	Small structures
Rental income	109.4	109.2
Total expense	106.4	107.9
Net operating income	115.8	113.1
Vacancy loss	0.1	0.6

28. Approximately one seventh of the married veterans in the area had homes, and of these owners, one fourth purchased following their discharge (U.S. Bureau of the Census, *Survey of World War II Veterans and Dwelling Unit Vacancy and Occupancy in the Boston Area, Massachusetts*, p. 2).

29. Sixteenth Census, U.S., 1940, *Housing*, Vol. 2, Second Series, Table 1, p. 7. Seventeenth Census, U.S., 1950, *Housing*, vol. 1, part 3, Table 17, p. 21:16.

30. U.S. Bureau of the Census, *1956 National Housing Inventory*, vol. 1, *Components of Change, 1950 to 1956*, part 3, "Boston," Table 2, p. 11.

31. *Ibid.*, Table 1, p. 11.

32. Seventeenth Census, U.S., 1950, *Housing*, vol. 1, part 3, Table 1, p. 21:23; Table 17, pp. 21: 14, 21:16. The data for two-family units apply to one-dwelling unit attached, one- and two-dwelling unit semidetached, and two-dwelling unit other, in the Census. There were comparatively few semidetached and these were not included in the percentages since they would not change the relative proportions.

33. The relevant figures on dwelling units built following both world wars, based on applications for permits, are

1919	481	1946	1023
1920	320	1947	890
1921	878	1948	1642
1922	3434	1949	1598
Total	5113		5153

Public housing units are not included in the data for the second postwar period, or the actual total would have been increased several fold. Data for the period following World War I were obtained from the "Annual Statistical Reports" of the Boston Building Department, Commonwealth of Massachusetts, 1918–1922; and data for the five years following World War II were obtained from the U.S. Bureau of the Census, *Statistical Abstract of the United States* for the relevant years.

34. These data were supplied by Mr. Richard Granara of the Building Department of the City of Boston.

35. Actually, 33,645 units were reported built between 1945 and 1950. But this total was based on 648,145 reporting units. If a proportionate adjustment is made to take account of the nonreporting units, the figure comes close to 35,000. See Seventeenth Census, U.S., 1950, *Housing*, vol. 1, part 3, Table 20, pp. 21–28. See also Housing Association of Metropolitan Boston, *Housing Action in Metropolitan Boston*. Actually, the sample census of 1947 indicates an increase of approximately 90,000 units between 1940 and 1947, or an average increase of 11,600 a year. The Boston regional office of the Bureau of Labor Statistics estimates 8,730 new dwelling units were started in 1947 in the Boston Industrial Area, which comprises Essex, Middlesex, Norfolk, and Suffolk counties. The record for 1956 was estimated as 5,200 starts; and the record for the second half of 1948, for which period data are available, was 15 per cent

higher than 1947 (U.S. Dept. of Labor, Bureau of Labor Statistics, "Progress of Housing Program in Boston," Press Release dated 2-10-48, with table attached; also a subsequent release on the same subject dated 1-30-49). On the basis of other studies and the proportion between units built in Boston City and the Boston metropolitan area, there is reason to suspect that the census figure is too high and that 7,000 to 8,000 represents a closer estimate. Therefore, the lower average of 7,000 units is employed to ensure a more conservative estimate.

36. Sixteenth Census, U.S., 1940, *Housing*, vol. 2, part 3, Table C-1, p. 161.

37. The data also contain some response errors, and they probably do not take full account of the number of converted units. Unfortunately, we have no way of gauging the extent of the underestimate. See Table 11; also *1956 National Housing Inventory*, vol. 1, *Components of Change, 1950 to 1956*, part 3, "Boston," Table 1, p. 13.

38. *Ibid.*

39. Households increased by 50,000 in the six and three-fourths years between April 1950 and December 1956. However, there are no direct data on the change in the number of households or families in the Boston metropolitan area between 1920 and 1930. Fortunately, there are data on the increase in the total population and on the average size of families. Population for the standard metropolitan area (excluding Lawrence and Lowell) increased from 2,108,082 to 2,426,624, or by a total of 318,542, during this period. The average number of persons per private family in the city of Boston was 4.5 in 1920, and the average number of persons per family was 4.1 in 1930. To ensure a conservative estimate, since the size of families would probably be larger for the metropolitan area, the total increase in population for the area between 1920 and 1930 was divided by 4.5 rather than the lower figure of 4.1. This calculation yields an estimated increase in the number of families of 71,000. On the assumption that there was an equal distribution of the increase for the decade, then the increase for the six and three-fourths years was roughly 48,000. However, there was probably a much larger increase in the number of families and households formed, during the first few years following World War I, and also a smaller family size because of migration to the area. It is probably reasonable, therefore, to assume that the increase in the number of families or households for the two periods was roughly the same or slightly larger for the earlier period.

See U.S. Bureau of the Census, *1956 National Housing Inventory*, vol. 3, *Characteristics of the 1956 Inventory*, part 3, "Boston," Table 1, p. 11; and Fifteenth Census, U.S., 1930, *Population*, vol. 6, Table 77, p. 71, and Table 66, p. 59. See also Rapkin, Winnick, and Blank, *Housing Market Analysis*, chap. vi; and Kristof, "Components of Change in the Nation's Housing Inventory in Relation to the 1960 Census."

It could be argued that following World War II one might have expected a greater volume of construction per family or household because of the more liberal provisions for financing housing made available by the Home Loan Bank System, the Federal Housing Administration, and the veterans' housing program. A counterclaim might be made, however, that the greater optimism and faith in land-value appreciation during the 1920's compared to later periods contributed to a greater volume of construction, particularly rental housing. It is probably impossible to estimate the strength of these two influences, and it was assumed that they roughly offset each other.

40. This estimate can be derived in one of two ways. We can apply the

estimated percentages used in determining the proportion of new units built for ownership as described on pp. 56–58 of this chapter. This procedure, which is deliberately biased to yield a higher proportion for ownership, yields a percentage of 46 per cent for rental units when applied to the total number of dwelling units built in the metropolitan district of Boston during the 1920's. The other approach is to assume that the rental units include half of the two-family units, all of the dwelling units in structures containing three or more units, and none of the units in one-family houses. On this basis the maximum number of rental units built in the 1920's comes to 40 per cent.

41. For an excellent analysis of this legislation, see "FHA's Impact on Financing and Designs in Apartments," *Architectural Forum*, vol. 92, no. 1 (January 1950), pp. 97–106. The FHA scandal in 1954 in handling Section 608 rental housing developments led to drastic revisions of the legislation. The investigations brought to light many large "windfall" profits which resulted from FHA appraisals often much in excess of cost. This practice enabled builders to "mortgage out," i.e., to retrieve all their funds and even substantial profits from the loan. Other abuses were found in the Title I home improvement program. See U.S. Senate, *Report of the Senate Committee on Banking and Currency on the FHA Investigation*, Jan. 6, 1955. For a more sympathetic interpretation, see Winnick, *Rental Housing: Opportunities for Private Investment*, pp. 187–190; also see U.S. Housing and Home Finance Agency, *Fifth Annual Report, 1954*, pp. 500–503.

42. Overcrowding refers to the number of people per household unit, and doubling-up refers to the number of married couples in private households who have not established their own households. Over-all averages, of course, do not imply that significant variations may not exist for special groups in the community. See U.S. Bureau of the Census, *Housing Characteristics of the Boston, Massachusetts, Metropolitan District: April, 1947*, Table 2, p. 6.

43. Seventeenth Census, U.S., 1950, *Housing*, vol. 1, part 3, Table 19, pp. 21–23.

44. For the statistics cited in this paragraph, see U.S. Bureau of the Census, *1956 National Housing Inventory*, vol. 3, *Characteristics of the 1956 Inventory*, part 3, "Boston," Table 1, p. 11.

Chapter 5. *Residential Growth and Development*

1. See Rutan, "Before the Invasion" in Woods, ed., *Americans in Process*, pp. 19–20; Stanwood, "Topography and Landmarks of the Last Hundred Years" in Winsor, ed., *Memorial History of Boston: 1630–1880*, vol. 4, pp. 603–644; Wright and Wadlin, "The Industries of the Last Hundred Years," *ibid.*, p. 79; Firey, *Land Use in Central Boston*, p. 42. The Mill Pond was later filled to form the present West End area of Boston. For an excellent recent study of Boston's growth and development, see W. M. Whitehill, *Boston: A Topographical History*.

2. Firey, p. 58; also "As the 'Little Transcript' Knew its Boston," *Boston Transcript Centenary*, pp. 1–4; and Stanwood, "Topography and Landmarks," p. 55.

3. Rutan, "Before the Invasion," pp. 30–33; Firey, *Land Use in Central Boston*, pp. 44–55.

4. Rutan, pp. 33 and 36. The West End really began to develop after the Mill Pond was filled, a process which took about twenty-five years (1804–1829); cf. Firey, pp. 42–55.

5. Chamberlin, *The Boston Transcript*, pp. 32–34. About 1800, the six wealthiest men of Boston were bankers, three of whom lived in the North End (Rutan, "Before the Invasion," p. 29).

6. Rutan, pp. 32–34; Handlin, *Boston's Immigrants, 1790–1865*, p. 17.

7. "Report and Tabular Statement of the Censors Appointed by the Board of Mayor and Aldermen to Obtain the State Census of Boston, May 1, 1850 . . .," pp. 24ff. (Also Chickering, "A Comparative View . . .," pp. 24ff.) See also J. T. Adams, "The Historical Background," in *New England's Prospect*, p. 9. Mr. Warner comments in the Massachusetts Census of 1865 that the population increase "has been confined almost entirely to the manufacturing towns or to those in the vicinity of Boston. In nearly all the counties, the smaller towns are losing population, the larger cities and towns at the same time increasing and the statement that all the larger towns are becoming manufacturing towns would be nearly the truth." (O. Warner in *Abstract of the Census of Massachusetts*, 1865, p. 273.)

8. Handlin, *Boston's Immigrants*, Table 5, p. 229. Between 1820 and 1830 Boston averaged about 1,000 immigrants per annum; and for the subsequent decade about 3,000. The number of Irish passengers entering Boston by sea for the five-year period from 1841 to 1845 was 10,157; from 1846 to 1850 it was 65,556; from 1851 to 1855, 63,831. A smaller movement of several thousand German immigrants followed the Irish peasants in the wake of the crop failure and changing patterns of land use, but this migration soon petered out. (*Ibid.*)

9. Beacon Hill was cut down to approximately half its size; Pemberton Square was cut and graded, and Cotton Hill was completely obliterated. Stanwood, "Topography and Landmarks," pp. 32, 63; Haynes, "Historical" in R. A. Woods, ed., *The City Wilderness*, p. 29.

10. Handlin, *Boston's Immigrants*, pp. 98–99, 106–112; and "Report to the Joint Special Committee of the City Government on the Census of Boston in 1855," p. 69. Unfortunately, there is only the most fragmentary data indicating how the housing crisis was met and who erected the houses for immigrants. Conversions, crowding, makeshift shacks, shanties, and tenements were some of the expedients employed. Also, leasing and subleasing of almost all buildings with four walls and a roof became a lucrative employment. Handlin contends that the converted buildings were generally superior to those directly built to house the foreign population because they had "some benefits of light, air and privacy. Whatever the intention of the proprietor or lessee, transformed buildings could not utilize space as carefully as those created specifically for immigrants. New dwellings completely free of restrictions displayed every stratagem for economy at the expense of the most humble amenities" (pp. 106–107). The Report of the Committee on the Expediency of Providing Better Tenements for the Poor tries to prove in one section that parts of Boston are "as crowded as the great work shops of the old world" (p. 51). If the vacancy ratio by wards is computed on the basis of data available in the 1845 Census, using 4 per cent as the minimum vacancy standard, an extremely tight housing situation is disclosed. For example, the vacancy ratios for Wards 1, 2, and 3 in the North End were 0.7 per cent, 1.6 per cent, and 2.8 per cent, respectively. The West End (Ward 5) and Fort Hill (Ward 8) had ratios of 1.3 per cent. The percentage for Beacon Hill, however, was 4.8 per cent, and for East Boston it was 5.6 per cent. These ratios, in the absence of any other information, appear to be generous because they do not exclude those units which were probably not fit to be lived in. (Shattuck, *Report to the Committee of*

the City Council . . ., Appendix M, pp. 22–23.) High rents in slum areas of $1–2 per week for a dark room or damp cellar are partially explained by these data.

11. Boston Superintendent of Streets, "Annual Report," p. 14. See also Wolfe, *The Lodging House Problem in Boston,* pp. 9, 24–26, 81–82; Stanwood, "Topography and Landmarks," pp. 63–64; Firey, *Land Use in Central Boston,* pp. 51–54, 59–70; Rutan, "Before the Invasion," pp. 36–39; Handlin, *Boston's Immigrants,* pp. 105 and 108.

12. Stanwood, "Topography and Landmarks," p. 63, note 2. About nine acres were filled by the Front Street Company in 1830, and approximately seven acres were added by 1860 as a result of the efforts of the South Cove Corporation. The filled portion covered the area from Beach Street to Dover Street. The town filled the rest. (Haynes, "Historical," pp. 20–30.) The commercial section greatly expanded, having invaded the Fort Hill district and much of the waterfront area of Boston Proper, South Boston, and East Boston. The business and financial zone still centered around the old State House and State Street, and the wholesale market area extended into the North End along and near Commercial, Fulton, and Blackstone streets. Most of Ward 10 was converted into a business and retail trade district. The latter was already pushing down Boylston Street and threatening dwellings along Beacon Street opposite the Public Garden. This pressure, as indicated above, had already eliminated the choice dwellings on Tremont Street facing the Common. (Herndon, *Boston of To-day,* pp. 101–110.) See also Wolfe, *The Lodging House Problem,* pp. 14–19; J. Ross McKeever, "Beacon Hill: A Thesis in Site Planning"; Firey, *Land Use in Central Boston,* pp. 118–121; and Chamberlain, *Beacon Hill: Its Ancient Pastures and Early Mansions,* p. 417.

13. Surprisingly enough, of the 766 buildings destroyed, "all but sixty-seven were of brick or stone . . ." (Stanwood, "Topography and Landmarks," p. 5).

14. For example, Dwight Porter, on the basis of his tenement house investigation, judged the probable "returns from the lowest class of wooden tenement houses proper in this city at from 15 to 20 per cent gross; from first-class brick tenement houses at from 10 to 12 per cent gross; while first-class business property yields from 6 to 8 per cent gross and 4½ or 5 per cent net. Even at the high rate mentioned for low-grade homes, it is probable that they often fail to net their owners much over 6 per cent on account of abuse of the property, repairs and bad debts. Still there are many other cases in which it is fair to suppose that the repairs, grudgingly made, cannot seriously reduce the gross income obtained from the property." (Porter, *Report upon a Sanitary Inspection of Certain Tenement-House Districts of Boston,* p. 17.) For another comparable, though less thorough, survey of income in such tenements, see the Bureau of Statistics of Labor, [First Annual] *Report,* 1870, pp. 164–185. See also Whitmore, "Real Estate Values in Boston," *Publications of the American Statistical Association,* pp. 1–5.

15. The legislation enacted after the 1872 fire was loosely drawn, and the administrative agencies were inadequately financed and staffed. Therefore, despite lot and height limitations, forty-foot lots with sixty-foot depths could be completely covered. Many of the new structures were built on the dumbbell plan with only two feet approximately of open land in the rear. (Paine, "The Housing Conditions in Boston," p. 128.) See also Wadlin, *A Tenement House Census of Boston,* p. 195. Many citizens rightly questioned "whether these vast tenement houses, sometimes called model houses, were not far worse in many

essentials for the health and welfare of their occupants than the little old houses often built of wood, which they displaced" (Paine, "The Housing Conditions in Boston," p. 128).

16. The depression of 1895 was partly responsible, of course. Yet it seems clear, as the Tenement House Commission observed, that building "of tenement houses in which low rents can be asked is quite impracticable. Such construction has largely ceased." (Commission to Investigate Tenement House Conditions, "Report," p. 3.) L. Veiller declared in 1900 that, allowing for variations in type, "after New York, Boston has the worst tenement house conditions of any American City" (Veiller, *Housing Conditions and Tenement Laws in Leading American Cities*, pp. 14–16).

17. "Report and Tabular Statement of the Censors Appointed by the Board of Mayor and Aldermen to Obtain the State Census of Boston," pp. 13–14. Between 1865 and 1870, Boston's population increased by 23,876; but "Boston Proper" (as defined by the Census) showed "a loss of 2,302 persons, while its annexed territory gained 10,065, Roxbury and Dorchester having been annexed in this period. In the territory not yet annexed, there was an increase of 4.811." (The Census of Massachusetts, 1885, vol. 1, part 1, pp. xxxix–xlii.) Even when increases occurred they were much smaller proportionately than in the peripheral areas. Cf. also U.S. Department of Labor, Bureau of Labor Statistics, *Forty-first Annual Report*, 1911, part 3, p. 231.

18. High prices were designed to discourage speculation as well as to promote and sustain only upper-class development. Sometimes also local public improvements were made on the land before public sale, presumably so that the community and not the speculator could benefit from the increment in value. By pursuing this policy it was felt that the speculator would not hold the land for too long a period. Inexpensive land, many thought, might well stimulate cheap or shoddy developments. Actually, cheap developments were not eliminated elsewhere in the city, for example, the slums or near slums erected in parts of Fort Hill, the West End, the North End, and Roxbury. Moreover, the number of exceptional upper-class developments was limited: the creation of the Back Bay development meant the hastened loss of values in the South End, South Boston, and to some extent even on Beacon Hill. To trace the precise losses and gains is not possible, but it was an illusory accounting policy for the community to reckon the new subdivisions as a complete gain, if municipal improvement costs, subsidies, and losses in real estate values elsewhere are considered.

This lesson, interestingly enough, was learned a little earlier by the federal government in the development of its policy for the disposition of the public domain. See, for example, Hibbard, *History of Public Land Policy*, chaps. viii, ix, and xiii; also Robbins, *Our Landed Heritage*, chaps. v, vi, and vii. In 1845 the city received a little more than $400,000 from the sale of public land and about the same amount the following year. In the period from 1847 to 1860 revenues were relatively low and uneven and prompted Mayor Bigelow's proposal to sell at a low price. Between 1860 and 1873, almost $2,000,000 was received from land sales, or about $153,000 a year. However, in 1894 Mayor Northrup in a valedictory pointed out that although $3,000,000 profit had been made from fiscal sales, it had cost the city over $4,000,000 in grading and selling the land with sewers. (Koren, *Boston: 1822–1922*, p. 133.)

19. Huse, *The Financial History of Boston*, p. 96. This land policy partly influenced the sale of real estate in the South End, particularly the cheaper

construction along Columbus Avenue and the New York Streets (Wolfe, *The Lodging House Problem*, pp. 14–15, and Firey, *Land Use in Central Boston*, pp. 63–64).

A Land Committee Report to the Mayor in 1852 emphasized that "many streets formerly occupied by some of our wealthiest and most respectable citizens are now wholly surrendered to foreigners. The older parts of the city are crowded, rents are exorbitant and it is with extreme difficulty that a comfortable apartment can be obtained. Many citizens of Boston are erecting houses in neighboring cities and villages and increasing the taxable property in these places from the profits of business transacted within our limits." (Land Committee, "Report on Petition of John S. Tyler . . .," pp. 3–5.)

20. "Report and Tabular Statement of the Censors Appointed by the Board of Mayor and Aldermen to Obtain the State Census of Boston," pp. 39–40; Handlin, *Boston's Immigrants*, pp. 99–106; The Census of Massachusetts, 1885, vol. 1, part 1, pp. xxxix–xlii. See also Rapid Transit Commission, *Report to the Massachusetts Legislature*, pp. 16–17. See also Pinanski, *The Street Railway System of Metropolitan Boston*, and Boston Elevated Railway Company, *Fifty Years of Unified Transportation in Metropolitan Boston*, pp. 4–43.

21. Chapter 298 of Massachusetts Labor Law (1900). Round trip fares of less than $0.10 per day became available to "healthful and uncrowded areas" such as Dorchester (Phelps, *South End Operatives, Employment and Residence*, pp. 9–26).

22. The Census of Massachusetts, 1875, vol. 1, part 1, pp. 39–42 (introduction); The Census of Massachusetts, 1895, vol. 1, p. 63; Handlin, *Boston's Immigrants*, p. 105; and Firey, *Land Use in Central Boston*, pp. 70–71.

23. Committee on Tenement Districts, "Report," 1895, pp. 1–5; Special Committee of Common Council Relative to the Improvement of Tenement Districts of the City of Boston, "Report," 1896, pp. 3–4; Estabrook, *Some Slums in Boston;* Commission to Investigate Tenement House Conditions, "Report," 1904, p. 3.

24. *Ibid.*, pp. 12–13 and 211; and Homestead Commission, *First Annual Report*, 1913, pp. 12–13. H. K. Estabrook reported in 1910 that in Wards 6 and 8, 20,000 out of approximately 44,000 people surveyed had less than 400 cubic feet of air in buildings covering 80 per cent of the land and in bad sanitary condition. The building of new and higher structures was probably relieved somewhat by the restrictive legislation, but room and apartment density as well as rentals had definitely increased. (Estabrook, "Congestion in the North and West End" in Housing Committee of Boston—1915, *Report*, Appendix A, 1910, pp. 1–2 and p. 137.) Cf. Bureau of Statistics of Labor, *Forty-first Annual Report*, 1911, part 3, pp. 136ff; R. A. Woods, *Americans in Process*, pp. 138–139. See also Jordan, "Room Overcrowding and the Lodger Evil Problem" in *Housing Problems in America*. In Boston the overcrowding occurred chiefly in the winter time, "commencing when the frost comes into the ground and the laborers flock into the city from the country and hire rooms from people who live in tenements. The only remedy . . . in Massachusetts is that the Board of Health can vacate these rooms" (*ibid.*, p. 171). Fantastic stories have been recounted of how three men slept on mattresses on the piano, of lines marking off family space, of four daughters sleeping feet to head, two on each side in a closet, of "hot bed" arrangements, and so on. The problem afflicted many cities, and there are many varying descriptions of the evils and the attempted solutions. See, for instance, Veiller, "The Housing Problem in American Cities," *Annals of the American Academy of Political and Social Science*, pp. 155–161.

25. Henry George's influence led many to protest against landlords and high land values. Others claimed that new, reasonably priced rental housing was impossible as long as the cheap, illegal competition of the slums was permitted. Decongestion was advocated, some even expressing interest in the Garden Cities movement in England. Others feared the effect of dispersal on property values, especially of immigrant investments in these areas. Such generous concern for the petty private investments overlooked somehow the shocked surprise of the 1895 Boston Council when it discovered the high social position and standing of many of those owning tenements in slum areas. Cf. Estabrook, "Congestion in the North and West End," p. 2; Veiller, "The Housing Problem in American Cities," pp. 4, 49; Special Committee of the Common Council on Improvement of Tenement Districts, "Report," 1895, p. 4. See also Hall, "The Menace of the Three Decker," p. 142.

26. Ward 5's population was 77,573 in 1915 and 63,267 in 1920.

27. Ballard, *Proposals for Downtown Boston*, p. 44; Boston, Mass., Finance Commission, *A Study of Certain of the Effects of Decentralization on Boston and Some Neighboring Cities and Towns;* Boston City Planning Board, *Building a Better Boston;* Special Commission on the Necessaries of Life, *Report,* January 1923, p. 90; McKeever, "Beacon Hill"; Firey, *Land Use in Central Boston,* chap. iii. The Boston City Planning Board, commenting on decentralization trends, dolefully observed that "The function of shopping, entertainment, and finance which had been concentrated in a central business district in the days of the first large department store, the legitimate theater and the large downtown bank were diffused by the chain store, the motion picture theater, the radio, and the suburban bank which furnished the same facilities at widely scattered centers. Likewise the functions of the wholesale district encircling the downtown business district shriveled because its function was supplanted by direct factory buying. Centrally located factories began a migration to outlying areas where the advantage of belt line transportation, ample light, air and cheap land plus a lower tax rate were available. The zone of low-rent housing formerly filled by successive batches of immigrants became a decaying slum. The areas adjacent to the slum belt became invaded by people moving away from the substandard area. Thus there was a process of change going on which renewed or rebuilt the older parts of the city." (Boston City Planning Board, *Building a Better Boston*, pp. 5–6.)

28. The restrictions were relaxed somewhat in the Displaced Persons Act of 1948. Between 1948 and 1959 about 400,000 victims of Nazi persecution and Communist pressure were permitted to immigrate to the United States under this act. According to the Office of Refugee and Migration Affairs in the Department of State, about 714,000 were admitted to the United States during this period under special immigration acts. The normal immigration quota admits about 155,000 persons annually, but about 60,000 national quota numbers expire annually unused. See Topping, "Displaced Persons of '48 Fulfill Their Hopes in the United States," *The New York Times,* Monday, Oct. 12, 1959, pp. 1, 3.

29. The losses occurred in Wards 1–10, 13, and 15. The other wards increased from 1 per cent in Ward 11 to over 50 per cent in Ward 20. The decentralization trends will be discussed in more detail later in this chapter. See Harris, *A Memorandum on the Population Trends in Metropolitan Boston,* pp. 3–5; Boston, Mass., Finance Commission, *A Study of Certain of the Effects of Decentralization . . .*, pp. 197–198.

30. The Commonwealth of Massachusetts, *The Decennial Census, 1955,*

Population and Legal Voters of Massachusetts. Note that even the better record enjoyed by Boston during 1900 to 1910 probably represented population additions attributable to changes of boundaries.

The 1960 census of population is not yet available; but current estimates indicate that the trend is continuing in the same direction. According to a preliminary report of the Bureau, Boston's population dropped to 677,626, a loss of about 15 per cent since 1950. Growth is still underway, however, in the metropolitan area, where the population in 1960 was 2,566,872, an increase of 15 per cent. (Note that the census definition of the standard metropolitan area of Boston is somewhat different from the definition employed in Table 17. On the basis of the census definition, the population in the Boston Standard Metropolitan Area was 2,233,448 in 1950.) See Bureau of the Census, Preliminary Report, Series P.O., PC (P2)–21, August 1960, p. 1; also Seventeenth Census, U.S., 1950, *Number of Inhabitants*, vol. i, chap. 21, Massachusetts, Table 2, p. 21: 5.

31. Greater Boston Economic Study Committee, *A Report for Downtown Boston.* See also Vernon, *The Changing Economic Function of the Central City.*

32. Handlin, *Boston's Immigrants,* pp. 94 and 99.

33. See Bushee, "Population" in R. A. Woods, ed., *The City Wilderness,* pp. 38–39; B. Rosen, "The Trend of Jewish Population in Boston" in Boston Federated Jewish Charities, *Monographs,* p. 111; Firey, *Land Use in Central Boston,* p. 210. Note that many immigrants and native residents did not leave, partly because of low income, partly because of attachment to the social values which these areas had acquired for those immigrants. These values sometimes even prevented the economic advancement of members of this group. (Whyte, *Street Corner Society,* chap. ii; Firey, chap. v and p. 45.)

34. Ascher, "The Suburb" in Carnovsky and Martin, eds., *The Library in the Community,* p. 63. Ascher provides evidence qualifying his thesis that "the suburban trend is in fact a series of familial cyclical movements" (p. 63) when he later points out in the same article that "workers in Bridgeport industries have money enough to get out of their three-decker tenements and get the same open space for their children that originally brought the wealthy to Stratford" (p. 64). The same holds for his reference to suburban postwar building induced by higher income (p. 71).

35. In 1846, A Committee on Tenement House Reform rejected cheaper suburban dwellings because of the added cost of transportation. Handlin also notes that most of the Irish immigrants were forced to remain in central Boston until cheaper transportation became available. See Committee on the Expediency of Providing Better Tenements, *Report,* pp. 14–17; Handlin, *Boston's Immigrants,* p. 96. Incidentally, the railroad officials in 1846, according to the Tenement Committee Report, were apparently not interested in providing trams for laborers. They believed it might depress land values because "The rich passengers might not like it" (pp. 14–17). Likewise, Josiah Quincy's proposal in 1871 to provide better housing in the suburbs for the workers assumed not only cheap transportation but also that the lowest-income groups could be helped only by helping those who earned more money. Only the workers in the higher-income group could be participants in this scheme. (Bureau of Statistics of Labor, [First Annual] *Report,* 1870, pp. 530–531.) Though the transit system later expanded rapidly, as late as 1903 R. F. Phelps noted that steam railroads were quite expensive and that few of the suburbanites

were workers. In 1900, however, the legislature passed Chapter 298 of the Massachusetts Labor Laws, establishing workingmen's trains to run six days a week for certain hours. Also special cars provided transport for $30 a year or less than $0.10 for a daily round trip. (Phelps, *South End Operatives*, pp. 8–12.) As a rule most of the studies (Phelps's included) only consider the travel costs of the principal wage earner. In poorer families there were usually one or two secondary wage earners and in that case costs tend to add up.

36. This factor is illustrated by the controversy over congestion in the North and West ends prior to World War I. Those who contended that cheap and illegal competition inhibited the building of houses elsewhere forgot that most of these people could not afford to secure better accommodations. That most of these residents would move when they could is reflected by their abrupt departure from their quarters during the war.

37. It is much easier to identify shifts of nationality groups because census data are available. There is every reason to believe that the native in-migrants followed similiar patterns, with gradations according to income and occupation and to a lesser extent social background.

38. Firey, *Land Use in Central Boston*, p. 210. Conversation with persons familiar with the Italian community indicates that certain areas of Brighton and Allston might possibly be included.

Chapter 6. *Residential Growth and Structure: Hypothesis and Generalizations*

1. This chapter is a substantially revised version of an article originally published in *The Appraisal Journal*, vol. 27, no. 3 (July 1950). For criticisms of this article by Homer Hoyt and Walter Firey, and a reply by the author, see *The Appraisal Journal*, vol. 28 no. 4 (October 1950), pp. 445–447.

2. Burgess, "The Growth of the City" in Park and Burgess, eds., *The City*, pp. 47–62.

3. Hoyt, *The Structure and Growth of Residential Neighborhoods in American Cities*.

4. *Ibid.*, p. 114.

5. *Ibid.*, p. 114.

6. *Ibid.*, p. 117.

7. *Ibid.*, p. 117.

8. *Ibid.*, p. 117.

9. *Ibid.*, p. 117.

10. *Ibid.*, p. 117.

11. *Ibid.*, pp. 117–118. The insert in the statement is based on Hoyt's important qualification made in the subsequent paragraph in the text.

12. *Ibid.*, p. 118.

13. Wolfe, *The Lodging House Problem in Boston*, p. 17.

14. Hoyt, *Structure and Growth of Residential Neighborhoods*. Hoyt explains that "the axial type of high-rent area rapidly became obsolete with the growth of the automobile. When the avenues became automobile speedways dangerous to children, noisy and filled with gasoline fumes, they ceased to be attractive as home sites for the well-to-do. No longer restricted to the upper classes, who alone could maintain prancing steeds and glittering broughams, but filled with hoi polloi jostling the limousines with their flivvers, the old avenues lost social caste. The rich then desired seclusion away from the 'madding crowd' whizzing by and honking their horns. Mansions were then built in wooded

areas, screened by trees. The very height of privacy is now attained by some millionaires whose homes are so protected from the public view by trees that they can be seen from the outside only from an airplane.

"The well-to-do who occupy most of the homes in the high-rent brackets have done likewise in segregated garden communities. The new type of high-grade area was thus not in the form of a long axial line, but in the form of a rectangular area, turning its back on the outside of the world, with widening streets, woods, and its own community centers. Such new square or rectangular areas are usually located along the line of the old axial high-grade areas. The once proud mansions still serve as a favorable approach to the new secluded spots. As some of the old axial type high-rent areas still maintain a waning prestige and may still be classed as high-rent areas, the new high-rent area takes a fan-shaped or funnel form expanding from a central stem as it reaches the periphery of the city" (p. 120).

15. *Ibid.*

16. Ballard, *Proposals for Downtown Boston*, p. 44. Note that Hoyt refers to upper-class districts in New York as being in existence for more than 100 years. Three generations or more is the bench-mark used here to judge existence for "a long time."

17. Hoyt, p. 118.

18. *Ibid.*, pp. 118–119.

19. These statements include the substance of three of the five conclusions reached in Chapter 6 dealing with the static pattern of residential areas rather than the growth pattern. They are (1) "the highest-rental areas are in every case located in one or more sectors on the side of the city"; (2) "high-rent areas take the form of wedges extending in certain sectors along radial lines from the center to the periphery"; (3) "intermediate rental areas or areas falling just below the highest-rental areas tend to surround the highest-rental areas on one side"; (4) "intermediate rental areas on the periphery of other sectors of the city besides the ones in which the highest-rental areas are located are found in certain cities"; (5) "low-rent areas extending from the center to the edge of settlement on one side or in certain sectors of the city are found in practically every city." The fourth generalization is discussed above and also in the section dealing with intermediate areas. The fifth statement is not discussed, but it is confirmed by Boston's land patterns, especially the sector to the northeast.

20. Hoyt, p. 114.

21. *Ibid.*, p. 116.

22. *Ibid.*, p. 75.

23. The same is true of the slums in the Fens prior to the building of de luxe apartments. Hoyt suggests that it also may be true of Providence, Rhode Island.

24. This point is partly anticipated by Hoyt in his introduction, where he observed that "In years to come, continued eradication of slum areas or cessation of population growth may foster conditions favoring a double back of high-grade residential areas rather than a continuation of growth in line with past experience" (Hoyt, p. 3).

25. A partial explanation is possible for both items. Coexistence of high- and low-rent areas may often indicate the desire or need for servant or service classes near the upper-income groups. Similarly, the short life of high-income residential areas may reflect the termination of a family cycle, i.e., the departure of the children and the failure of new upper- or high-income groups to take up residence in this area.

26. Note that this analysis is confined to the residential aspects. Moreover,

though Hoyt also develops the thesis with regard to other land uses, he was mainly interested in this aspect. He states, for example, that "having segregated the home areas from the general urban mass for study, the third major step in the technique differentiates the several types of residential areas on the basis of their essential housing characteristics. The analysis of these home areas and the formulation of generalizations apparently governing the distribution of the several types of residential urban areas are the main subjects of this monograph." (Hoyt, p. 4.)

27. *Ibid.*, p. 75.

28. I am indebted to George Duggar for this insight.

29. Hoyt believes that zones should be so described. He indicated that "zones or sections are determined by the predominance of one use, not by its exclusive presence" (Hoyt, p. 5).

30. A recent study of Newburyport, for example, indicates that the lowest-rent areas are "high in social prestige despite the low rentals. Their low rentals are in part due to their peripheral location." (Warner and Lunt, *The Social Life of a Modern Community*, p. 232.)

31. As an example, Hoyt states: "Thus in many cities there is a circular or rectangular area of a few blocks in which is located the peak rental area from which rents of all other blocks slope downward. *Apparently each income group tries to get as close as possible to the next higher group in the economic scale.*" (p. 74. Italics added.) Earlier, Hoyt refers to the desire of people of the same nationality "to live together" and also of "the segregation of sectors populated by different races," but these facts are in no way incorporated in his analysis (p. 62). When he comments on the movements of these groups, there is again no reference to class and ecological patterns within these groups (pp. 120–121). Firey also checked some of Hoyt's propositions by using names in the Social Register as an index and found considerable dispersion as well as concentration (Firey, *Land Use in Central Boston*, pp. 56 and 75, Figs. 2 and 5). Incidentally, it is somewhat surprising that Firey, as a sociologist, did not challenge Hoyt's conception of class structure.

32. Warner and Lunt concluded that "On the whole . . . both class and ethnic factors operate in the ecological distribution of the Yankee City population" (*The Social Life of a Modern Community*, p. 237).

33. Warner and Lunt's study provides evidence of a similar tendency (pp. 234–238).

34. Hoyt did suggest repeatedly that the research techniques must be adapted by different analysts to the problem under consideration (Hoyt, *Structure and Growth of Residential Neighborhoods*, pp. 57–58). The sector thesis, however, is an interpretation based on the studies of the cities surveyed, and this formulation presumably was not subject to such modifications.

There may be some question whether such detailed data were available for the 142 cities studied. The 1940 Census data could have been used to some extent, supplemented by several more careful field studies for special cities. If that was not feasible, the study might have underlined the necessity for more refined analyses of individual cities to take account of these important variations.

35. Hoyt observed that in several cities intermediate-income sectors were found on other sides of the city than where the "highest-rental groups" resided. This fact should have indicated the need for some qualification or refinement of the assumption or hypothesis concerning the drawing powers of the fashionable area.

36. One exception illustrating the point may be the frequent absence of "shading-off" in central areas. High-cost land frequently results in low-cost slums adjacent to upper-income residences. Most middle-income families apparently prefer the advantages of better and cheaper suburban residences to the opportunity of living adjacent to Park Avenue or Beacon Hill socialites.

37. The emphasis of this factor may also be quite significant for Firey's analysis as well. The goal of a better environment tends to be greatly under-emphasized in his study. That is because Firey, to develop his points more sharply, picks very visible but not altogether representative areas, like the North and South ends, Beacon Hill, Back Bay, and the Common, rather than middle- and low-income areas such as Dorchester, Brighton, and parts of Jamaica Plain. Even for those areas selected by Firey, such as the North End and Back Bay, part of the explanation of the departure from the area is the desire to change the physical environment. The shift, of course, may be explained on the basis of the acceptance of new social relationships and ideals and can be described and analyzed as such. Nonetheless, it is important to emphasize that the merits of any analysis, even in terms of social and cultural systems, depends upon proper appraisal of the component elements within these systems.

For further evidence supporting the hypothesis that a functionally adequate environment is important in shaping decisions of families to move, see Leo Grebler, *Housing Market Behavior in a Declining Area*, pp. 121–127; and P. H. Rossi, *Why Families Move*, pp. 8–9, 13–15, and chap. viii.

38. "It is in the twilight zone where members of different races live together that racial mixtures tend to have depressing effects upon land values and therefore upon rents" (Hoyt, p. 62). Hoyt nowhere suggests a policy of exclusion, yet this conclusion is inescapable given these assumptions and emphases.

Appendix A. *Derivation of Data on Income and Housing Costs: 1846–1956*

1. Bureau of Statistics of Labor, *Seventeenth Annual Report*, 1885, pp. 283–285.

2. Bureau of Statistics of Labor, *Sixth Annual Report*, 1875, indicates after a careful study that "fathers rely or are forced to depend upon their children for one quarter to one third of the entire family earnings" (p. 384). Incidentally, Oscar Handlin assumed 260 days' employment in preparing estimates of the wages of laborers and master masons in Boston (*Boston's Immigrants*, Table 5, p. 91). Handlin's income estimate for the wages of a master mason during this period are lower than ours because he uses a lower average working period and does not include an allowance for supplementary wage earners.

3. Data available in surveys of wages in Massachusetts and Boston indicate a difference of 15 to 18 per cent in wages and total family income between the state average and the Boston average for earnings. This is the basis for the assumption of a one-sixth differential for this and the two subsequent periods. (Bureau of Statistics of Labor, *Seventh Annual Report*, 1876. See Tables 69 and 100.)

4. The Bureau of Statistics of Labor in its 1874 survey indicates that skilled workingmen in Massachusetts paid 16 per cent of their income for rent (*Sixth Annual Report*, 1875, p. 388). Also, an expenditure study in 1876 of Boston's skilled workers indicated a 15 per cent average of rent to income (*Seventh Annual Report*, 1876).

5. Characteristic advertisements for this and subsequent periods are listed

in Lloyd Rodwin, "Middle Income Housing Problems in Boston," Appendix E.

6. Bureau of Statistics of Labor, *Seventh Annual Report,* 1876, p. 100 (Table).

7. *Ibid.,* p. 252 (Table).

8. For example, the survey included bank officials, chemists, civil engineers, dentists, journalists, lawyers, managing editor, and so on (*ibid.,* pp. 2–5).

9. *Ibid.,* pp. 4–14.

10. Bureau of Statistics of Labor, *Sixth Annual Report,* 1875, Table 10, p. 368.

11. A sixty-hour week generally prevailed. Bureau of Statistics of Labor, *Sixteenth Annual Report,* 1884, pp. 121–122; also *Tenth Annual Report,* 1879, pp. 67–77; and *Fifteenth Annual Report,* 1884, p. 296.

12. Bureau of Statistics of Labor, *Sixth Annual Report,* 1875, Table 18, pp. 380–384.

13. Bureau of Statistics of Labor, *Seventh Annual Report,* 1876, pp. 221–254. J. Quincy employed $175 per annum as an average rental for the "best tenements" ([Second Annual] *Report,* 1871, pp. 530–531). Also R. T. Paine, analyzing the possibility of building a home through cooperative banks for workingmen, estimated average tenement rents for this group to be $204 per annum (Paine, "Homes for the People" in *Contributions to the Science of Society,* p. 16).

14. Bureau of Statistics of Labor, *Sixteenth Annual Report,* 1885, Table 5 and pp. 489–490.

15. Woods, ed., *The City Wilderness,* pp. 101–102. Cf. Eleventh Census, U.S., *Report on Manufacturing Industries in the United States,* part 2, pp. xxii–xxiii. The income range used above is probably generous. However, it is supported by the testimony of a fairly reliable contemporary observer. The federal census data are useful, however, in gauging the direction of error.

16. The adjustments for total family income employed the assumption again of one-third additional income for supplementary wage earners.

17. Woods, ed., *The City Wilderness,* pp. 101–102.

18. Wright, *Comparative Wages and Prices: 1860–1883,* "Massachusetts and Great Britain," p. 50, Table entitled Workingmen's Budget Averages, Massachusetts and Great Britain.

19. The Census of Massachusetts, 1895, vol. 5, p. 279. Inclusion of high-income salaried employees probably inflates the average. The mode would probably be somewhat lower. Approximately one third has been added for supplementary earnings.

20. Phelps, *South End Operatives,* pp. 35–36.

21. Wadlin, *A Tenement House Census of Boston,* p. 437 (Table).

22. This stringency is evidenced also in the discouraged observations of philanthropic company reports. For example, the *Twenty-Ninth Annual Report* (1900) of the Boston Cooperative Building Company said, "Since 1892, no new work has been undertaken by the Company . . . [we] have come reluctantly to the conclusion that the price of desirable property . . . almost precludes the erection of new dwellings according to the provisions of the law, which would afford good tenements at moderate rents." (Cited in Miles, "The Boston Housing Situation," *Charities and the Commons,* p. 97.)

23. Estabrook, "Congestion in the North and West End," Appendix A. Actually per capita rents were about $0.60 and the reduction, of course, was secured through crowding, p. 2.

24. The British Board of Trade conducted a survey in 1909 to compare

the standard and cost of living of workers in European, American, and British cities. The data have been summarized in the Bureau of the Statistics of Labor, *Forty-first Annual Report*, 1911, part 3. The rents in Table 20 are somewhat lower than they would have been a few years earlier because of the panic of 1907.

25. Hall, "The Menace of the Three Decker," pp. 148–150.

26. Commission on the Cost of Living, *Report*, May 1910, pp. 134–136.

27. This range is based partly on the table of weekly wages of skilled workers which Wolfe indicated in his book *The Lodging House Problem in Boston*, p. 98 (Table) and pp. 87–99. It is likewise in accord with the prevailing wage rates of $14–$26 (ca.) for skilled workers published in 1911 Bureau of Statistics of Labor, (*Forty-first Annual Report*, 1911, Tables 1–12, pp. 7–77). It also concurs with the declaration of a Treasury report indicating that two thirds to three fourths of the male workers in the principal industries of the United States earn less than $15 a week" (Warner and Sydenstridker, *Health Insurance: Its Relation to Public Health*, cited in E. E. Wood, *The Housing of the Unskilled Wage Earner*, p. 15).

28. E. E. Wood, *Recent Trends in American Housing*, pp. 50–51.

29. The following studies provide rent statistics for different types of three-deckers: Bureau of Statistics of Labor, *Forty-first Annual Report*, 1911, pp. 243, 249–250; Hall, "The Menace of the Three Decker," pp. 147–150; Marble, "The Menace of the Three Decker," p. 324.

30. See, for example, Bureau of Statistics of Labor, *Annual Reports* for the years 1921, 1923, 1925, 1926, and 1928.

31. National income distributions were used as a base with upward adjustments for New York City.

32. Special Commission on the Necessaries of Life, Commonwealth of Massachusetts, *Report*, January 1925, p. 36.

33. *Ibid.*

34. An adjustment of the percentages in Table 21 is required because of the higher rents prevailing earlier in the decade.

35. U.S. Dept. of Labor, Bureau of Labor Statistics, *Consumer's Price Index for Moderate Income Families: Boston, Massachusetts: 1914–1960*. The base years for this index were 1947 to 1949.

36. Special Commission on the Necessaries of Life, *Report*, January 1925, pp. 42–43.

37. Table 21. The percentages of families in this and the following sentence are derived by interpolation. Equal distribution of families throughout the rent class is assumed.

38. U.S. National Resources Committee, *Consumer Incomes in the United States*, Table 3, p. 18. This distribution excludes the earnings of adult sons and daughters who live at home and pay board.

39. This range is somewhat lower than the wage rates of $0.75–$1.25 for diverse skilled trades in Boston. Most of these rates were "temporarily inoperative," however, "because of business conditions." Also the yearly earnings are quite different from the actual rates. (Massachusetts Department of Labor and Industries, *Time Rates of Wages and Hours of Labor in Massachusetts, 1935*, Labor Bulletin no. 173, pp. 3–4 and pp. 5–48.)

40. Sixteenth Census, U.S., 1940, *Population and Housing, Families, General Characteristics*, Table 59, p. 270. The distribution is based on families without other income, since the data for families with other income include income up to $50 and thus are misleading. Adjustments were made in the

1939 income distribution to conform to the above class ranges. Equal distribution throughout the class limits was assumed.

41. Roterus, "Stability of Annual Employment, Cincinnati and Selected Cities," *Economic Geography*, pp. 130–131; and Winston and Smith, "Sensitivity of State Income Payments to Nation's Total," *Survey of Current Business*, pp. 6–19.

42. WPA Division of Social Research, "Intercity Differences in Cost of Living in March, 1935 (59 cities)," cited in E. E. Wood, *Introduction to Housing*, Chart 18, p. 110.

43. U.S. National Resources Committee, *Consumer Income in the United States*, pp. 23–25 and Tables 7 and 8.

44. Boston Housing Authority, *Rehousing the Low Income Families of Boston: 1936–1940*, Schedule of Rents and Income Allowances (no page numbers).

45. *Ibid.* This represents the highest rents for the largest units and families. These rents, it is true, include utilities, but there is usually a gap between the housing market served by public housing and those families adequately provided for by private enterprise.

46. Sixteenth Census, U.S., 1940, *Housing*, vol. 3, part 2, Table B-1, p. 13. Note that these rents, unlike the rents for public housing apartments, do not include utilities such as gas, electricity, and heat.

47. "Good" units are the residual number of dwellings after the number needing minor repairs and structural repairs and those not fit for habitation (as well as those not reporting) are deducted (Boston City Planning Board, "Report on Real Property Inventory," vol. 1, Table 2, p. 2).

48. *Ibid.*, p. 6.

49. Townsend, "Some Economic Aspects of Urban Housing with Special Reference to Metropolitan Boston," pp. 50–51.

50. Census reports on surveys of the total money income level for families for the Northeastern region are fairly consistent with the above distribution. The Census breakdown is somewhat lower, i.e., 41.2 per cent below $2500; 30.3 per cent between $2500 and $4000; and 28.6 per cent over $4000. (U.S. Bureau of the Census, *Income of Nonfarm Families and Individuals: 1946*, Table 4, p. 10.)

51. Mr. John Carroll has pointed out that in September 1947 the average earnings of 117,790 wage earners in Boston, according to a survey by the Massachusetts Department of Labor and Industries, were $46.30 a week, or $2407.60 per year. This average, however, may be a little low because it includes single persons, making the average income lower than that of married workers. Mr. Carroll did point out, however, that the middle-income group probably earned between $3000 and $4000 per annum. (U.S. Senate, *Hearings Before the Joint Committee on Housing*, pp. 2488 and 2479.)

52. These figures are consistent with the 1946 Census survey of veterans' needs in the Boston area, which indicated that veterans planning to rent reported that they were able to pay $44 for a 5-room apartment, their average weekly income being approximately $45. Those veterans who would buy or build (our top stratum of the middle-income group) reported an ability to make a gross monthly payment of $65 a month for a six-room house, with an average weekly income from all sources of $57. (See U.S. Bureau of the Census, *Survey of World War II Veterans*, p. 1.)

53. U.S. Bureau of the Census, *Housing Characteristics of the Boston, Massachusetts Metropolitan District: April 1947*, Table 2, p. 6.

54. Cf. Maisel, "Have We Underestimated Increases in Rent and Shelter Expenditures?" *Journal of Political Economy*, pp. 107–118.

55. U.S. Bureau of the Census, *1956 National Housing Inventory*, vol. 3, *Characteristics of the 1956 Inventory*, part 3, "Boston," Table 2, p. 13.

56. *Ibid.*, Table 12, pp. 13 and 21. There are about 45,000 dwelling units in the categories of $49 and under, but approximately 7,000 of these units lacked facilities and another 6,500 were dilapidated. About 23,000 of these dwelling units also had three rooms or less. Thus, there are only a negligible number of standard dwellings of the right size which could serve the middle-income families.

57. *Ibid.*, Table 13.

58. Ratcliff, "Filtering Down," *Journal of Land and Public Utility Economics*. See also Colean, *American Housing: Problems and Prospects*, pp. 182–185. Note that more intensive use of the structure might also be a factor which would produce surplus accommodations.

59. Boston Cooperative Building Company, *Fourth and Fifth Annual Reports*, p. 3. The average cost of thirteen houses built by this company in Dorchester for "American mechanics and those in sympathy with them" was $1840. A down payment of $200 was required, plus $25 a month, and the company hoped to serve those earning between $800 and $1000. (*Ibid.*, pp. 5–6.)

60. Paine, "The Housing Conditions in Boston," p. 25. J. Quincy also referred to the possibility of building cheap houses in the country for the poor at a cost of $1000 (Bureau of Statistics of Labor, [Second Annual] *Report*, 1871, pp. 530–531). In an analysis of the problem of building homes for workers through building and loan associations (cooperative banks), Mr. Paine estimated tenement rents for 5 rooms in 1880 at $17 a month, whereas he hoped to bring it down to $14. If we use this as the range, it would amount to $168 to $204. (Paine, "Homes for the People," pp. 16–17.)

61. *Ibid.*, p. 129.

62. Phelps, *South End Operatives*, pp. 35–36.

63. Bureau of Statistics of Labor, *Forty-First Annual Report*, 1911, part 3, pp. 240, 249–250; also Hall, "The Menace of the Three Decker," pp. 147–159; and Marble, "The Menace of the Three Decker," p. 324.

64. Special Commission on the Necessaries of Life, *Report*, January 1925, pp. 36, 37.

65. The average FHA value of property for one-family homes in the Boston Metropolitan District was $6437 in 1938 and $6134 in 1939. The average mortgage value from 1935 to 1939 was $5970. Also the average gross monthly payments for one-family homes in 1938 and 1939 were $47.86 and $47.00, respectively. (U.S. Federal Housing Administration, *FHA Homes in Metropolitan Districts*, p. 39, Table 2 and Table 10.)

66. U.S. Senate, *High Cost of Housing*, Tables 15, 16, and 17, and pp. 41, 43, and 54. See also Special Commission Relative to the Immediate Relief of Traffic, Housing, . . . *Partial and Preliminary Report*, p. 12; and U.S. House of Representatives, *Final Majority Report of the Joint Committee on Housing, Housing Study and Investigation*, part 2, "Statistics of Housing," Table 53, p. 149.

Appendix B. *Rent Control and Housing*

1. This appendix is a revised version of an article previously published in *Social Research*, vol. 17, no 3 (September 1950). Following the earlier publication, two thoughtful studies were published. Readers interested in examining

the somewhat similar, and in some cases sharply different, conclusions of these studies should see Grebler, "Implications of Rent Control in the United States," *International Labour Review*, pp. 1–24; and Winnick, *American Housing and Its Use,* chap. v.

2. There are many other bases for distinguishing housing submarkets, such as classifications of dwelling units according to neighborhoods, or quality, or size of dwelling unit. The most careful statement on the structure and behavior of the housing market, admittedly tentative and exploratory, may be found in Rapkin, Winnick, and Blank, *Housing Market Analysis,* chap. iii. The substance of the material of that chapter appeared as an article by Blank and Winnick on "The Structure of the Housing Market," *The Quarterly Journal of Economics.*

3. Of course, this tenure characteristic is not necessarily a permanent condition.

4. Winnick, *American Housing and Its Use,* chap. iv.

5. Colean, "The Rental Housing Mystery," *Architectural Record,* pp. 81–85; Friedman and Stigler, *Roofs or Ceilings,* condensed for and issued by the National Association of Real Estate Boards, Washington, D.C. See also, as a representative though small sample of the groups presenting these views at congressional inquiries, U.S. Senate, *Hearings before the Joint Committee on Housing,* part 3, and U.S. Senate, *Hearings before a Subcommittee of the Committee on Banking and Currency.*

6. There are almost no studies on this subject.

7. This effect follows from the assumption that rental housing is a "poor man's good."

8. A useful but difficult research project would be to analyze historically the relative importance of the motives influencing the ownership and production of rental housing.

9. Foreclosed properties held by banks and not previously disposed of would probably be put on sale during this period. However, John Lintner found in his study of Massachusetts mutual savings banks that "the proportion of foreclosed properties sold continued to decline for a period of four years beyond the upturn in the general real estate market." (*Mutual Savings Banks in the Savings and Mortgage Markets,* p. 276.)

10. Colean, *American Housing,* pp. 200–203.

11. See Chap. 4, note 41.

12. Winnick, *Rental Housing.*

13. Friedman and Stigler, *Roofs or Ceilings,* pp. 10–14.

14. See, for example, Lerner, *The Economics of Control,* pp. 14–17, 43–45.

15. Friedman and Stigler, *Roofs or Ceilings,* pp. 10–11.

16. Control of prices and allocations of materials existed during World War II, as did controls on prices and rents of new houses. Both were abandoned after the war.

17. For a discussion of some increases in the *over-all average* of rents that might occur even under controls, see Maisel, "Have We Underestimated Increases in Rents and Shelter Expenditures?" pp. 106–118.

18. It might be argued that this problem does not occur because other families are accommodated as vacancies occur. In point of fact, many who were previously desperate will have purchased homes, and the same pattern will occur for the new batch of evictees. For example, before rent increases there may be a thousand families needing housing. Two hundred may buy homes

reluctantly. If five hundred families are evicted because of rent increases, their quarters may be taken by those who had doubled up. An additional hundred families, however, might be pushed into ownership.

19. In the event that rent rolls were not yielding satisfactory returns, purchasers at controlled rents would not be easy to find, unless prices reflected this situation or unless buyers wished to speculate on the possibility of revised control policies.

20. For evidence that this tendency has occurred, see Winnick, *American Housing and Its Use*, p. 10.

21. If it were true, as some economists have maintained, that controls permitted an excessive use of space, an even greater demand would exist for new rental housing. On the other hand, the free market, by distributing space according to capacity to pay, might lower the demand because the higher-income groups would generally get the better accommodations and would therefore not be so interested in the new high-cost construction, often flimsily built and inconveniently located, while many lower-income families would not be able to afford the new housing.

22. Social objections also exist. Moreover, as Lerner and others have indicated, rationing, though justified in some circumstances, results in inefficient distribution, because it prevents the use of goods in varying proportions to needs and tastes, thus precluding maximum satisfaction (Lerner, *The Economics of Control*, pp. 50–52).

23. Bloomberg, "Rent Control and the Housing Shortage," *Journal of Land and Public Utility Economics*, p. 28. Note that underprivileged minorities will likewise tend to be more adversely affected, since the proportion of owners in such groups is smaller.

Appendix C. *Notes on Firey's Critique of the Sector Hypothesis*

1. This appendix was originally part of an article published in *The Appraisal Journal* entitled "The Theory of Residential Growth and Structure." For more detail see Chap. 6, note 1.

2. Firey, *Land Use in Central Boston*, chaps. i, ii and ix. Firey's criticisms are also applied to the locational theories of Weber, Burgess, Predohl, Park, Haig, and others.

Some of Firey's definitions ought to be noted. A social system is defined as "the organization of particular concrete persons and groups into regularized interaction," and a cultural system as "the integration of ends and meanings with respect to generalized types of persons and non-human externalities" (*ibid.*, p. 32). The "nonintrinsic society space nexus" involves a symbolic relationship in which "the characteristics of space are not those belonging to it as a natural object of the physical world but rather are those which result from its being a symbol for a cultural system . . . the properties attaching to physical space and the ends by which a social system orients itself to space have their being in a cultural system. In contrast to this an intrinsic society space relationship would be one in which the properties of space were natural givens and in which the ends orienting a social system to space had their only being in the system itself, as a long disparate unit seeking maintenance of identity." (*Ibid.*, p. 133.)

3. Firey analyzes these and other areas in great detail and much of his contribution lies in the skill and ingenuity with which he develops this point.

4. Such selectivity undoubtedly existed for Beacon Hill—but Firey does not

explain why an entirely different pattern held for an area like the South End, when it started to decline.

5. Firey's writing at best employs considerable technical sociological terminology and at worst is astonishingly prolix and obscure. The summary above is really an interpretation; and though this writer reluctantly assumes responsibility for the statements, it may be wise for the more interested reader to consult the original source. It is a pity that much of what Firey has to contribute may well be lost or misinterpreted by his potential audience.

6. Hoyt, in reviewing Firey's book in the *Journal of the American Institute of Planners,* dubbed it "an outstanding contribution to urban land economics and human ecology" (p. 36).

7. Firey limits his interpretation of determinism to "the premise that social activities, in their territorial layouts, always constitute the dependent, 'caused' variable, with physical space being the independent and 'causing' factor. It is only in this sense that the expression 'determinism' is to be used in the present study." A little earlier, Firey also declares that most of the ecological theories "ascribe to space a determinate and invariant influence upon the distribution of human activities. The socially relevant qualities of space are thought to reside in the very nature of space itself, and the territorial patterns assumed by social activities are regarded as wholly determined by these qualities. There is no recognition, except in occasional fleeting insights, that social values may endow space with qualities that are quite extraneous to it as a social phenomenon. Moreover, there is no indication of what pre-conditions there may be to social activities becoming in any way linked with physical space." (Firey, *Land Use in Central Boston,* pp. 1–2.)

Firey does acknowledge in a footnote that Hoyt's analysis allows for many deviations and is not "doctrinaire," but contends that "the scientific adequacy of his idealized scheme may legitimately be evaluated and criticized" (*ibid.,* p. 78, note 100).

8. See Hoyt, *Structure and Growth of Residential Neighborhoods,* p. 114.

9. Several times, as a matter of fact, Firey commits the double injustice of choosing portions of Hoyt's text which do not correspond to Firey's views of what Hoyt should be saying and thereupon rebukes him for "deviationism." Thus, when Hoyt points out the practice of inflating land prices in order to maintain upper-class development, Firey insists that neither the raising nor lowering of prices to limit or multiply sales was "an ecological necessity. . . . To the extent that Hoyt relies upon this variable in his theory, then he is unwittingly introducing a volitional element which in its logical implications completely vitiates the determinancy of his scheme" (Firey, *Land Use in Central Boston.* pp. 64–65). It is obviously not a necessity that merchants reduce prices on overstocked goods or raise prices for merchandise serving a special clientele. The effects and practice are still subjects for economic as well as sociological analysis. Firey does not seem to realize that Hoyt takes the sociological significance for granted, and explores the economic mechanism and effects solely to see how the locational characteristics emerge. Provided that the limitations of the model are grasped, it is perfectly proper for the economist to explore the impact of economic forces alone. Failure of the economist to realize these limitations is a different kind of criticism and often more warranted.

10. Hoyt in fact states at the beginning of his inquiry that "the techniques suggested and employed in this study, and the principles of urban structure and

growth suggested are not set forth as the only method of attack upon the difficult question of the nature of the structure and growth of cities. There are innumerable roads by which the subject may be approached" (*Structure and Growth of Residential Neighborhoods*, p. 3).

11. *Ibid.*, pp. 112, 114. Firey in fact mentions this himself (*Land Use in Central Boston*, p. 8). Hoyt also indicates several sectors in his rent maps. See Firey, pp. 44, 50, 55, and 62.

12. *Ibid.*, p. 44.

13. There was apparently another cluster along Summer Street from the Common to the river. Note that Hoyt points out that in the early period of a city's growth there is "considerable choice of direction in which to move but that range of choice is narrowed as the city grows and begins to be filled up on one or more sides by low-rent structures" (p. 119).

14. Firey, p. 50 and Figure 2 on p. 56.

15. *Ibid.*, pp. 62–63.

16. On page 60, Firey says, "With business encroaching upon their homes, residents of the area lying south of the business district began to look elsewhere for places in which to live. Many moved to the suburbs. Others looked to South Boston." A writer in the *Boston Almanac* for 1853 wrote: "South Boston from present appearance is predestined to be the magnificent section of the city in respect to costly residences, fashionable society and the influence of wealth." Yet on pages 62–63 Firey says: "Hoyt does not mean to rest his case on such geographically determined processes. . . . The imperious necessity of finding new land for residential expansion made the South End the only possible direction of growth. But this is not the kind of determinacy to which Hoyt would himself attribute his asserted radial extensions of land uses."

17. Firey includes in this band, in addition to Beacon Hill and Back Bay, the following communities: Brookline, Newton, Wellesley, Weston, and perhaps Dedham (pp. 77 and 78).

18. Hoyt, p. 117. Actually the southwest trend (Dedham, Dover, Medford, and Westwood) can be attributed to the increasingly advantageous location of the South and Back Bay stations in relation to "big business" centers; and the west-northwest trend (northern Wellesley, Weston, and Lincoln) is correspondingly related to ease of access along the Charles by auto. To this extent, the sectors correspond to Hoyt's thesis, particularly the emphasis of the roles of transportation routes in determining the shape of the residential pattern. I am indebted to Prof. R. B. Greeley (Department of City and Regional Planning, M.I.T.) for sharpening my thinking on this point.

19. See Chap. 6, pp. 115–116.

20. Firey describes the proportionalization of ends as follows:

"Let us then imagine a city that is made of certain ends defined for it by the value system of the society in which that city exists. We can postulate that there will be an hypothetical point at which the amount and 'kind' of space devoted to a particular end or function balances off with the spatial requirements of each other end or function comprising the city. At this point the total deprivation of all the ends comprising the system is at a minimum. It is important to recognize that this 'end deprivation' is not synonymous with 'cost' in the economic sense of the word, since it refers not only to dearth of scarce goods but also to thwarting of intangible and non-empirical ends which are just as real functional requirements of a city. All of these ends and functional requirements must be attained, yet none of them can be pursued to an unlimited degree lest others be unduly deprived. That point along the 'deprivation continuum' of a particular end, at which point the degree of deprivation comports with a minimal deprivation of all other ends comprising the community may be called point x. Now by definition, any deviation away from x will entail increased deprivation to one or more of the other ends comprising the community as a system. Thus an allocation of too much space to park and recreational facilities will obstruct certain other requirements of the city as a functioning social system, such as commerce or manufacturing. Likewise the allocation of too little space to park and recreational facilities will obstruct the 'best' functioning of the community as a system. Reasoning deductively, then, it may be suggested that departure from point x in either direction as to degree of a deprivation of a particular end is accompanied by a progressive increase in deprivation to the system as a whole—more specifically, to one or more of the other ends comprising the system" (pp. 326–327).

Firey also translates this into algebraic symbols, but, as he indicates, the significance of the proposition is not thereby changed.

21. Firey, p. 340.

22. *Ibid.*, p. 23. Moreover, his theory is apparently not useful for this purpose.

Acknowledgments

It is a pleasant duty to record my appreciation for the help I received from the Center for Urban and Regional Studies of the Massachusetts Institute of Technology and from the Joint Center for Urban Studies of the Massachusetts Institute of Technology and Harvard University, an agency which has grown out of the urban research activities of these two institutions. Both Centers provided assistance in the final typing of the manuscript, in the preparation of the charts, maps, and index, and in the review of the galleys.

I am also much obliged to Mr. Walter Muir Whitehill for permission to reproduce the Boynton map of 1844 of Boston which is owned by the Boston Athenaeum and which appeared in his handsome book "Boston: A Topographical History."

For valuable comments on all or parts of the manuscript I am indebted to Charles Abrams, Leo Grebler, Roland B. Greeley, John T. Howard, Kevin Lynch, Martin Meyerson, Chester Rapkin, Robert M. Solow, and William L. C. Wheaton. Some of this assistance was provided a decade ago when an earlier version of this study was in the form of a dissertation; some was given during the past year after I decided to reorganize substantially the main ideas and to add new materials. I am especially grateful to Hilbert Fefferman and Aaron Fleisher, whose assiduous criticisms of the manuscript spurred me to clarify my ideas and presentation; and I owe more than the usual accolade to my wife for lavish assistance on all phases of the research effort.

I had the good fortune to have the services of Mrs. Judith Verrill and, in the final weeks, of Miss Juliet Masters in coping with the laborious task of typing and retyping the manuscript. In addition, Lowell Stroom helped me to read the galleys and made many useful suggestions while preparing the charts and maps. Finally, Caroline Shillaber's extraordinary patience and skill in ferreting out elusive source materials saved me many precious hours.

Needless to say, I alone am responsible for errors of fact and judgment.

Lloyd Rodwin

September 1960
Joint Center for Urban Studies
of MIT and Harvard University
Cambridge, Massachusetts

INDEX

Index

224   INDEX

Cost of living: Special Commission index, 20; WPA study, *1935*, 139
Cotton Hill, 85, 199n
Credit. *See* Mortgage finance

Dedham, 110, 111, 216n
Demand: rising standards of, 1, 2, 5, 8, 125, 127; and oversupply, 39; and high prices, 63–64; of minority groups, 122; and increase in households and income, 146–147
Depression, 5, 52; of *1921*, 54; of *1873*, 120
Discrimination, 64, 151; and Hoyt's thesis, 122
Dividends, policy of building and loan associations on, 28–29
Dock Square, 85
Dorchester, 36, 37, 91, 92, 93, 102, 103, 111, 114, 118, 121, 189n, 201n
Doubling-up, 54, 64, 66, 155, 198n
Douglas, Paul, quoted, 183n
Dover, 115, 216n
Dover St., 200n

East Boston, 36, 88, 91, 93, 102, 103, 111, 118, 121, 189n, 199n, 200n
East Cambridge, 91
East Canton houses, 142
Employment: and rental investment, 39; shift in, and population migration, 94–95; and family cycle thesis, 102
Engels, F., 185n; quoted, 27
Engle, C. L. L., 183n
Environment, improvement of, 7, 8; and increased income, 22; as determining factor, 94, 103, 119–120, 122
Equipment, housing, 22, 25
Estabrook, H. A., 135
Ethnic groups: housing patterns, 7–8, 86, 90, 91, 92, 93, 101–103; in Hoyt's thesis, 116–117
Everett, 102, 103
Evictees, 152
Evictions, 48, 54
Existing housing: rent-income data, 15, 18, 19, 21, 131–140; rise in price, after World War I, 54, 58; rent controls on, 65, 152, 154

Families: growth of, 1; size, 22, 71, 145, 197n; and number of rooms, 23; and sub-families, 72; migration of, 94–95; new, 152. *See also* Population
Family cycle thesis, 7, 204n, 206n; modification of, 102–103
Faneuil Hall, 85
Federal Housing Administration, 198n;

insurance, 65, 149; and Hoyt's study, 118, 121
Fens, the, 161, 206n
Fenway, the, 93, 110
Fields Corner, 103
Filtration process, 120, 127, 142, 183n; retardation of, 18; and three-decker, 38
Financial institutions, 121
Fire hazard, and three-decker, 36–37
Firey, Walter, 108n, 208n; critique of Hoyt's thesis, 158–163, 207n, 215n–217n; definitions, 214n
Fort Hill, 85, 86, 88, 112, 120, 159, 160, 199n, 200n, 201n
Franklin St., 85
Friedman, M., 150, 151
Fulton St., 85, 200n

G.I. bill. *See* Veterans
Greeks, 92

Hall, P. F., 136
Handlin, Oscar, 208n; quoted, 102, 199n
Hanover St., 88
High-income groups: and housing shortage after World War I, 47, 61, 64; and family cycle thesis, 102; in Hoyt's thesis, 109; movement of, 120–121. *See also* Income
High-rent residential areas. *See* Hoyt
High St., 85
Home Loan Bank System, 32–33
Home Owners Loan Corporation, 33
Households: space utilization and rent controls, 6–7, 72–73, 77–81, 198n; total new units, after World War II, 71; increase in, and demand, 146–147, 197n
Housing costs: and rent-income ratios, 21; inflation, 26, 49, 125. *See also* Construction; Ownership; Rents
Housing policies: shift in, 4; public intervention and market mechanism, 8–9, 125–127; nineteenth-century, 35, 88, 90–91; tenure issue, 45, 47; in *1920's*, 47–50; broadened, 51–52, 65; and Hoyt's thesis, 108, 113, 114, 118–119, 121–122; government subsidies, 113, 122, 154; and minority groups, 122; in shortage periods, 145. *See also* Rent controls
Housing shortage, 1, 4, 6, 20, 21, 33, 125; after World War I, 38, 47–50, 51–52, 53–54, 64, 65, 94, 136, 139; and free market, 63, 64, 146, 148, 150, 151; and rent controls, 53, 65,